THE
CHARLOTTE DYMOND
MURDER

© PAT MUNN, 1978   I.S.B.N.   0 9501732 5 8 (hardback)
                              0 9501732 4 X (softback)

ALL RIGHTS RESERVED   No part of this publication may be reproduced, stored in a retrieval system or transmitted in any form or by any means electronic, chemical, mechanical, photocopying, recording or otherwise without the prior permission in writing of the publishers - **BODMIN BOOKS LIMITED.**

CONDITIONS OF SALE   This book shall not by way of trade or otherwise be lent, re-sold, hired out or otherwise circulated in any form of binding or cover other than that in which it is published without the publishers' prior permission in writing and without a similar condition including this condition being imposed upon the subsequent purchaser

Cover illustration by Elizabeth Arch

The publishers thank Munn's Leathercraft, Bodmin, for sponsoring this publication

FIRST PUBLISHED · APRIL 14, 1978
(the 134th anniversary of the murder)

Printed in Falmouth, Cornwall, by
CENTURY LITHO (TRURO) LIMITED
for Bodmin Books Limited

PAT MUNN B.A.

THE
CHARLOTTE DYMOND
MURDER
CORNWALL 1844

BODMIN BOOKS LIMITED
The Cornish County Town Publishers
45 Fore Street, Bodmin, Cornwall, PL31 2JA, U.K.

(photo: C. R. Clemens, Bodmin)

The author

Pat Munn graduated from the University of London in 1961.

Professionally, she has lectured in English and Religion at the Cornwall Technical College, where she was also responsible for drama; and she has been a political agent in the Falmouth-Camborne parliamentary constituency.

Having served various organisations in a voluntary capacity, she has - since returning to her home town, Bodmin, in 1966 - been secretary to the Chamber of Commerce (1966-67), a borough councillor (1967-72); and is, at present, a comprehensive school governor.

As a Cornish historian, she contributes to periodicals on a variety of subjects; has lectured to academic bodies and under the auspices of the W.E.A.; and has been a television regional quiz panellist.

Recreationally, she has written and directed for the amateur stage, specialising in pantomime productions with youth companies.

Married to Tom Munn, the leather craftsman, she partners him in business; and they have a son, Simon.

This is her fourth non-fiction publication; previous works having been *Bodmin Moor* (1972), *The Cornish Capital* (1973), and *Bodmin Riding* (1975). They have all, including the present work, featured in television and radio programmes.

Charlotte Dymond

Contents

Frontispiece		6
Introduction		7
1.	The Ghost Of Charlotte	9
2.	What They Belonged To Do	10
3.	All Worthy & All Drunkard	15
4.	A Letter In His Hand	21
5.	Her Mother Would Kill Her	26
6.	The Neighbours Are Saying	31
7.	Small Marks Of Blood	35
8.	The Body Of A Woman	39
9.	Seduced By The Devil	42
10.	Across The Tamar To Plymouth	51
11.	King John, The Doctor, & The Master Of The Hounds	57
12.	The Constable Denied It	62
13.	The Road To Bodmin Gaol	65
14.	Something Black Showing	70
15.	Dropped Into The Grave	75
16.	This Fire Of Iniquity	80
17.	The Case Requires Management	83
	Illustrations centre pages	89-104
18.	A Strong Opinion	105
19.	His Wretched Position	111
20.	There Is No Hope	119
21.	All But Cut Off	124
22.	Firmly Grasped In Death	133
23.	Strange To Say	135
24.	To Lay The Ghost	145
Relationship of case personnel		164
Acknowledgments		168
Bibliography		170
Source Notes		171
Index		184

Charlotte Dymond

Murder

From the dramatised documentary screened on B.B.C. Television, Jan. 9, 1978, Charlotte Dymond played by Jenny Tucker, and Matthew Weeks by Tony Hale. Note the shawl, bonnet and boots which had to be taken off for this re-enactment of Weeks's confession.
[photo: John Wood; director, Peter Hercombe. By courtesy: Pebble Mill, B.B.C. Birmingham]
BBC copyright

Introduction

Late in an afternoon, towards the end of June in 1973, I was putting the finishing touches to a room I had just redecorated, when the bell on my telephone rang.

It was the author, Colin Wilson. And so began the sequence of strange events that culminated in the publication of this book.

He was writing a series of articles on jealousy murders, he said, and wanted to include the Cornish example of that genre. So could I, he asked, having mentioned the case in my first work, *BODMIN MOOR*, tell him exactly how Charlotte Dymond had met her death.

Paint brushes still in hand, I apologised for lack of immediate knowledge. And, if the truth had been told, murder was neither my subject nor concern at that time. But I would consult my files, I said, and ring him back after dinner should there be anything that could help.

I did ring back. There was nothing. In any case, as he was working to a deadline, it would have been too late. So that was that.

About a fortnight later, I had been talking to L. E. Long, author of the essay-and-anecdote series of books under the general title, *AN OLD CORNISH TOWN*. And, as I was leaving, I just happened to mention Colin Wilson's query.

'You've looked up the brief, no doubt', said Mr. Long.

'What brief, and where?' I asked.

'The brief to prosecuting counsel, in the guildhall', came his reply.

I was stunned. An original 1844 document in Bodmin's guildhall?

It was under lock and key, admittedly. But, as part of the local Old Cornwall Society's lending library collection, it could be borrowed one day and lost for ever, I felt.

With one object in mind, to ensure that another copy existed, I found the custodian, collected the key, borrowed the document, and had it photographed - all fifty-six foolscap pages of it, recto and verso. As far as I was concerned, it was £6.25p well spent and an interesting addition to my files.

Then I remembered my promise to Colin Wilson that, if I ever came across anything on the Charlotte Dymond case, I'd let him know. Accordingly, I made notes on the brief which, two years later, he used in his introduction to *MURDER IN THE WEST-COUNTRY*.

Yet, by the time that version of the case was published, I had grave reservations as to its acceptibility. I was also aware that a series of coincidences persuaded me to write this book.

It is not every day that an author receives seventy-seven school essays out of the blue, albeit on a subject she's known to be studying. Neither is it usual for a writer to be visited by an employee of the Public Record Office in London, whose routine work is to locate documents for the photographic department to supply researchers all over the world. But she remembered the Charlotte Dymond records and sought me out in Cornwall to discover my progress on the case.

These two things, following in natural succession it now appears, from Colin Wilson's query and L. E. Long's drawing my attention to the brief, did happen. They made me realise that something, beyond the normal forces of curiosity and interest, urged me to re-investigate this case. When I came to write up my findings, even the style was not really mine. This may be apparent in chapter two, where the formal lapses into the vernacular; and that way it stayed for the rest of the book.

It has been a strenuous and expensive project involving thousands of hours of searching, reading, decyphering, analysing, discussing with experts, walking, driving and writing. It has also entailed hundreds of telephone calls and letters.

I could not have undertaken the task without the help of those I've acknowledged. To them all, particularly the people of North Cornwall whose story this is, I reiterate my gratitude. Few writers, surely, have received more ready and generous co-operation and my appreciation is profound.

THIS I STRESS - no allegations are made against any person or persons, living or dead, in this book. The facts, as I have been given to understand them, are set out for readers to draw their own conclusions.

This is essentially a study in social history, a look at a rural community in a remote part of the British Isles during the first half of the nineteenth century. So much is known about the upper crust of early Victorian society; but it is only when this is broken open, usually by violence, that we are permitted a glimpse of the lower levels.

The Charlotte Dymond murder case placed a Cornish community on record. To study the affair is to discover the ways in which that community reacted to something extraordinary taking place in its midst.

If some idea of the life and times of the people of Bodmin Moor in 1844 is gained by reading this work, the years of its research and writing will be justified. Should anyone be thanked for the book's appearance, I think it must be - Charlotte Dymond!

Bodmin, 1978   **Pat Munn**

THE CHARLOTTE DYMOND MURDER

Cornwall 1844

The ghost of Charlotte

1. Close by the Helland bridge over the River Camel, on the edge of Bodmin Moor in Cornwall, there stands an old house called Tredethy. [1]
    One morning early in the twentieth century, a guest at the house set off by himself to follow the river in pursuit of fish. The Camel was famed for salmon. In pre-Reformation times there had been countless disputes between local folk who poached them and the Bodmin prior whose right to them was chartered.
    This day, however, the house guest did not follow the river to its head in Davidstow parish but wandered along a tributary called the Alan.[2] By the time he neared its source on Bodmin Moor and looked up at Roughtor, Cornwall's second highest hill, the sun must have been low in the sky.
    The moor is a desolate place in any season. It is dangerous, too, for marshes lurk beneath the heathland. So the best way through for a stranger is by following the course of a granite strewn stream.
    He must therefore have wondered on his homeward journey why a young woman dared cross the moor on her own that day. She had been, he reported upon his return to Tredethy, the only living thing he'd seen apart from the sheep and ponies loose on the slopes.
    A woman on the moor!
    His host was curious. 'What was she like?' he asked.
    'She was wearing a gown of different colours, a red cloth shawl and bonnet of silk', the guest replied. 'I watched her and she kept stopping and shading her eyes from the sun with her hand', he went on, 'as if looking for someone'.
    Then 'you have seen the ghost of Charlotte', he was told. [3]
    The guest's response is unrecorded. But he was by no means the first, or last, to experience the supernatural in the Roughtor area.
    James Noble, a cook sergeant with the Callington 5th Corps, the Cornwall Rifle Volunteers, told his grandson that night-time guard duty was unpop-

ular when camps were held there towards the end of the nineteenth century. Several of those who had been posted alleged that they had seen the ghost of Charlotte crossing the moor. [4]

Stout-hearted moorlanders employed at the Stannon clay works, an industry in operation adjacent to Roughtor since the 1860s,[5] have reported glimpsing 'a light figure'. When asked if it might have been an animal, they have sworn it was a woman. [6]

An animal is on record, though, as having behaved strangely in the area. This was on a September morning in the early 1970s when two men took a small dog on a climb to the Roughtor peak.

The higher they went, the more apprehensive it became until, reaching the top, the dog took refuge in a crevice and seemed unwilling to go further. So the owner carried it back down the slope towards Roughtor Ford and, halfway there, the animal struggled to the ground, then scampered off as though nothing had happened. [7]

Other men have returned from a day's fishing in the moorland streams saying they have seen 'a white figure with best clothes on'.[8] April has been a month when people have gone to the area in the hope of glimpsing such an apparition. And a Liskeard man is on record as having made regular visits in order to shoot the ghost; but it never appeared. [9]

There is something, then, that is out of the ordinary on this side of Bodmin Moor.

The area has been holy ground. A chapel once stood on top of Roughtor and, as a record of 1419 shows it was dedicated to St. Michael, it is among those places that have been regarded as having been possible energy fields of ancient man. [10]

A white witch told me that the place has power, enthusiasts having apparently gathered there to charge themselves. And geothermal experts are actually reviewing the 'hot rock power' possibilities of areas such as this.

It was a cloudless, hot and sunny afternoon when my husband, Tom, and I paid a visit there. We climbed up Roughtor and walked across the top of it and Showery Tor to Lanlary Rock, then turned again and made for Roughtor Ford.

Suddenly Tom felt cold. An inexplicable shiver went up his spine. Then I guessed we'd found the route, the path a couple took in 1844.

It ended with one lying dead at Roughtor Ford, and another suspended from a rope in Bodmin.

What they belonged to do

2. Britain was enjoying its seventh year under the young queen, Victoria, in 1844. As she awaited the birth of her fourth child, Alfred, her country was the envy of the world. Unlike many of its continental neighbours, it was a unified state and had not been over-run during the Napoleonic wars. An enormous second empire was being gained and protected by a navy without equal. Russian advances in the Balkans and Mediterranean, which worried the reorganising or emerging nation states of Europe, were but opportunities for the gun-boat dip-

lomacy of such as Palmerston. As the only internal and real revolutions it had known in recent times had been agrarian and industrial, it had great commercial wealth. And, were all this not enough, Britain had vast resources of coal upon which to draw.

Yet, although the country appeared to enjoy peace and prosperity, there were those within it who felt that they missed out. The eyes of the ordinary people of Britain had been opened by the French Revolution at the end of the eighteenth century; and their so-called betters were getting the message that, unless they improved the lot of those who depended upon them, the fate of the French upper classes could be theirs. So, while the working classes made their feelings known through riots and other disturbances in the first half of the nineteenth century, and to a certain extent change for the good was brought about by them, it was the reforms and innovations of their governors which better served their cause.

The abolition of slavery in the empire by 1833, through the efforts of such as William Molesworth of Pencarrow in Cornwall, supported the case for an end to slavery at home. Prisons were gradually improved and regularly inspected; and, by 1838, all except murderers escaped the rope. A series of factory acts had lessened the exploitation of children and, by 1844, had given a measure of protection to women as well.

The railway mania, made possible by the engineering of Trevithick and the steam jet of Gurney - of Pool and Padstow in Cornwall respectively - enabled people to see that parliamentary boroughs were villages compared with their cities, which had little or no representation, and that industrialisation had rendered the land and its owners out of date. So Parliament and the municipal corporations had been reformed in the 1830s; and, when the union workhouses replaced the parish relief system, guardians were elected rather than appointed.

Even the postal system, pioneered the previous century by Cornwall's Ralph Allen of St. Blazey, furthered the cause of the lower classes. The prepaid penny stamp of 1840 widened the propaganda circulation of such as the unions, Free Traders, anti-Corn Law Leaguers, and the Chartists, the last-named counting among their leaders yet another Cornishman, William Lovett of Newlyn.

If those in power were beginning to heed the will of the people, there was still a long way to go and one above all others knew the cost. Sir Robert Peel had already been accused of betraying his conservative party for assisting the cause of Catholic emancipation in 1829. Now, in 1844, he was mid-way through his second administration which turned out to be one of the most memorable of the nineteenth century. Britain was not involved in a major skirmish abroad this year, this ministry of Peel was the only prolonged period between 1830 and 1865 that Palmerston was out of foreign affairs.

1844 is remembered, instead, as a year of home affairs. The year when the first long-distance telegram was sent by means of Morse code over an electric wire, when the Bank of England was given precedence which led to its eventual monopoly of issuing notes, when the Co-operative movement was founded, and when the Corn Laws were modified.

Yet, as a result of one of the three worst trade depressions of the nineteenth century and a series of bad harvests, the year was one of what came to be called the Hungry Forties. And Peel's downfall was already foreshadowed as the potato blight crept across North America; and Ireland could be next. Too many people were helpless at this desperate time. Almost two million, of some sixteen million people in England and Wales, were on the pauper roll; and it has been estimated that only one in twenty-four of the population could vote.[1]

This would have meant that, in a county like Cornwall with some three hundred and forty thousand people,[2] only about fourteen thousand had a say in electing fourteen M.P.s. And, in any case, fourteen equal-size areas were not represented, as the boroughs of Bodmin, Truro and Penryn-Falmouth had two Members each, those of Helston, Launceston-Dunheved, St. Ives and Liskeard had one each, and the county at large was divided into two divisions with two Members each.[3]

But Cornwall could hardly grumble about representation, as it had been well known in Parliament before the 1832 Reform Act. No fewer than forty-four M.P.s had been returned from its 1,407 square miles.[4] Great names from the pages of history had featured in manifestos at Cornish elections, names like Raleigh, Wentworth, Gibbon and Huskisson for, as the county had been favoured with so many seats by virtue of being a royal duchy, it was one of the safest launch-pads into parliamentary orbit.

Yet this county in the far south west is virtually cut off from the British mainland by the River Tamar, an island but for four windswept miles of heath between its source and storm-lashed cliffs at Marsland on the north coast. From there, the arm of land, some forty-five miles across at its widest part and only seven at its narrowest, points out into the Atlantic for eighty miles towards America.[5]

It is a wild and lovely country of extremes - majestic rock formations, lapped by the Channel on the southern side and pounded by breakers on the northern shore; steep wooded valleys carved by tumbling streams and wide, lush estuaries where mellow air wafts lazy water. And, giving them substance, four granite moorlands roll down the interior from the Tamar to Land's End.

Like their land, the Cornish have a character moulded by dint of circumstance and climate. Their livings have been earned as fishermen on tossing boats at night, as miners crouched in hot and dripping tunnels, as quarriers of slate and hardest moorstone, and as farmers on a tough and hilly terrain.

So, in 1844, their talk was of the Corn Laws first and foremost. It was high time they were done away with. They had served their purpose since the end of the wars in 1815 and protected local growers from foreign competition. But now, with service-men back and the birth rate rising, there were too many people for home-grown stuffs to feed. The greater the demand, the higher the prices. And soon, the people would not be able to pay; farmers would cease producing if they couldn't sell. Already labourers had been laid off and had emigrated; even farmers themselves were going, 280 had sailed from Plymouth on the *Spermaceti* alone in February of 1843.[6] That was last year, when John Bright had spoken against the Corn Laws over to Liskeard and the place had been packed out in his favour. Better fit Peel got on with the job instead of biding his time with modifying.[7]

Yet, if the Cornish believed in free trade as far as corn was concerned, they were afraid of it when it came to minerals. Already, in 1838, Peel had reduced the import duty on foreign tin ore and the signs were that he would abolish it altogether. This could spell ruin to the local tin trade. It was already hampered with smelters stockpiling for the East India Company, at a contracted price often lower than could be fetched on the growing home market; and, if Peel let in foreign tin duty-free, what was happening abroad would happen here, Malayan alluvial tin worked by cheap labour would snatch the market from the Cornish.[8]

Not only tin would be affected if foreign ore took over, but copper would be too. Cornwall had become the world's main producer of this metal since Anglesey deposits had declined some years before, so many depended upon it for their livings.

It was all very worrying, especially at a time of general trade recession. For hundreds of laid-off miners, emigration was the only solution, their passages paid by colonies in need of populations. So, to Africa, America and Australia the Cornish Jacks and Jennys sailed from little ports like Fowey and Padstow. These were no voyages of discovery in adventure spirit, even although some who made them were better off than many who stayed behind. In foreign parts, the tempting higher wages in the new mines of the 1820's had gone and the rushes of gold and tin were yet to come.

They were, rather, journeys of necessity, a change in a way of life through force of circumstance.

The Cornish hated change unless its benefits were obvious. Their disdain for the re-introduced income tax, about 2¾p in the £ on incomes over £150 per year, had been evident at Falmouth in 1843. Having walked 104 miles in an area which should have yielded between £100 and £200, the local assessor had returned with the equivalent of 57½p for his trouble.[9]

They'd liked the changeover from parish relief to workhouses even less. Some four to five hundred Delabole slate quarriers had assembled at Camelford in 1837 to prevent the Poor Law commissioner enforcing the new provisions. Six of the new London policemen and sixty soldiers had been required to restore the peace.[10]

The Cornish were by no means alone in resenting the changes of the 1830s and 1840s, there was trouble elsewhere in the country. On the other hand, they were not all in favour of resisting what was new, Cornishmen were amongst the pioneers of the period. But the ordinary Cornish did tend to be conservative at heart.

The reason was because they were a people apart. They were not of Saxon blood in general, but Celtic. Smatterings of the ancient Cornish language, akin to Welsh and Breton, had been spoken naturally within living memory. If the tongue were almost forgotten now, an echo nevertheless remained in the sentence construction and intonation of the Cornishmen's speech which was foreign to the English ear.

Besides, the Cornish were not yet linked to England by a main line railway. Their clocks were set some twenty minutes later than Greenwich mean time.[11] Neither was there a county police force to keep them up to scratch.[12]

The Cornish 'belonged to do' what they 'belonged to do'. Country folk walked everywhere if they couldn't afford a mount or a seat on a cart. When offered what they thought of as charity, they refused in memorable style like the lady who declined a lift on the Bodmin-Wadebridge railway because she 'wanted to make haste'. [13]

Their spirit of independence came from a self-reliant way of life. Their fuel was the peat they cut from the moors. Their food was grown and raised on patches of land. Their clothes were made by themselves, or a local tailor or dressmaker, from Cornish cloth such as Pearce's turned out in Camelford from merino wool. [14]

On high days and holidays they went to fairs and markets in the towns, smallholders taking with them produce surplus to their own needs for the townsfolk to buy. To a certain extent, the townsfolk were dependent upon shops and tradesmen; but even they could hold out if supplies were cut off by such as a blizzard for they preserved the harvest of substantial gardens. When the Cornish had to buy, they tended to buy big, their flour in bushels and lard in wooden buckets. [15]

Their thrift was born of necessity. By most living standards, those of the small self-employed were low; and their attitude, in turn, governed the fate of the employed. In mining areas, 28 per cent of the male workers could expect to die through violence, lung disease, malnutrition or exhaustion by the time they were thirty.[16] In agricultural districts, life was hardly less harsh. Youngsters were put out to service, having had little or no education, and expected to stay with their masters.

Under such as the Master And Servant Act, rewards were advertised for the arrest of apprentices who escaped or labourers who broke contract. If they managed to get far enough away in time so that potential employers were ignorant of their circumstances, they were fortunate. Alternatives were a fine and a return to what they had run away from, imprisonment, or punishment for vagrancy.[17] There being only parish and borough constables, rather than county police forces, society itself was the brake on so-called crime and operated a system not far removed from the Saxon hue and cry.

In Cornwall, the system was aided by the discipline imposed upon members of the Methodist sect, which had a large following of the lower orders of society. Wesley hadn't had it all his own way when first arriving in the county back in 1743. He had been stoned and shouted down by the people and cold-shouldered by fellow Anglicans. But he had persisted, visiting Cornwall thirty-one times in all, and by the time he died in 1791 its people were singing his hymns, as only Celts can, and building chapels in every hamlet. [18]

It was also assisted by the advertising power of the newspapers. By 1844, the Cornish had the whig *West Briton*, the *Falmouth Packet*, and the tory *Royal Cornwall Gazette*. By and large, they were filled with the exploits of those who could not read. Ordinary people were illiterate unless they had attended a Sunday or dame school, or had been incarcerated in a workhouse or gaol, where instruction was given.[19] Newspapers were the lively entertainment of those lucky enough to have been born with silver spoons in their mouths, reading material and education were expensive luxuries. [20]

By courtesy of the local press which circulated scoops of information, Cornish news also appeared in the regional and London papers. In fact, had

Queen Victoria herself been scanning the *Morning Chronicle* on April 30, 1844, she might have noticed a piece sent up by the *Falmouth Packet* on page six.

It was headlined DREADFUL MURDER IN CORNWALL and featured a place called Davidstow.

All worthy & all drunkard

3. Davidstow was the forty-fourth largest parish in Cornwall, out of 209, when the Reverend John Wallis, assiduous vicar of Bodmin, was compiling his *Cornwall Register* in the 1840s. But, as only 408 persons lived on its 6,260 statute acres, it occupied forty-first place from the bottom in the county's population chart, according to the parson. [1]

Such statistics were of utmost importance to the Cornish for, as the county was largely rural and its scattered hamlets so small, it was necessary to give the name of a parish if asked where one came from; and, as the names of parishes generally coincided with the names of towns, it was also very convenient. There were exceptions like Camelford, which was in Lanteglos parish; but this was a good illustration of the fact that the Cornish had rarely taken to towns in the past.

They had developed in the middle ages, encouraged by earls of Cornwall or local lords, for the sake of commerce. The English and Norman-French had been the main settlers in the towns, while the Cornish had preferred to stay in their isolated farmsteads and tiny hamlets until fair times came round. It was not until the fourteenth century that Cornish names had appeared on the subsidy rolls of the towns in any number. [2]

Yet the Cornish never felt small. The boundaries of their minds were their parish ones; and these could encompass as many statute acres as St. Neot's 14,540 or as few as Tregoney St. Jameses 70.[3] What mattered was that they belonged to a community, a recognised unit of local government, church organisation and, until the workhouses, poor relief. So if a person were asked where he came from and answered Davidstow in reply, he would mean that he came from the *parish* on the northern side of Bodmin Moor and not necessarily from the *place* called Davidstow.

For that was Davidstow *churchtown* and he hadn't said that at all. That was the place centred upon the church, some 2¼ miles from Camelford, which had given the parish its name. The name showed that it was originally a Celtic settlement in honour of St. David of Wales; and when the Saxons had found this place called Dew in the Cornish language, they'd tacked on 'stowe' to make Dewstowe or Davidstow meaning 'place of David'. The churchtown - and 'town' to the Cornish could mean as little as a home or field - was the churchstead comprising essentially the church, its glebe lands and the rectory.

In Davidstow's case, it had hardly mattered if there were a rectory for the incumbent rarely used it. Way back in about 1230 it had become a vicarage because the tithes had been appropriated to the hospital of St. John at Bridgwater in Somerset. And, by 1385, those in charge of the parish were so remote that, when someone reported the vicar dead and another was put in his place, it was not until the death of the real one that the fraud was discovered. Most who held the office in the eighteenth century had lived elsewhere.[4] Even in 1844, there was no resident vicar at Davidstow. The Reverend John Glanville, who had the living, was also rector of Jacobstow. So, as he had preferred to live in that parish since 1833,[5] the vicarage was left to the curate, John Gillard, a forty-five-year old Devon-born cleric.[6]

The church tended to be the business of the gentry, anyway, the likes of those who sat on the bench at Lesnewth Division petty sessions on the first Monday every other month. The magistrates met in the long, low-ceilinged parlour of the inn at Halworthy, 1¾ miles up the road towards Launceston from Davidstow churchtown, on the edge of Wilsey Down. And it was said that prisoners who stood before them, from the seventeen parishes of the Division,[7] were handcuffed to a metal bar that reached from the floor to the ceiling of the room.

That could have been no joke to those involved. But Halworthy itself was something of a joke because, by 1844, it was also known as Alldrunkard and there were several stories as to how this name had come about. One maintained that the magistrates were all drunkards, during the sessions, instead of all worthy; another that Wesley had converted all the inn's drunkards and made the hamlet all worthy; and yet another reckoned that, when the soldiers of the Somerset and Cheshire militias had frequented the inn, while encamped near Camelford during the French invasion scare of the 1790s, it might as well have been called Alldrunkard.

In fact, the name seems to have derived from 'hal drümyow', meaning 'moorland ridges' in the Cornish language, the alternative Halworthy having apparently come from 'hal wortha' meaning 'higher moor'.[8]

If the church were the religious hub of the parish establishment, its secular life revolved around the inn at Halworthy, although it was on the edge of Davidstow and alongside the gutter separating it from Treneglos parish. Horses, feeding from nosebags, stood between carriage and van shafts near the upping stock in front of the stable, while business was conducted by their owners in the saloon or the yards. And talk in the skittle alley would turn to work in the marshes - as to how much sedge had been collected for use as packing between Delabole slates transported by boat, or the quality of down which was ready for the pillow makers, and as to the suitability of the weather for the cutting of peat.

Once a year, the inspectors of weights and measures would hire a room at the Halworthy inn; and the farmers' wives would turn up with their scales to be tested and stamped to ensure that the butter they sold to the dealers and markets was standard measure. Twice yearly, a small sheep market was held in the yard called fair plot. And, in the autumn, merchants from Wadebridge and Boscastle would hold dinners at the inn so that farmers who had afforded to buy Welsh coal, lime dressing and feed stuffs during the season, could pay their bills.[9] For thirty-three-year old William Northam and his family, who kept the inn, it was a constant round of parish activity.[10]

Come the Sabbath, however, and it was church or chapel in the afternoon and preaching in the evening at Davidstow, even although most of those expected to attend had livestock to see to as well. Proof enough of Lord's Day observance in the area had been when Camelford's mayor and aldermen back in 1820 enforced an Act to ensure that those carrying Sunday dinners from the common bakehouses would not waft them under the noses of others returning from Divine Service.[11]

Fair distances were covered on foot and horseback around Bodmin Moor on the Sabbath. One minister was erecting half-mile posts so that preachers and worshippers could find their way across the moorland between Watergate and Five Lanes. And that was five or six miles as the crow flies.[12]

With Methodism being a comparatively new denomination, people were still attending a parish church for one service and a Wesleyan chapel for the next. There had been chapels in Camelford and Altarnon and preaching places at Fentonadle and Tremail prior to 1815. Then Bible Christian chapels and more meeting houses had opened at Camelford and Advent in the following two decades. And, by 1844, Wesleyan Methodist (Reform) chapels had been built and yet more preaching places had opened in St. Breward, Camelford, Advent and Davidstow, so that there was a variety of Methodist alternatives to the parish churches on this side of Bodmin Moor.

As far as Davidstow parish was concerned, members of the new sect met at Trewassa (Bible Christian), Treseat (Wesleyan), and at Tremail, where the Reform Association had built a chapel in 1838.[13] And, as it was customary for farm servants to attend church or chapel with their masters and mistresses whether they liked to or not, services here would have been more popular than those of the church because they were simpler. But, wherever the serving lads and lasses met in 1844, there was an added interest for this was a leap year and it was anyone's guess who would be keeping company with whom by the end of the twelve-month.

* * * *

Amongst the worshippers of Davidstow parish were members of the household of Penhale farm, a sizeable holding about a mile and a quarter from Tremail chapel, adjoining the moor. There was its mistress, Phillipa Peter, a sixty-one-year old St. Breward-born widow.[14] Next was an unmarried son, John, who, although born in Davidstow almost thirty-eight years before, was regarded as being rather soft and desirous of stating more than he really knew when asked anything.[15]

Next to him was Matthew Weeks, a twenty-three-year old bachelor from Larrick, in Lezant parish, over Launceston way. Mrs. Peter was kindly disposed towards him, he was in his seventh year of service with her and dressed in a manner superior to the generality of farm servants, which gave him a very decent appearance.

It was just as well, because Matthew had not been especially endowed with good looks. He was about five feet four inches in height, and rather lame in his right leg so that he dipped a mite in walking. His face was pock-marked, his brows hung over his eyes to give him a sullen and dogged appearance and, even when he smiled, a toothless top left gum gave his mouth a peculiar conformation so that he seemed to smirk.

Nevertheless, Matthew had a good head of light-brown , curly hair, he conducted himself in a very becoming manner, and he looked younger than his years. The census enumerator had put him down as fifteen in 1841, although he'd been baptised nearly twenty-one years before. And, now, everyone thought he was a young-looking twenty-two when he was approaching twenty-four. But, as he could neither read nor write, he was whatever age anyone fancied.[16]

John Stevens was in a similar predicament. His age had been put down as twenty in 1841, when he was working for the Haynes at Trenewth. But now, three years later, when he *was* that age, his intelligence did not match his years. Yet he was honest enough presumably Mrs. Peter had thought when she'd taken him on at Penhale last Monday, March 25."That was Lady Day, which marked the end of winter and beginning of spring in the farming calendar, the quarter day that servants and casual labourers were taken on or laid off, according to need.

A girl who went by the name of Charlotte Dymond had been paid off on Lady Day by Mrs. Peter. And, with her notice to quit Penhale, she'd received four shillings in change which had included two silver fourpenny pieces.

Yet, despite the warning, Charlotte remained at Penhale where she had lived and worked for the past eighteen months. There was little alternative, unless she found a new position, because she wasn't wanted at home.

Known as a bastard child from Boscastle, on the north coast, Charlotte had first arrived at Penhale some six years before and had stayed for three years. Then she had left to work for the Haynes at Tremail for about a year and a half. And, since she had been back at the farm, Elias Bettinson of Davidstow had heard that her mother was against her. It was even rumoured that, rather than Charlotte should come inside her door, her mother would kill her. She was, as Elias put it, a poor friendless creature.

They thought she was about eighteen, she was a middle sized woman. But, if the census of 1841 was anything to go on, she was only sixteen, as she'd been been put down as thirteen then. Probably, the census enumerator had reckoned that she must have been born around 1828, the year that Charlotte, the Princess Royal, had died because that would have accounted for her forename. *Charlotte* was un-usual for her class, the name being generally given to children of such as clergymen and teachers - the literate people.

Whether she was sixteen or eighteen - and she might have known, as she could read and write - Charlotte Dymond made up the household at Penhale. Apparently possessed of considerable personal attractions, she was known to be pleased with admiration and was not insensible to the attentions that came her way. In fact, report had it that she was coquettish, a flirt.

For some time, however, she had been keeping company with Matthew Weeks. The two had first arrived at Penhale about the same time in 1838, when she was a child of ten or twelve and he a young man of eighteen. But it had been while Charlotte was working at Tremail, in 1841 and 1842, that the courtship had begun. And it had so flourished, since her return to join him in Mrs. Peter's service, that Matthew was in the habit of keeping Charlotte's best clothes in his bedroom box at Penhale.[18]

The Cornish-stone farmhouse with a steep slate roof was built as a north north-east, south south-west rectangle, its long frontage with a south south-easterly aspect allowing for a lean-to porch to protect the main entrance.

The ground floor was largely given over to a substantial kitchen, the window overlooking the front yard having a built-in seat. In the south south-westerly wall was a doorway, which led out into the mowhay or meadow that extended along the side and across the back of the farmhouse. And, across the kitchen from the front entrance, was the staircase.

The first floor was divided into four rooms, there being a back bedroom with a window overlooking the mowhay, and two front bedrooms either side of a middle chamber with a connecting door into one of them. In one of the four slept Mrs. Peter. Another was shared by her son John, who had his own bed, and her servants Matthew Weeks and John Stevens who slept together. And a third room was occupied by Charlotte Dymond.

Adjoining the farmhouse, on its north north-easterly side, was the barn which was slightly higher than, but with as long a frontage as, the house itself. And, leaning to its end wall, was the stable. Across the farmyard from the house, barn and stable was a terrace of single-storey out buildings which gave shelter to the cart, cattle and pigs.

Penhale was a fairly typical example of the thirty or forty farmsteads that made up Davidstow parish. Tithable acreages had varied from the eighteen of the church glebe to several hundred of a husbandman; and households usually comprised a farmer and wife, often a grandparent or other independent relative, an average of five children, and three or four servants. In 1841, when the Davidstow tithe map was completed, Penhale was assessed as 147 acres. And these, with the fifty-one acres of the adjoining Rosebenault holding, were run by a widow and son with the help of three resident servants in 1844.

* * * *

As the Penhale farmhouse was completely surrounded by its land, access to the outside world was achieved by following one or other of two main routes. Leaving the farmyard by the lane in a north-easterly direction, there was a choice of two ways when Penhale Field was reached: either of bearing left through Five Acres Field to a track which eventually joined the Davidstow churchtown to Moorhead road, or of bearing right through Trevanters to the lane between Trevilian's Gate and Halworthy. Alternatively, by following the lane from the farmyard in a north-westerly direction, then bearing south-west through four fields, Higher Down Gate at Moorhead was reached.[19]

The way up to the Gate was a climb, because Penhale was one of the Inney Valley farms. But, once at the top and across a strip of common, there was the Altarnon-Camelford road and, beyond it, Bodmin Moor - one hundred square miles of lonely tors and treacherous marshes, where mists swirled in from both coasts and the rainfall on the Camelford side was a third more than the Cornish average.[20]

About a quarter of a mile from Higher Down Gate, in the Altarnon direction, was a settlement on the moorland side of the road called Trevilian's Gate.

This, because of its name and position opposite the turning to Halworthy, seems originally to have been a toll gate. But the easternmost property, which had probably been the turnpike house, had been rebuilt in 1836 by Humphrey Craddock Vosper, a then fifty-one-year old carpenter who hailed from the parish of Northill near Launceston.

As the work undertaken by Vosper was within six years of the 1830 Beer Act, which removed taxes from ale and cyder for the two-fold purpose of boosting agriculture out of depression and of discouraging spirit drinking, he apparently took advantage of the opportunity it afforded. Any ratepayer could open his property as a public house upon payment of the equivalent of £2.10p to an excise officer for a licence. So, when Vosper's house was complete, he opened it as the *Brittannia Inn*.

Its sign, set into the wall above the front door, was noteworthy in that it was a stone taken from the doorway of the ruinous chapel of St. Michael on top of Roughtor. To its arch over a fleur-de-lis embellishment Vosper added his own initials, H.C.V., and the year in which the house was rebuilt, 1836.[21]

In 1844, he and his Cardinham-born second wife were running not only the inn but a small holding comprised of two cultivated fields behind the house and a garden across the road.[22] Adjoining the main property was the holding of Isaac Cory consisting of a house and three arable fields stretching westward along the moorland side of the road. And, opposite the furthest field, lived Sampson Prout and his family at Downhead or Moorhead, a tenement between Penhale's Higher Down Field and the Altarnon-Camelford road. [23]

Isaac Cory, who was about sixty-three, was a native of Jacobstow parish. In 1814 he had worked as an herdsman at Fernacre, on the moor near Roughtor in St. Breward parish; but, by 1818, he and his wife Maria had moved to live at Trevilian's Gate and, until at least 1841, he had worked as an agricultural labourer. It was only now, in 1844, that he felt able to describe himself as a small farmer.[24]

It is possible, because he and Matthew Weeks had once been colleagues, that Cory had laboured for Mrs. Peter at Penhale farm since arriving in Davidstow parish. When the 1841 census was taken, his son William was certainly a servant at Penhale with Matthew.

Since that time, however, there had apparently been a quarrel between Weeks and Isaac Cory over some lost bullocks, although Cory denied there had been an altercation. And Weeks seems to have made little of it, or John Stevens would have known.

Stevens, who had been taken on by Mrs. Peter at Lady Day, appears to have watched her right-hand man like a hawk, Matthew Weeks could not move for him. But, being so unintelligent, Stevens did not always get the hang of Matthew's business.

One day, for instance, he thought he saw him buy a knife from Charles Parsons. He saw money pass between the two and watched Matthew take something to his box. But, when he later investigated and found new braces instead, Stevens reckoned Matthew had merely looked at the knife then not purchased it. Had he mentioned the incident to Mrs. Peter, he would have been told that Matthew was never without a knife, his job required that he carried one, surely, and it would have been unremarkable had he bought a new one.

Undaunted, Stevens considered it significant that Matthew returned from visiting his widowed mother in Lezant with a paper about a murder. This was about a week after Lady Day, a week after Stevens had arrived at Penhale, and he had overheard Matthew mention the paper. But, as Matthew was unable to read, it was hardly material.

It was when it came to the relationship between the Penhale household and Thomas Prout, however, that Stevens's interest really quickened. [25]

A letter in his hand

4. Thomas Prout was subsequently to be described by Mrs. Peter as 'a servant man, about the same age as Matthew Weeks, of Helset in the parish of Lesnewth.' [1]

But, as there was neither a person of that name at Helset, when the census was taken in 1841 nor a family of that surname in Lesnewth parish during the early nineteenth century, the Thomas Prout in question must have been the one baptised at Davidstow in 1814. If so, he would have been Matthew's senior by six years, the son of a family that lived at Rosebenote, a tenement two fields away from Penhale farmhouse on the lane between Trevilian's Gate and Halworthy, and a brother of Sampson Prout who lived at Moorhead. [2]

In this case, it explains why he, like Isaac Cory, had once worked with Matthew Weeks; and why he visited Penhale although it was four miles as the crow flies, and considerably more by road, from where he now lived in Lesnewth.

But, that Matthew had no time for Prout, took barely a week for John Stevens to discover. Mrs. Peter was not the only one to overhear what happened in the Penhale mowhay a few days after Lady Day. Voices were raised. And Stevens tuned in.

Thomas Prout had apparently come upon Matthew in the meadow at the back of the farmhouse and, during the course of conversation, had announced that he was thinking of moving to live at Penhale. If he decided to, he informed Matthew, he would deprive him of his girlfriend, Charlotte Dymond.

Matthew gave a saucy retort. Prout goaded further. And, eventually, Weeks called him a few choice names.

When later asked what all the noise had been about in the mowhay that day, Prout admitted that he had had some words with Weeks. But he could not recollect, he said, if they had been about Charlotte.

John Stevens could have refreshed his memory. He had taken in every word. In fact, when Prout had gone, he himself had had a go at Matthew. He had heard, he said, that Prout might be moving in to Penhale; and, if that came about, Matthew would be losing Charlotte.

In his reply to this, Weeks was adamant about one thing. If Prout moved in to Penhale, he would move out. And the reason was, said Matthew, that he and Prout could never agree when they had lived together last time.

* * * *

Charlotte Dymond

Easter Sunday in 1844 fell on April 7.

On Easter Monday, Charlotte and Matthew were paid their dues by Mrs. Peter, there being a silver fourpenny piece (almost 1¾p) in Charlotte's five shillings (25p) but none in Matthew's wages. And, as people bought new things when money was around, Charlotte had evidently ordered a new bonnet cap. At any rate, on the evening of the following Saturday, April 13, Mrs. Peter noticed that one was delivered for her from a dress-maker.

That day, however, John Stevens was minding Matthew's business rather than Charlotte's. He had been at Penhale for almost three weeks by then and had never noticed Matthew shave, nor had he seen him with a razor. Yet there, outside the door, stood Weeks with a hone and a razor.

Phillipa Peter would hardly have noticed because she knew that he had a razor amongst his possessions. But Stevens was fascinated and engaged Matthew in conversation regarding the hone. And that was the trouble, Matthew told him, the hone was too hard to made a sweet edge on the blade. [3]

* * * *

The next day, Sunday, April 14, was a very dirty day as far as the weather was concerned. It was noticeable because, although three or four inches of rain had fallen during each of the first three months of 1844, the early part of April had been exceptionally fine. [4]

Whatever the weather, Sunday was changing day at Penhale, members of the household being expected to exchange the clothes they had worn all the week for clean ones, so that the dirty linen was ready for the wash on Monday morning. Accordingly, Mrs. Peter placed Matthew's best blue cotton stockings by his bedside; and, later on, sent Charlotte up to the bedroom he shared with her son and John Stevens with a clean shirt for him.

Although it was fairly new, the shirt had had a piece let into the shoulder during mending and the collar button's stitching had been re-newed with white cotton. It was probably while Charlotte was delivering the garment to Matthew that Mrs. Peter overheard him ask her to wash his waistcoat. [5]

Members of the household were in the kitchen by about half past ten that morning when Thomas Prout paid Penhale another visit. He sat on the settle by the fire for a while. Then, when he got up to go, Charlotte fetched her bonnet and followed him outside. It is unclear whether Matthew was already in the farmyard, followed the two outside, or stayed in the kitchen. Whatever, Mrs. Peter saw Prout in the yard at about eleven o'clock and, soon after, Matthew was saying, according to her, 'I cannot think what Charlotte and Thomas Prout can be talking of. What can they have to say to one another?'

'I cannot tell', replied Phillipa Peter. And Matthew left it at that.

Some time later, Mrs. Peter noticed Matthew outside the door with something like a letter in his hand. Then she saw that Charlotte was with him; and she thought how fond of each other the couple were, even although he seemed to be teasing Charlotte by preventing her catching the letter which she could read but he could not. Eventually, they came into the kitchen, still playing with the letter, and went upstairs.

Charlotte Dymond

* * * *

It was about five to four in the afternoon when they came down again. And Mrs. Peter was rather surprised to see that they had changed into their best clothes. Although Matthew had passed through the kitchen and into the porch, she did catch Charlotte before she joined him.

'Charlotte. Where are you going at this time?' Asked Mrs. Peter. 'You are too late for church or chapel in the afternoon and too early for preaching in the evening'.

There was no reply. Charlotte continued on her way. And John Peter, who was outside, saw her standing with Matthew in the front porch.

After about a minute, Charlotte returned to the kitchen to tell Mrs. Peter that, although she herself would not be back in time to milk the cows, Matthew would. To this, Mrs. Peter replied that, as Charlotte had been in the habit of staying out on Sunday evenings until after milking time and she, the mistress of Penhale, had done the milking for four Sundays up to then, she supposed she could milk the cows that evening.

Meanwhile, John Stevens was making his way towards the stable when he noticed Matthew in the front porch. And, taking the tail of his velvet jacket in his hand, Stevens said ''twas very foolish for you to be throwing away so much money in buying a new cloth coat for best, Matthew, when you had got such a good velvet one for Sundays.'

Matthew made no reply. He was very smart on Sundays in his best blue cotton stockings and short boots, his clean shirt, fancy waistcoat, and his greyish trousers newly cleaned and pressed. No wonder Stevens seemed worried by his appearance for the short, dark, velvet frock-coat which set it off was only his second best.

Then out came Charlotte in her Sunday finery. Mrs. Peter had taken it all in - the multi-coloured, green-striped gown, a darkish red cloth diamondy shawl, the brown silk bonnet with light ribbons, oval-ringed pattens to protect her shoes, and a black silk handbag trimmed with rusty lace.

But although her son and her servant watched the couple's progress through the farmyard and around the corner up the lane in the direction of Higher Down Gate, they were not quite as observant as Mrs. Peter. John Peter took in her bonnet and shawl and thought she had gloves on, while Stevens noticed only the shawl.

Despite the bad weather, however, no-one noticed an umbrella between the two. They appeared very friendly towards each other; and neither had said where they were going. It was as nigh as could be to four o'clock in the afternoon of Sunday, April 14, 1844 that Charlotte Dymond and Matthew Weeks set off for an unknown destination from Penhale farm.

* * * *

Some time later that evening, between half past five and half past nine, Isaac Cory of Trevilian's Gate arrived at Penhale. He had been, he said, to the afternoon service at Davidstow church. And, having stayed for a short time after it ended at half past three, it must have been about twenty to five by the time he reached his wheat field at Moor Lane, a quarter of a mile from his home.

'Whilst stopping to look at my wheat, I could see the moor just beyond Higher Down Gate to Lanlary Rock', Cory told Philippa Peter. 'From the place where I stood, I saw Matthew Weeks going along the moor. I knew him by the going of him, he walked upon the twist, his usual walk,'

'A woman was with him', Cory continued, 'going the right side of him, walking on with him. She was a young woman, with a red shawl on, and she had an umbrella which was up so that I could not see her bonnet. When I first saw them, they were about sixty yards from the corner of a field of mine adjoining the moor. They were on the moor side of the Davidstow (Altarnon-Camelford) road and that by a good bit.'

The mentioned field would have been at Trevilian's Gate so that the couple, when Cory first saw them, would have been some 500 yards away from him.

The farmer went on 'I stayed there, occasionally looking at them, for about twenty minutes. When I last saw them, they were about a quarter of a mile further out and in the direction of Lanlary Rock. I got back to my house at Vivian's (Trevilian's) Gate at about five o'clock. It had been foggy but I could see Roughtor and Lanlary Rock and Brown Willy plain.'

What Mrs. Peter was saying to all this is not recorded; but Cory went on with his tale. Upon reaching Trevilian's Gate, he said, 'I stopped. They were going on very steady, they did not stop, they were not going very fast.'

'The woman I saw on the moor with Matthew Weeks had pattens on', Cory assured Mrs. Peter, 'I say this from their having come in the direction from Higher Down Gate and my having followed the same track, in which there were recent marks of pattens.'

* * * *

By half past nine that evening, the time that Phillipa Peter's servants were expected to be in, Isaac Cory had left Penhale. Phillipa and her son, John, were seated at the kitchen table, reading in the candle light; and John Stevens was on the settle, a long bench with a high back.

The door opened and in came Matthew.

'Where's Charlotte?' Mrs. Peter asked him, as he eased himself onto the window seat inside the table.

'I don't know', Matthew replied.

'Matthew, you always say so, and then Charlotte comes in in a minute or two', his mistress smiled, 'I dare say she's outside.'

'I don't know any thing about her', Matthew insisted.

'She ought to have come in and fitted your supper', said Mrs. Peter, realising his ignorance of Charlotte's whereabouts was in earnest.

'Never mind, I'll go without supper', Matthew volunteered.

'tis not worth while to do that', Phillipa Peter replied, 'I'll get a little supper for thee' and she made a move to prepare a meal.

John Peter dropped his reading and looked at Matthew in the shadow of the window.

Charlotte Dymond

'Where is Charlotte, then?' he asked.

'I dare say she is gone to the moor to meet Tom Prout or else his brother, John', answered Matthew as his meal was served.

It was then, while he made a hearty supper as usual, that the other two men went upstairs to bed. After he had finished eating, he remained in the window seat for a while longer than he generally did, Mrs. Peter thought. But, at about half past ten, he unlaced his boots, put them under a chair at the bottom of the stairs, and went up to the bedroom he shared with John Peter and John Stevens.

Stevens was still undressing, in the dark, his version of the conversation since Matthew had come in alone doubtless turning over in his mind. Mrs. Peter had asked where Charlotte was. Matthew had replied that 'he had not seed her'. Mrs. Peter had said 'how not have seed her when you went away together?' And he couldn't recollect if Matthew had answered, or that Mrs. Peter had said anything more. Stevens got into the bed he shared with Matthew. And Matthew was soon undressed and into his side.

* * * *

Downstairs in the kitchen, Phillipa Peter waited up for Charlotte.

For an hour she was alone with her thoughts which were never divulged. But they may well have centred upon the events of that Sunday.....what had Charlotte been up to, running out after Thomas Prout like that; what was the letter she and Matthew had been playing with and where had it come from?

Where was Charlotte planning to go that afternoon, she'd never answered; and why had she said Matthew would be back for milking, when he probably had no idea he was expected to be. Whatever was Isaac Cory doing, watching a couple on the moor for twenty minutes and then only naming Matthew as the man and not Charlotte as the woman?

That didn't stand to reason. Everyone knew Matthew by his limp, sure enough, but they also knew he'd been keeping company with Charlotte for at least two years, they were continually together; and she belonged to wear her red shawl on Sundays. Besides, if Cory followed fresh patten marks to Penhale, they had obviously been made by Charlotte. It was strange that he could not name her as the woman on the moor.

And then Matthew had come in on his own saying he didn't know where Charlotte was. He always did; but, this time he'd meant it, and Charlotte hadn't appeared. She'd observed nothing remarkable in his manner or appearance, although she had been surprised at his sitting so long in the window seat.

Where *was* Charlotte? It was half past eleven at night. She would go to bed for there was a busy week ahead. But Matthew would answer for it in the morning.

The candle was snuffed. Penhale was in darkness by midnight on that Sunday, April 14, 1844.

* * * *

Charlotte Dymond

Her mother would kill her

5. The next day, Monday, April 15, Matthew Weeks was first out of the bed he shared with John Stevens. As he was in the habit of sleeping in his shirt, he was still in the one that Charlotte had brought up to him the previous morning, although the other clothes he now put on were different from those he wore on Sunday.

Stevens knew Matthew's habits and noticed his Sunday best on the bedroom box for, although he got up after Matthew, he beat him to it downstairs. There, in the kitchen, Mrs. Peter had been up and about for some time. It was wash day. There was a busy week ahead. Charlotte, her assistant, was missing. And Matthew was still not down to help her milk the cows.

She went to the bottom of the stairs and shouted up for him. Then she added 'for it's your work you've put away the maid (Charlotte) in this clandestine way.'

She heard no answer from Matthew. But, soon, he appeared; and together they did the milking. Phillipa Peter made no secret of her annoyance. She expected her servants to be in by half past nine, she said; she had never known Charlotte to stay out until eleven o'clock, let alone all night; Matthew must know where she was. He, however, expressed no surprise at her absence and insisted that he knew nothing about her.

Some time later, while Mrs. Peter was in her bedroom, Matthew appeared at the door and asked if he might have Charlotte's clothes; and, as he had been in the habit of keeping them in his box, she let him have Charlotte's trunk. This, he took into the middle chamber where he left it; but, into his bedroom, he took the better items of clothing from it - Charlotte's best yellow gown, a black silk whiff or kerchief, two collars, and a bonnet cap. [1]

Then Mrs. Peter's twenty-nine-year old married daughter, Mary Westlake, arrived from Halworthy where she lived.[2] And, naturally, she asked where Charlotte was.

'It's no use for to ask me', her mother replied, 'you must ask of Matthee'.

Mary did ask of Matthew. But he repeated, what he had been saying ever since he had come in without her the night before, that he knew nothing of her whereabouts.

'Don't you provoke me again', Phillipa Peter warned him, 'for you do know,'

Matthew made no reply. Then, as though to turn the subject, Mary Westlake thought, he asked her mother if she were going to change his bed.

After the 12 - 1 p.m. mid-day meal, it was, that Mrs. Peter went up to make, rather than change Matthew's and Stevens's bed; and soon she was tackling Matthew again, for, by it, she found the blue cotton stockings she had put there clean on the Sunday morning, but now they were dirty and wet.

She was, she said, frightened to find them covered with mud up to the knees, the same as if Matthew had been cutting turfs. When this was done on the moor for peat, the pits from which the fuel was cut were at least two feet deep and very soggy.

'I'm very surprised to have to wash the stockings again, Matthee', she remarked.

'It was very dirty (weather)', he explained.
" ' tis turfy mud", Mrs. Peter scolded, 'there was some little rain yesterday, but nothing like enough to get the stockings in the mess they are'.

That evening or the next morning, Phillipa Peter was too confused to remember exactly, she washed the stockings. And then she had another go at Matthew with regard to Charlotte's whereabouts; and, this time, he was forthcoming.

He had gone with her, he said, as far as Higher Down Gate. There, she had left him and gone to the moor while he had made for Halworthy, three miles in the opposite direction. At Halworthy, he had seen a light in Mr. Northam's window but had not called at his inn; instead, and as Mrs. Peter's daughter, Mary, and her husband, John Westlake, had not been in, he had called at John Westlake's mother's, Sarah Westlake's, house.

What Phillipa Peter made of this is not recorded. It certainly did not tally with Isaac Cory's tale of having seen Weeks on the moor with a woman.

One day without Charlotte was over. And the Penhale household went to bed uneasy in her absence.

* * * *

It was the following day, Tuesday, April 16, that John Stevens first noticed that Matthew's shirt was ripped at the collar and a button was missing. How he had failed to remark upon this on Sunday 14 and Monday 15, when he worked with Matthew all day and slept in a bed with him at night while in the shirt, defies explanation. Matthew's every movement seems to have been under the closest scrutiny since he had returned alone on the Sunday evening, yet other members of the household also appear to have overlooked the state of the shirt.

However, it was Tuesday when Stevens noticed it and remarked to Matthew that the shirt must have been badly sewn to have torn so early in the week, when it was almost new; yet he did admit, he said, that it had been mended once before. Matthew nodded.

Opposite, and in view of, the side door of the kitchen was the shute that supplied the farmhouse with water; and, above the place where it ran into a trough, a thorn tree grew. There, sometime during the Tuesday morning, Phillipa Peter noticed Charlotte's bonnet cap as though it had been hung up to dry.

'Matthew', she said, 'how came Charlotte to go away and leave that pretty lace in the thorn; surely she did not. You come and take it in.'

'I'll come up and drag it in', came Matthew's reply.

'Don't you do that for to tear it', warned Mrs. Peter, 'I'll send up the little maid to pick it off.'

Upon inspecting the bonnet cap after its recovery from the thorn, Mrs. Peter pronounced it 'very badly washed'. And this day or some other, she could not be sure, she came upon Matthew's best light waistcoat, which had never been washed, hanging on the hedge. She remembered having heard Matthew ask Charlotte to wash it for him; but, judging it not to be up to her standard, she took it in and washed it again. [3]

Charlotte Dymond

Meanwhile, Elias Bettinson arrived at Penhale. As there were three of that name in Davidstow parish - the seventy-four-year old grandfather at Tremail, the forty-seven-year old father at Trewassa, and his son in his late teens - it is unclear which one encountered Matthew in the garden. Whichever it was, he was well acquainted with Charlotte Dymond, so it was probably the eldest who who had lived nearby where she had worked at Tremail. [4]

'Matthee, they tell me she's gone.' Elias said. 'Where's she gone to?'

'I don't know', Matthew replied. 'Can you tell me where we can get a maid?'

'No', replied Elias; and then went on 'a poor friendless young creature, they say her mother's against her.'

'They tell me so too', agreed Matthew, 'and rather than she should come inside her door, the mother would kill her. If Charlotte's found dead, her mother would have to hold her hand at the bar and be tried for her life.'

Whether or not Elias advised Philippa Peter of this conversation or she overheard it herself, she became even more determined to have it out with Matthew that day. So, in the afternoon, she tackled him. She would insist, she told him, on his telling her where Charlotte was. And, if he did not tell her, he would be made to. She would apply to a magistrate before she slept.

'If I must tell you the truth', began Matthew, 'she's gone to Blisland to service.' And then, as Phillipa Peter listened, he explained that Charlotte had told him that she had been given a week's notice by Mrs. Peter and that Rebecca Lanxon, Mrs. Peter's eighteen-year old niece, had got an easier place for Charlotte in the parish of Blisland. [5]

'How could Charlotte go to Blisland Sunday night?' asked Mrs. Peter, " 'tis ten miles away and she couldn't get there before dark."

Matthew replied that Charlotte had said that she intended sleeping at Hezekiah Spear's at Brown Willy, Cornwall's highest hill, the first night and going on from there to Blisland the following day.

'What did she say then?' asked Phillipa Peter in amazement. 'And when did the week's notice expire? Hardly on a Sunday, I should think! I never give notice on a Sunday, yet I must have done if the notice was up last Sunday.'

There seemed no answer to this, so she continued, 'why did she not go away at Lady Day, Matthew? I gave her warning (notice) for Lady Day and she did not go.[6] I had not given Charlotte warning (Sunday 14), nor she me, and I had no idea of her leaving my service.'

Matthew volunteered no more.

It was all very disturbing for Phillipa Peter. Even although she had overheard him ask Charlotte to wash his waistcoat, she suspected that the bad washing of this and of her bonnet cap had been his doing. And the thought that Charlotte might have been murdered, had she known of the conversation between Matthew and Elias Bettinson, was probably the cause of her threatening him with a magistrate.

But his latest yarn did tally with Cory's tale about a woman on the moor making for Lanlary Rock, that was certainly in the direction of Spear's at Brown Willy. Yet Cory had maintained that Matthew was on the moor, while he himself had said he was at Halworthy. It still didn't add up.

Charlotte Dymond

That evening, Phillipa Peter was in the kitchen where John Stevens and Matthew sat at the table. And she overheard Matthew ask Stevens for his needle and thread.

'What for?' enquired Stevens.

'I want to sew in a button to the collar of my shirt', came the reply.

'I've got some thread, but it is too dark', Stevens apologised, 'it would not look well and my needle is very rusty and not fitting for it.'

'Let me see the needle and I'll scour it', Matthew persisted.

At this point, Mrs. Peter broke into the conversation.'Matthee, if you'll help milk, I'll sew it in with white (cotton) and do it well.'

Matthew neither answered nor offered her the needle and thread, as she thought he might have. Instead, he sewed on his button with Stevens's rusty needle and black thread.

* * * *

Matthew's obstinacy obviously did not improve Phillipa Peter's temper for the next morning, Wednesday, April 17, she was at him again.

" 'twas your work to put away Charlotte", she told him as they finished the milking, " 'twas a very bad trick. Jealousy made you do it. 'tis no use putting her down to Blisland to keep her from men, there are men there as well as at home."

'I never put her up to go', protested Matthew, 'I never slocked her away. She had a letter for her to go from Rebecca Lanxon, who was here some time before and promised to get a place for her and to let her know.' [7]

Phillipa Peter remembered that her niece had, indeed, stayed at Penhale during the winter; and, if she would but admit it, she had noticed something like a letter in Charlotte's bag.[8] But, not being satisfied, 'which way did this letter come?' she asked.

'I don't know which way it came', said Matthew, 'but she had a letter.'

But there was no pleasing the household now. As soon as Mrs. Peter had finished, John Stevens started with 'Charlotte is not come back, then, Matthee; wherever is she gone?

'I don't know', said Matthew.

'It's a very curious thing you don't know', persisted Stevens, 'for you and she went away together and we have not seen anything of her since.'

'It is', agreed Matthew.

'Where did you leave her?' Stevens asked, as though he had not already heard.

"I went a little way out along with her" , Matthew explained, "and she said to me 'I don't want you to go any further now'. I then turned and came back and I have not seen her since."

'You was seen going out over the moor together'. Stevens knew; and had probably awaited his chance to say this for Matthew's reaction. Yet he received nothing but silence in reply.

It was not long before Mrs. Peter's soft son John was baiting Matthew, also, with -

'Where's Charlotte, Matthew?' And then 'you were seed going out Higher

Charlotte Dymond

Down Gate together.'

'No-one saw me beyond the gate', Matthew assured him.

'Isaac Cory saw you', John Peter retaliated.

'No-one saw me', said Matthew, ' and no-one spoke to me.'

* * * *

On Thursday, April 18, nothing particular passed, as far as Phillipa Peter was concerned, more than that she again found fault with Matthew 'for putting away the maid (Charlotte) at this time, when 'tis a busy week'. But he only replied that he'd had nothing to do with her going away.

Although he had denied that he knew anything about Charlotte on the Sunday evening and Monday, he had, since Phillipa Peter had pressed him, stuck to his story of leaving her at Higher Down Gate and going himself to Halworthy, while she made for an easier position at Blisland. Mrs. Peter admitted this.

To other people, Matthew had not told all. But to his employer, 'if I must tell you the truth', he had said, he had outlined what he had been told by Charlotte and what he himself had done. Yet Phillipa Peter just could not reconcile his story with the fact that Charlotte had taken with her nothing more than she'd stood up in on Sunday, April 14.

* * * *

On Friday, April 19, however, attention turned to the pig which was to be killed. And Phillipa Peter had arranged for the thirty-two-year old farmer and butcher of nearby Trevivian to undertake the job.[9] John Chapman duly arrived and was accompanied to the pig shed, across the farmyard from the house, by Matthew, John Peter and John Stevens.

Stevens could recite Matthew's wardrobe by heart: three pairs of trousers, which were a light fustian pair, his greyish Sunday pair, and the week-day cord ones; two pairs of boots, which included his common skuted and nailed pair and a best pair with heel skutes and toe plates; and two jackets, the new cloth coat and the second best velvet frock coat. For the pig kill, Stevens noted, Matthew wore his cord trousers, common boots, and the shirt that Charlotte had taken up to him on the morning of Sunday 14. Trousers and boots were optional, but the shirt had to be worn until a clean one was received on the coming Sunday morning.

All was ready in the pig shed, when Matthew asked the butcher if he might kill the animal. As Chapman agreed, Matthew took a knife and made towards the pig.

His first thrust was unsuccessful. In fact, John Peter maintained that Matthew put it down to its having given him 'a turn' and he seemed surprised at this because, as Matthew was subject to occasional nose bleeds, it could not have been the sight of blood.

But as far as Chapman, the butcher, was concerned, it was because Matthew had the wrong knife for the job; and he provided him with another.

With this, Matthew struck the pig with great force and the creature fell dead at his feet. [10]

Charlotte Dymond

The neighbours are saying

6. By Saturday, April 20, Charlotte Dymond had been missing from Penhale farm for six days. But nothing had been done to discover the girl's whereabouts or to establish the truth or otherwise of Weeks's story. In 1844 there was no county constabulary, neither public information nor telephone systems. Penhale was virtually cut off from the world.

Yet news of Charlotte's disappearance was spreading around Davidstow parish. Mary Westlake had taken it back to Halworthy. Elias Bettinson, if he had not already known and called at Penhale to find out more, had returned with it to the Tremail area. And Isaac Cory was doubtless telling callers at the *Brittannia Inn,* Trevilian's Gate, that he had seen Matthew Weeks on the moor with a woman on the Sunday that Charlotte had vanished.

This obviously affected the attitude of the locals towards Matthew. It was most noticeable as far as John Peter was concerned for it was he who told or reminded Matthew that Cory had seen him beyond Higher Down Gate and, being soft, he could not let it be with one telling.

John Chapman, the butcher, had returned to Trevivian with the latest details after the pig kill. And as William Hocken, his twenty-nine-year old neighbour, had a field adjoining Penhale's Higher Down Field, it was hardly by chance that he ran into Matthew there on the Saturday. The conversation that ensued was carefully remembered by him.

'What has become of Charlotte?' Hocken asked Matthew.

'I can't tell, I believe she's run away', said Matthew.

'How can't you tell?' enquired Hocken, 'I am informed that you went away with her.'

'It's true, I did go away with her', Matthew readily admitted, 'but I do not know what has become of her now.'

At this, John Peter arrived on the scene and Hocken turned to him and said: 'I've been joking Matthew about what has happened to Charlotte'

'He put her away out of the way of Thomas Prout', replied Peter.

'How put her out of the way?' Hocken asked. 'Where has he put her to?'

'Out on the moors', John Peter answered.

'How put her to the moors?' persisted Hocken. 'It is rather too cold to put her out summering yet'.

Evidently, and in the belief that the neighbouring farmer was joking, Matthew joined in the exchange with 'who knows that?'

'People saw you go out at this (Higher Down) Gate', John Peter replied; but his tone told Matthew that *he* was not joking, although Hocken had tried to sound light-hearted.

'They could not swear to (its being) me', said Matthew, 'they never spoke to me.'

'If *they* cannot swear to you', retorted John Peter, 'Isaac Cory can for he saw you go by his wheat field hedge.'

'Cory cannot swear to me. He never spoke to me', Matthew was adamant.

'I don't like to hear so much about this swearing', Hocken broke in. He had been fishing for details when he'd first encountered Matthew; now, with Peter's help, the bait had been swallowed and he could wind up. 'It appears evident to me', he told Matthew, 'that there is something serious and amiss in the matter. To be sure, Matthew, you have not put her out on the moor and destroyed her.'

'No, I have not', said Matthew, 'they cannot swear anything against me'.

'I don't like to hear so much about your swearing', Hocken told Matthew again; then, turning to his neighbour, he said 'it appears plain to me, Mr. Peter, that this girl is destroyed. The girl has now been wanting a week'.

'They can't swear anything against me', Matthew repeated. And Hocken had afterwards to admit that an innocent man might have said the same. [1]

But Matthew's behaviour that week had demonstrated his belief that the household and society, of which he had been a member for some six years, had little faith in his word. He had accounted for his movements on Sunday 14 to an obviously disbelieving mistress and so he had miserably refused to take in the bad washing on the Tuesday. He had divulged Charlotte's intention to take up new employment, yet seen the doubt in Mrs. Peter's face and so he had obstinately rejected her offer to mend his shirt.

He had shown willing to participate in normal conversation ; but it must have seemed that everyone was out to trick him into confession. John Stevens caught him with his money on this Saturday and talked to him about it. Matthew mentioned that Charlotte had asked if she might borrow half-a-crown (12½p) but he had said he could lend only eighteen pence (7½p). Then, what had become of the three silver fourpenny pieces (5p altogether) Matthew had been seen with recently, Stevens wanted to know. Charlotte had had such coins in her wages and Matthew had had none, was inferred. Didn't Matthew remember having said they would do to pass as sixpences (2½p)?

Things were drawing to a head.

'Matthee, there's very bad talk about you, about the maid (Charlotte)', Mrs. Peter told him that evening as he sat in the kitchen window-seat. 'The neighbours are saying that you've certainly destroyed the maid. You are a very bad man if you've done it, you were always so loving together, you ought to be hung in chains.' [2]

This allusion to a former practice, of covering a hanged body with pitch and placing it in a metal frame to swing from a wayside gibbet as a warning to passers-by, must have shaken Matthew coming, as it did, from his mistress. He had depended on her.

He got up from the window seat without a word, went over to the dresser on the far side of the kitchen, and stood there with bowed head. [3]

John Peter and John Stevens, who had been listening and watching, moved out of the room and upstairs to bed.

Phillipa Peter and Matthew were left alone in the kitchen.

'Matthee', she said, 'I want you a minute, here, to talk with you.'

Matthew said nothing. He undid his shoes.

And then he went right up over the stairs as quickly as he could.

* * * *

Charlotte Dymond

The morning of the next day, Sunday, April 21, was very fine. The Penhale household was up early as usual. And, as Matthew was dressing, Phillipa Peter entered his bedroom.

'I think I ought to have Charlotte's clothes', she told him, 'I do not like the talk (in the neighbourhood) and I think I should have them until it's settled'.

Matthew handed Charlotte's clothes to her without a word. And then Mrs. Peter noticed his greyish trousers, which he'd worn out with Charlotte the Sunday before.

'I observe your trousers are dirty', she said in surprise, 'how have they become so, when they were cleaned and ironed for last Sunday?'

Matthew picked up the trousers and looked at the back of them. 'They are not very dirty', he said.

'It is not at the back they are dirty', scolded Phillipa Peter, 'but at the knees'.

'It was very dirty weather', explained Matthew.

'Not so dirty as to bring the dirt up to your knees', Mrs. Peter replied.

Very soon, Mrs. Peter, her son John, John Stevens and Matthew were breakfasting in the kitchen in their working clothes. And, afterwards, Matthew went out to see to the bullocks. When he'd gone, it was arranged that John Peter and John Stevens should ride to Brown Willy to enquire at Hezekiah Spear's if Charlotte had been expected there and had, in fact, stayed the night on the previous Sunday. They were then to go on to the parish of Blisland and discover whether or not Rebecca Lanxon had written to Charlotte and she had arrived there to take up a new position on the Monday.

John Peter and Stevens thereupon made ready to go. By 9 a.m., according to Mrs. Peter, or 10 a.m. according to Stevens, they were setting off in the direction of Higher Down Gate when Stevens saw Matthew in the doorway, having returned from the bullocks.

With the two men gone, Matthew went into the kitchen where Phillipa Peter was. And, without a word, went upstairs. Within a short time, he was down again, and Mrs. Peter saw that he had changed from his working clothes into his very best cloth frock coat, his best waistcoat, and the greyish trousers and best boots he'd worn on the previous Sunday. She also noticed that he carried his umbrella.

'You must mind to be back to dinner in time', she warned him, as he was going out, 'I shall not wait'.

'I'll be back to dinner, or directly after', she heard him say.

'What be you going to do with your umbrella this fine weather?' she enquired.

But Matthew had left her without an answer.

It was not long before Mary Westlake, her daughter, arrived from Halworthy. And, soon, the two had decided to take advantage of Matthew's being out until dinner time to search his bedroom.

Coming upon the second best velvet jacket that Matthew had worn out with Charlotte the previous Sunday, Mary Westlake searched the pockets. In one on the outside, she found Matthew's red cotton handkerchief which, like his umbrella, Mrs. Peter remembered Charlotte sometimes borrowed. In the inside, breast pocket of the jacket, Phillipa Peter found a green gauze handkerchief, which Mary Westlake recollected having borrowed to wear home one night and therefore identified as having been Charlotte's property.

It was assumed by the women that, as the handkerchiefs had not been amongst the clothes Matthew had collected from Mrs. Peter the previous Monday and she had retrieved from him earlier that Sunday morning, one or both of them had been worn by Charlotte when she had left the farmhouse with Matthew. But, presumably to allay any suspicions Matthew might have had that his privacy had been violated, they left the articles in the pockets of the jacket.

It was probably this morning, or it might have been the next, that the two also looked into Matthew's bedroom box. Phillipa Peter was anxious to find the razor she knew he possessed, and any knives. Nothing of this nature was found. But they did come across the paper about a murder, that Stevens had overheard Matthew mention having brought back from his mother's three weeks before. It was a story about a man in prison being supported by his daughter.

The mid-day meal time came around and Matthew had not returned. But he had, of course, said that he might be slightly later.

During the afternoon, John Peter arrived back at the farm on his own. John Stevens had apparently ridden on the to Lanxons in Blisland parish alone, while he brought the news from Hezekiah Spear at Brown Willy. As in the case of the Bettinsons of Davidstow, there were three who went by the name of Hezekiah Spear in St. Breward parish - the sixty-five-year old grandfather at Poladrick, the thirty-one-year old father, and his ten-year old son in the churchtown.

The one in question was probably the middle-aged who, at the time of the 1841 census, was a shoemaker and by the 1851 return had become a grocer and miller. In the meantime and now in 1844, it seems, he described himself as an herdsman. The tithe map of 1840 showed no-one of that name with a holding at Brown Willy but he had probably rented a plot there since.

On Sunday, April 14, he had told John Peter, he had returned from chapel at about five o'clock . This would have meant that he had attended the afternoon service in the churchtown or at Treswallock, a hamlet between it and Brown Willy.

Hezekiah, otherwise known as Ezekias or Caius, had also told Mrs. Peter's son that he had slept at home that night; and that Charlotte Dymond 'did not come there either that night or the next day'.*And, having heard this, the mistress of Penhale must have been truly perplexed.

Perhaps Matthew had made up the tale that Charlotte had said she was going to stay there, or maybe Charlotte had said so but had not kept her word. Perhaps Charlotte had not been the woman Isaac Cory was supposed to have seen making towards Lanlary Rock in the direction of Caius Spear's, or maybe it had been Charlotte but with someone other than Matthew, despite the mystery man's limp. Perhaps Isaac Cory had seen nothing at all, or maybe Spear was not telling the truth.

And still Matthew Weeks had not come back to Penhale for his dinner, or anything else.

At about six o'clock in the evening , John Stevens returned from the parish of Blisland. There, he had visited Mrs. Peter's niece, Rebecca, who lived at Metherin. And the message he brought from her and her husband, George Lanxon, who was almost thirteen years her senior, confirmed the worst fears and suspicions. The Lanxons had denied sending either Matthew or Charlotte a letter and had neither expected nor received her on the previous Sunday or Monday. Rebecca had maintained, moreover, that she had had no idea that Charlotte intended to leave Mrs. Peter's service and had therefore never looked for, let alone found, a new position for the girl.

* * * *

So Matthew Weeks had been guilty of something and had fled the district. He must have guessed that John Peter and John Stevens were headed for Brown Willy and Blisland that morning and known that they would break his story on returning. Allaying suspicion by taking nothing with him and saying he'd be back to dinner, he'd made off.

This was right, to a point. Matthew *had* left the district. But to say that he went, as a thief in the night or a murderer on the run, would be to press the evidence too far. He had been given to understand what Charlotte had intended by the girl herself; and he had explained what he had been doing. His own alibi still stood, unchallenged; he had, when he left, no knowledge of the news which would come from Brown Willy and Blisland. Davidstow, also, knew nothing until the return of Mrs. Peter's son and servant. Yet, during the past week, the parish had pointed an accusing finger; and an air of suspicion had pervaded the household where he lived and worked.

Thus, having completed his usual chores, Matthew had walked out of Penhale in broad daylight on that fine Sunday morning of April 21. He had left his dirty linen at his bedside, as was the custom every Sabbath in the farmhouse, when he changed from his working clothes. And he went from the place that had been his home for the past six years in his Sunday best, the umbrella serving a purpose no more sinister than of aiding his lameness.

He had a long walk ahead, at least eleven miles, to the parish of Lezant where his widowed mother and family lived.

Small marks of blood

7. The day after Matthew walked out of Penhale, Monday, April 22, was the eighth day of Charlotte's disappearance. Yet still no-one had really looked for her and rumour continued to be rife, particularly as word spread that Weeks had absconded.

Wash day had come around again. And Phillipa Peter went into Matthew's bedroom in search of dirty linen, as usual. By his and Stevens's bed, she found the shirt which she had given Charlotte to take up to him on the morning of Sunday 14. The shirt which Matthew had worn for the past seven days, through the pig kill and perhaps nose bleeds, to which he was occasionally subject, and on which she had watched him sew a button the previous Tuesday evening.

Inspecting it closely, she found that its breast pleats were 'unripped', the collar was partly torn from the body of the shirt and that there were several small marks of blood on it, some having deeper stains than others. From the state of the shirt, she deduced that great violence must have taken place to make it so. This, together with other evidence against Matthew, and Charlotte's disappearance, added up to one thing in her mind. He had premeditated and carried out her murder.[1]

Stevens had thought he saw Matthew buy a knife from Charles Parsons; and had watched him hone a razor on Saturday, April 13. She herself had heard Thomas Prout goad Matthew into saying he'd leave Penhale if Prout came to work there and took Charlotte away. Matthew had asked her what Prout and Charlotte were talking about on the Sunday morning; and she had personally accused him of being jealous and getting rid of Charlotte to keep her from other men.

Matthew had set out with Charlotte. Isaac Cory had watched a couple on the moor. Matthew had returned without Charlotte and cooked up the Brown Willy and Blisland yarn when threatened with a magistrate; and it *had* been a yarn because Spear and the Lanxons had refuted it.

His stockings and trousers had been muddied to the knees, as though he'd been in a marsh. Charlotte's bonnet cap and his waistcoat had been found badly washed. He'd insisted upon sewing a button on his shirt himself, doubtless so that she did not see that it was torn; and he'd asked to kill the pig, although she'd engaged John Chapman, the butcher, obviously to account for the blood spots. And, according to her son, John, Matthew had said that his first thrust with the knife had given him a turn.

She'd found Charlotte's handkerchief in his velvet jacket pocket, and a murder story in his box. And Matthew had mentioned the possible murder of Charlotte to Elias Bettinson.

John Stevens had seen Matthew with three silver fourpenny pieces. She had given Matthew none, that she could remember. But Charlotte had had two in her Lady Day pay four weeks before and one in her Easter wages a fortnight ago and had not been known to have spent money lately.

There had been no answer from Matthew when she had said he ought to be hung in chains. He had vehemently denied putting Charlotte away through jealousy, yet his explanations of her disappearance to everyone else had conflicted with what he had told her. Finally, he had run off in that sly manner so as not to arouse suspicion until it was too late to catch up with him.

* * * *

Despite church or chapel in the afternoon and preaching in the evening every Sunday, Phillipa Peter and her household, Davidstow and its parishioners, had collected circumstantial evidence against Matthew Weeks, had tried him in their minds, and had found him guilty of a pre-arranged and violent crime.

It all added up very neatly, give or take a few convenient lapses of memory and a slight discrepancy here and there. Yet all that was known to have taken place up to then was that a girl had disappeared; and, as far as anyone would admit, Weeks had been the last person seen with her.

The knife Stevens thought he saw Matthew buy turned out to have been braces. Weeks had said nothing about taking it out on Charlotte if Prout moved into Penhale but merely that he himself would move out.

As Charlotte and Matthew had been courting for some time, it was only natural that he should be curious as to her conversation with Prout on the Sunday morning. And, as for jealousy, it is evident that several were jealous of Matthew rather than he of them. Thomas Prout obviously coveted his girlfriend Charlotte. John Stevens envied Matthew's wardrobe. And Isaac Cory had apparently quarrelled with him, despite his denial. These three men, at least, could not be counted admirers of Matthew Weeks.

Matthew had, indeed, set out with Charlotte. Cory's tale conflicted with his, regarding his whereabouts on Sunday 14; and Spear and the Lanxons denied knowledge of Charlotte's movements that day. It was their word against Weeks's. Yet it was not his, if he were telling the truth, but Charlotte's; for he maintained that he divulged only what she had told him she intended to do.

Had he been guilty of something, he would surely have hidden or tried to wash his muddied stockings and trousers instead of allowing them to be found. He would hardly have honed a razor openly. His knife, had it already killed a girl, should have been more effective on the pig even if he momentarily suffered from loss of nerve.

Similarly, if his shirt were evidence of a violent struggle, he would hardly have mended it so nonchalantly in front of witnesses. It had already been repaired; and Stevens's surprise, that it had ripped 'so early in the week' showed that it was quite usual for shirts to be torn by wash day during work on the farm. As for the blood spots Mrs. Peter discovered on the Monday, April 22, they had obviously got on the shirt at the pig kill on Friday, 19, because Stevens did not notice them the previous Tuesday, whereas he *had* remarked on the rip and the missing button. And Matthew's volunteering to kill the animal, despite the butcher's being there, was probably in order to re-ingratiate himself with a suddenly hostile household.

The fact that Matthew had Charlotte's handkerchief in his pocket was as significant as Charlotte's having been known to borrow his umbrella and handkerchief, or his being in the habit of keeping her clothes in his box. They were courting. It was share and share alike.

As for the badly washed waistcoat and bonnet cap, Mrs. Peter had heard Matthew ask Charlotte to wash his waistcoat; and, as a new bonnet cap had been delivered, she had probably decided to wash the old one. The fact that she had hurriedly swirled the garments around in the outside trough, instead of washing them properly, was hardly Matthew's fault. There was the difficulty, of course, of explaining why Charlotte had worn no bonnet cap at all on Sunday 14, because one was in her trunk and the other found on the thorn and she possessed only two. But it would be just as hard to explain why, if he had murdered her, he had troubled to bring back her cap, wash it, and hang it up for all to see in the most public place on the farm. The place where, if water were needed, everyone went at some time every day.

The murder story in his box was immaterial, Matthew could not read. His mention of murder to Elias Bettinson was but a repetition of common rumour. Bettinson himself must have been aware of it because he prompted Matthew's remark. In any case, there was only one possible source of that rumour, Charlotte Dymond. No-one appears to have known who the mother was, only that she had threatened to kill the girl. Her name was never mentioned throughout the case; nor her locality. Neither did she show up at any time. As for the father, it was anyone's guess who and where he was.

Matthew had been seen with three silver fourpenny pieces, coins which were not amongst those in his latest wages but were known to have been part of Charlotte's and she was supposed not to have spent any. Yet she must have spent some money on her new bonnet cap; and, according to Matthew, she wanted to borrow 2/6d from him. If, as he said, he offered to lend only 1/6d, he might well have given her a 2/6d piece and received the 1/-d change in fourpenny pieces, three of them. [2]

The story he told his mistress had not, in fact, conflicted with what he had told other people. He had been forced by threat of legal action to tell Mrs. Peter 'the truth'. And, if it were the truth, he should not have told anyone else. Mrs. Peter denied having given Charlotte notice to leave. The girl had therefore absconded from her mistress, it must have occurred to Matthew, and it was no longer his business to involve himself.[3] Doubtless, Charlotte had asked Matthew to send on the rest of her clothes when she was settled into her new position; and he had collected them awaiting her word.

If that were the case and he had consented to help, it had been on the understanding that everything was above board. Yet now, not only was there a rumpus over her leaving but he was actually being accused of having murdered her. The whole thing was turning sour and his only real recourse was to get out while the going was still good.

* * * *

Just assuming that Charlotte had not intended to disappear and that Weeks was guilty, however, what kind of murderer might he have been?

He could have been simple-minded, had he not kept to a plausible story under constant interrogation by quite clever conversationalists.

He would have been the calculating type, had he not left tell-tale clothes around and prepared his deadly weapons in front of others.

He must have been a cold-blooded blackguard but for his shock at being told he was worthy of hanging in chains, when nothing had then been known to have happened at all.

He might have been an ultra-righteous man bent upon ridding the world of evil, in the form of the temptress, Charlotte, but then he would not have announced that fourpenny pieces would do to pass as sixpences.

And, if he had been capable of murder because he was a man of sudden passion, the gossips who had goaded him during the past week would surely have been struck down.

Phillipa Peter's right-hand man at Penhale farm in Davidstow fitted none of these descriptions. He had little background, no education, and a limp. But what he had, he made the most of.

Unlike many of those around him, he had stuck to one job for at least six years so that, until these unfortunate events, his employer regarded him highly. Being a sensible sort of a fellow, he had not wasted his money but had used it to dress as well as was possible.

This meagre show of wealth had probably won him Charlotte. He had little else to offer a girl of her popularity. But it was enough for any serving girl let alone for a bastard child unwanted by her family and therefore without a home except the one she worked in. Matthew Weeks with money was a catch.

Yet the means and the girl seem to have made him the object of local jealousy. And the envy appears to have been the more intense because he was so close a character.

Penhale could be any household, Davidstow any parish and 1844 any time - and Matthew's personality in that kind of community and circumstance could spell disaster.

Society does not like the secretive smug.

There is no evidence to suggest that Matthew was smug, although he had cause to be. But it is apparent that he kept a secret.

The body of a woman

8. With the dawn of Tuesday, April 23, Charlotte Dymond had been missing from Penhale for nine days and Matthew Weeks had been gone for two. As it had, by then, been established that nothing he had said regarding Charlotte's movements on Sunday 14 had come true, it was decided that the moor should be searched.

Accordingly, William Northam of the Halworthy inn turned up to help with John Westlake, his neighbour, Phillipa Peter's thirty-nine-year old son-in-law.[1] And these two set off from the Penhale farmyard with John Peter and John Stevens.

Westlake and Northam had been walking together, along the lane that Charlotte and Matthew had taken on April 14, and it must have been as they crossed Corner Down field - the third field after leaving the lane, and about three quarters of the way from the farmhouse to Higher Down Gate[2] - that they noticed they'd been following prints on the ground. But it was not until they entered Higher Down field that they stopped to investigate them.

They decided the marks had been made by pattens, undershoes worn by women, which raised their height by one or two inches, because the wooden soles were set on iron ovals to keep the shoes up off the mud and wet. William Northam bent down and placed his stick across a print made by an iron oval, while Westlake cut a notch in the wood. Then, measuring between the end of the stick and the notch, they found that the iron stand of the patten had made a mark some 4½ inches in length.

The two men thereupon proceeded through Higher Down field, occasionally stooping to test other patten marks against their notched stick. When they found that all the prints corresponded with their measurement, they felt satisfied they had been made by the same pair of pattens.

Out through Higher Down Gate, just over three quarters of a mile from the

Penhale farmhouse, they went; and across the strip of common and the Altarnon-Camelford road, still following the marks. But, as the Davidstow heathland inclined towards Bodmin Moor by Trevilian's Gate, the patten prints ran out. And, search though they did, Northam and Westlake could find no more. The ground was apparently too grassy.

Meanwhile, John Peter seems to have left the party and returned to Penhale, his place being taken by Humphrey Vosper of the *Britannia Inn* at Trevilian's Gate. He, with fellow publican William Northam, John Westlake and John Stevens, made for Lanlary Rock, a mile and a quarter across the moor from the inn, towards which Isaac Cory was believed to have seen Weeks walking with a woman on Sunday, April 14.

For anyone walking across the rolling brown and green Davidstow heath from Trevilian's Gate, Lanlary Rock is a landmark. To the left and southwards of the white stone outcrop is the way to Brown Willy and on to Blisland. But, if the rock is reached then the walker keeps to the foot of the ridge it is part of, that way leads through Crowdy Marsh beneath Showery Tor and Roughtor, to the ford where the path comes out from Camelford. This was in the parish of Simonward or St. Breward, part of the highest, bleakest and most desolate region of Bodmin Moor. [3]

On the way to Lanlary Rock, Simon Baker joined Vosper, Northam, Westlake and Stevens in their search. So now there were three licensees in the party as fifty-five-year old Baker kept a beer shop at Trevalga churchtown, [4] some seven miles as the crow flies from Penhale and adjacent to Charlotte Dymond's native Boscastle on the north coast.

The five men watched the ground as they walked; but it was not until reaching the boggy area beneath Lanlary Rock that they came upon prints. These, upon inspection and comparison with the measurement on William Northam's stick, were judged to have been made by the pattens that had left marks between Higher Down Field and Trevilian's Gate.

Following the patten prints along the foot of Showery Tor in the direction of Roughtor Ford, Northam noticed that two prints were together at one point, as though the wearer had stood still on the spot. And, a little further towards the ford, the innkeeper found a man's boot mark which he reckoned was an impression of some days' standing. After he had bent down, placed his stick across the mark and notched its length on the wood, he found a patten print close by.

By now the men had reached the marshy area around Roughtor Ford and the five-strong team had become a twelve-man party. Word of the search had obviously spread; some, like Vosper and Baker, had joined it as it progressed across the moor while others, like Christopher Arnold of Camelford, appear to have come out from the town by the lane that crosses the ford. [5]

As no more prints were to be found, the men decided to separate into two groups. The larger party kept to the left bank of the little River Alan, in St. Breward parish; but Simon Baker, the Trevalga beershop-keeper, and William Northam, the Halworthy publican, took the right bank in Advent parish. Down from the ford, they followed the little stream as it made its way around chunks of granite, until they reached a place that was washed with water when the level rose in bad weather.

And there, beneath Simon Baker and William Northam, was the body of a woman.

Baker was first to catch sight of it, face upwards in the cutting and looking as though it had recently been washed with river water, although it was about a foot from the present flow. One of the arms was by the woman's side, the other was extended. One of the legs was bent while the other was almost straight; and the stockings were in place although a garter seemed to be missing. But the most noticeable thing was that the throat was cut.

Very soon, the other men had joined Baker and Northam to look down at the body from the river bank. There were no shoes, pattens, bonnet, bonnet cap, handkerchief, bag, shawl, nor gloves to be seen. But John Stevens recognised the gown on the body, open to the stomach, and up to the middle of the thigh on one leg and just above the knee on the other.

Charlotte Dymond had been found.

A search of the river bank was made. There was no blood about the place nor sign of a struggle. No weapon was to be seen. And, as the ground was firm and grassy on this Advent parish side, there were neither boot nor patten prints. But, just behind the head of the body and on the slope, a broken coral necklace was found and Christopher Arnold of Camelford picked up some of the beads.

Word of the discovery of the body must have been taken back to Penhale, as Phillipa Peter's daughter, Mary Westlake, eventually arrived on the moor with a cart to collect it. Before it could be moved, however, a professional was required to view it where it lay in the river pit; so, while a suitable person was being found, Mary Westlake took charge of the beads that Christopher Arnold had picked up and she herself collected some more from the bank.

*   *   *   *

In the meantime, too, John Westlake, Humphrey Vosper and William Northam retraced their steps, on the St. Breward side of the river, to the spot where they had lost the patten prints they had been following. And, around the foot of Showery Tor where the ground was moist and clayey, they found boot and patten prints.

Northam judged the place to be about a gun shot from where the body lay, which was about sixty or seventy yards from the site according to Vosper and seventy or eighty according to Westlake. There were two prints of a man's boots and two of a woman's pattens; and, as the pairs were toe to toe, the three men guessed that the couple who had left them had stood face to face on that spot.

One of the patten marks was less distinct than the other but both boot prints were clear. Humphrey Vosper studied the print of the right boot, which was particularly distinct and came to the conclusion that the wearer had nailed toe plates and heel skutes to his boots. A skute was a metal shield, in the shape of a horse-shoe, which was attached to the heel of a boot by nails that were hammered in to the swedge or outer edge of the skute. And, as the nail heads were proud of the metal, they left a stronger impression in the ground than the skute itself or its swedge.

To the undiscerning observer, little of this might have registered. But, to a countryman of even recent times, such prints would have meant that the wearer had been in his best boots. Had they been working boots, the sole would have been nailed all over rather than plain with just a toe plate, although the heel skute would have resembled that on a Sunday pair.

* * * *

Then, four hours after the body had been found, Thomas Good arrived on the scene. The thirty-nine-year old bachelor, who lived with his mother and sister at Hicks Mill in Lewannick some nine miles away, was a Somerset-born Member of the Royal College of Surgeons of England and a Licentiate of the Apothecaries' Company.[7] Whether or not, as was usual when a body was discovered in suspicious circumstances, a coroner had been called to the place where the corpse lay was unstated. But Thomas Good, it was, who attended the scene of death to make the required preliminary pathological examination before the body was moved,[8] even although there were medical practitioners much nearer at hand who might have arrived more quickly.

Upon inspecting the body in the water course, he found that the undergarments were wet although, as the gown was not, it was presumed it had dried as the water level dropped. And, although John Stevens had noticed no blood, the experienced eye of the surgeon picked out pale stains on the clothes, their pallid appearance being accounted for by the body's having been washed by the river water, he thought.[9]

The preliminary inspection over, Good and the moorland searchers escorted the body back to Penhale on the cart. There, in the farmyard, the sorry procession was received by Phillipa Peter and her son, John. The body was then taken to rest in the barn adjoining the house.[10]

Nine days after she had left in her Sunday finery, Charlotte Dymond had returned to the place where she had lived and worked on and off for the past six years.

But her throat was cut.

Seduced by the devil

9. The day after Charlotte Dymond's body had been found, on the Advent parish side of the little River Alan, just below Roughtor Ford on Bodmin Moor, was Wednesday, April 24. And, in all probability, as many people visited Penhale farm that day as had ever been there before or have been there since. It was the day of the post mortem examination of the body and of the inquest as to whose it was and as to when, where, how and by what means the person met with death.

The role of pathologist was played by Thomas Good, the Lewannick surgeon, who had viewed the body where it was found on the previous day as the law required, and who had seen it into the Penhale barn to rest overnight. Now, on the Wednesday, he had returned to conduct the autopsy.[1]

John Stevens's preliminary identification of the body as Charlotte's was confirmed by one of the constables of Davidstow parish, Thomas Rickard. Ordinarily, Rickard, who was in his mid-50s, farmed three hundred acres at Hendraburnick, to the west of the Davidstow churchtown-Camelford road. Now, he had been called in to act in his unpaid and part-time capacity as a parish policeman for which he was answerable to the local magistrates and received expenses.[3]

The body of Charlotte was stripped of clothes by Surgeon Good in Rickard's presence. And, while the constable took possession of such as the multi-coloured green-striped gown, the pathologist compiled his report:

I found a wound in the neck 8 inches and a ½ in length, commencing from about the middle of the neck behind, continued on the left side to the front of the neck and extending as far as the middle of the neck on the right side, passing 2 inches and a half below the ear, and being in the middle of the cut 2 inches and a half in depth.

The whole of the soft parts on the left side were divided down to the bone of the neck, the windpipe completely divided at its upper part, including a small portion of the larynx. The small portion of the larynx was attached to the windpipe; the oesophagus was partly divided and the instrument had not only gone through the soft part but had partially separated two of the vertibrae by entering a little way into the cartilage between them.

Much force must have been used in giving the wound, which was deeper in the left side. The wound was the cause of death. It appeared from the common carotid that there had been two cuts, I do not think that the instrument used was a very sharp one and this because of the roughness of the sides of the wound. I do not think it possible that she could have inflicted the wound herself.

Dr. Good then went on to say 'I examined the rest of the body which was healthy. The bladder was empty, but this might have happened after death. The uterus was healthy and there were no signs of pregnancy or of violation.'

The under-garments on the body were inspected by the pathologist during the post mortem examination - and he was subsequently to consider them again, but his final conclusion was to be - 'I see nothing in them to lead me to suppose that there had been any violence although, had any person had recent connection (sexual intercourse) with her, the time which had elapsed and her exposure to water would have prevented its being discovered. The hymen was ruptured but the rupture did not appear to be recent.'[4]

* * * *

Meanwhile, more people were arriving at Penhale to attend the inquest which was to follow the autopsy. Among them were four other part-time constables who had come to assist Thomas Rickard, the Davidstow policeman. Sixty-three-year old Constable John Bennett hailed from Hicks Mill in South Petherwin parish, which adjoined Matthew Weeks's native parish of Lezant. Forty-three-year old William Dingle, a butcher by trade and excessively deaf, came from the adjoining parish of Northill. Irishman, John FitzGerald, who was about thirty-three was the Camelford borough constable. And John Brooming was the Launceston borough policeman, aged about thirty-eight.[5]

In fact, the two borough constables might have been properly paid and disciplined, as the 1835 Municipal Corporations Act had provided for the setting up of borough police forces under Watch Committees of the local authorities.[6] But, as far as John Brooming was concerned, he held no regular appointment for it was not until 1846 that he became Launceston's first salaried and full-time constable.[7]

However, the parish and borough policemen carried out what they saw as their duty; and, in this case, it was to collect the available evidence. Accordingly, Thomas Rickard issued forth from the autopsy with the clothes from Charlotte's body; and received from Mary Westlake, Mrs. Peter's daughter who had arrived by then, the broken coral necklace which had been found near the body by her and Christopher Arnold of Camelford. In the meantime, Mrs. Peter had brought Matthew's torn and blood-stained shirt from the farmhouse and handed it over to Constable John Brooming of Launceston.

Before the 1926 Coroners Amendment Act, an inquest relating to a suspected murder was more than the present identification of a body and medical cause of death. It was a public court of enquiry, in the presence of a body, with a jury charged to reach a conclusion, after witnesses had given evidence to the coroner. But, as no strict rules of evidence were necessarily observed and the verdict was publicised by the press, the procedure was unfair to anyone suspected of having committed a crime, whether rightly or wrongly.

A coroner was appointed by the county or a borough authority. But, although he was paid by one or the other, he was answerable only to the Lord Chancellor and generally held office for life. He could be either a medical practitioner or a lawyer and his deputy would usually be a junior partner.[8] In the Charlotte Dymond case they were county appointees, the coroner being a surgeon and his deputy a solicitor. They were, in fact, father and son; and they had ridden to Penhale farm from Bodmin, the county town of Cornwall.

Sixty-two-year old Joseph Hamley, the coroner, and twenty-seven-year old Edmund Gilbert Hamley, his son and deputy, were members of an ancient Cornish family which emanated from the parish of St. Mabyn, on the south western side of Bodmin Moor. But a branch had settled in Bodmin and several of the coroners' ancestors had served as mayors and Members of Parliament for the borough.

Joseph Hamley had himself been mayor in 1818, 1826 and 1837; and, by following the profession of surgeon, he kept up a family tradition from the time of his great grandfather, William Wymond. For some years, he had been cared for by his third wife; but his second wife had been the mother of his son and deputy.

She was the late sister of Walter Raleigh Gilbert, the soldier, who had distinguished himself in India under Lord Lake and was destined to become a hero of the Sikh Wars. It was after his father that the deputy coroner had been named. And, if he did but guess as he stood in the Penhale farmyard that day, Edmund Gilbert Hamley would see his name carved on the 144 ft. high national monument to his, by then, celebrated uncle for he would be mayor when it was erected on Bodmin beacon in 1856.[9]

According to the record, the inquest was held 'at the house of Phillipa Peter'. But, as there was then a doorway between the ground floor of the farmhouse and that of the adjoining barn, it probably took place in the latter where Charlotte's body had rested overnight. For, although the lower part of the barn was divided into two rooms, neither of which could have accommodated a crowd, the upper room stretched the length of the building.

This, reached by means of a flight of granite steps from the mowhay, was furnished with an enormous table that was used for harvest suppers.[10] And in that room it, doubtless, was that the coroners Hamley, the five constables, twelve jurors, nineteen witnesses and representatives of the press and public assembled to begin -

> *an inquisition taken for Our Sovereign Lady, the Queen, at the house of Phillipa Peter in the parish of Davidstow, in the county of Cornwall the twenty-fourth day of April, in the seventh year of the reign of our Sovereign Lady, Victoria, by the grace of God, of the United Kingdom of Great Britain and Ireland, Queen, Defender of the Faith, and in the year of our Lord, one thousand eight hundred and forty-four, before Joseph Hamley, gentleman, one of the coroners for our said Lady the Queen, for the said county, on view of the body of Charlotte Dymond then and there lying dead, upon the oaths of (twelve named) good and lawful men of the said county duly chosen, and who being then and there duly sworn and charged to enquire for our said Lady, the Queen, when, where, how and by what means the said Charlotte Dymond came to her death...* [11]

The twelve jurors duly sworn and charged appear to have been some good and lawful farmers of Davidstow, with the exception of one, each of whom signed the official document. They were-

Digory Hayne, of Tremail, about fifty-four
Richard Ford, of Trehane, about sixty
William Hocken, of Hendraburnick, about thirty
George Hayne, of Tremail, fifty-two
John Bennett, of Treslay, about thirty-three
John Chapman, of Trevivian, thirty-two
John Pethick - either of Treworra, sixty-eight; or of Trewassa, forty-three
Robert Earl, of Tremail, forty-seven
Edward Jollow, of Tresoke, about forty-three
James Baker, of Trewinnow, about thirty-eight
Gerrance Pethick - probably of Treworra, sixty-three; rather than of
　　　　　　　　　Trewassa, thirty- six
John Westlake, unclear which of several namesakes. [12]

Preliminaries over, witnesses proceeded to give evidence. The Penhale household was represented by its remaining members, Mrs. Phillipa Peter, her son John, and John Stevens, who recounted the events to date. The various articles were produced by the five constables, Rickard, Bennett, Dingle, Fitzgerald and Brooming, who themselves were now learning the details of the case. Isaac Cory told his story of having seen Weeks on the moor with a woman and of having followed patten prints to Penhale on Sunday, April 14. And Spear and the Lanxons repeated their denials of having expected or received Charlotte on that day or the following.

A report of the autopsy findings was given by Surgeon Thomas Good. William Hocken of Trevivian outlined his conversation with Weeks, over the hedge dividing Higher Down and Long Valderns fields, on Saturday 20. And details of the moorland search on the day before the inquest were given by the three publicans, Simon Baker, William Northam and Humphrey Vosper, and Mrs. Peter's son-in-law and daughter, John and Mary Westlake.

The Westlakes did not stop at the search, however. They proceeded to give evidence relating to Weeks's alibi that, after he had left Charlotte at Higher Down Gate, he had gone to Halworthy and, as John and Mary Westlake had not been in, he had called upon Sarah Westlake.

'I was at home at my house at Halworthy, otherwise Alldrunkard, during the whole of that Sunday', Mary Westlake explained, 'I was not well. We dined shortly after the middle of the day and I did not leave my house afterward other than by stepping just outside the door (probably to a lavatory); but, if anyone had come, I should have seen him. I did not go into any neighbour's house after the middle of the day. I did not see Matthew Weeks on that day or hear anything of him.'

Her evidence was followed by Mrs. Peter's son-in-law's. He knew Matthew Weeks well, John Westlake told the inquest, he had been occasionally in the habit of coming to his house. 'About five o'clock in the evening of Sunday 14, I came back from a marsh[13] I rent and had tea in my own house', he continued. 'I stayed home for the rest of the night. I might have just gone outside my door, but not for any time. I did not see Weeks that evening and I do not know that he came to my house.'

Then came Sarah Westlake of Halworthy, who was about sixty-eight and described herself as a widow. 'I was home all the day, having been very unwell', she said. 'I might have gone just outside my door, but never left it or locked up my house. I did not, during the day, see or hear anything of Matthew Weeks. No-one, after I was gone to bed, came and asked if John Westlake (my son) was home. No-one from my room said that they did not know whether he was home or not. I went to bed about nine o'clock that night.'

'My house consists of one room under and one room over, the windows of each room face the same way', Mrs. Westlake explained. 'There were with me that night three children only, who all slept in my bedroom, the eldest being ten years old only. I don't think I've seen Matthew for a quarter of a year'.

The three children would have been those of her son and daughter-in-law, John and Mary Westlake.[14] And, by 'a quarter of a year', the seasonal measurement among rural communities, she would have meant that she had not seen Weeks since about Christmas.

But what most interested the inquest was that the three from Halworthy had broken Matthew's alibi. This, coupled with the denials of Spear and the Lanxons, posed the problems as to where in fact Charlotte and Matthew were, on Sunday April 14, if she were not making her way via Brown Willy to Blisland and he were not at Halworthy.

Charlotte Dymond

According to the press, *the town and neighbourhood of Camelford had been thrown into considerable excitement by the discovery of the body of a female* on Tuesday April 23.[15] Possibly as a result of this, two new witnesses had come forward. And they were now available to give evidence which might solve the mystery.

One was Richard Pethick, a cattle farmer of Tresinney in Advent parish, who was about twenty. The other was forty-eight-year old William Gard, of Minster parish, who was a Wesleyan Methodist (Reform) local preacher.[16]

On Sunday April 14, William Gard had crossed the moor to Butters Tor, south west of Brown Willy, at about two o'clock.[17] Several hours later, he retraced his steps in the direction of Tresinney in Advent.

'About half past five of the clock of that day', he told the inquest, 'I had to pass Roughtor Ford. Just before coming to it, I saw a man and a woman. They were on the Lanlary Rock side of the ford and were walking at a very slow pace, as if *from* the direction of the ford *towards* Lanlary Rock. They were about two gun shots from me (140yds.) and three from the ford. I did not know who they were.'

'The man had on a short, dark, frock coat', the preacher continued, 'the woman had an umbrella open over her head, I did not take notice of any shawl, her dress appeared to be dark. The man was a little man. I cannot say whether he walked lame. They walked very slow. I saw them for about five minutes at this time. Occasionally, the man would stop and stand up, standing rather back and with his hand either to his side or his pocket, and look about. And the woman would walk on and stop. And then the man would get up to her again. This was done several times.'

'I had before seen them at a greater distance and they then appeared walking on *to* the ford. I was not near enough to discover their features. It was very foggy and wet. I did not speak to them but went on my way. I occasionally looked back at them and observed that they would occasionally go a few steps and then stop. When I last saw them, the man and woman were standing still and he was looking towards the ford. He was then about another gun shot (70 yds.) further *from* the ford. (It was) not foggy then, (although it) had been so (and) mist was hanging about Roughtor'.

The coroner and jury had already heard, from Isaac Cory, that Matthew Weeks was seen walking in the direction of Lanlary Rock in the company of a woman from about twenty to five on the afternoon in question. And, although it had been foggy, Cory had noticed a red shawl and could identify Weeks because he 'walked upon the twist, his usual walk'.

Now they had heard from Gard that, just before half past five, he had seen a man and a woman walking from Lanlary Rock towards Roughtor Ford when it was foggy and wet. By the time he reached the ford, the couple had turned back and the fog had cleared; but, although he watched them for at least five minutes, he did not take notice of any shawl and could not say whether the man walked lame.

Then followed the evidence of Richard Pethick, the Tresinney farmer, who said that, at about six o'clock in the evening of the Sunday, he was riding towards Fox Hole (Catshole Tor) in search of his cattle. And, when he first came within sight of Lanlary Rock, he was about a mile from it.

'I saw two people coming from Lanlary Rock, aiming towards me', he continued, 'I watched them go between Showery Tor and the new piece of hedging leading to the (Roughtor) ford. They were walking together and they continued walking on towards me. I observed them so walking on for about a quarter of an hour. They occasionally stopped and turned about and stood in front of each other, it appeared as if face to face.'

'In turning back over the moor, I lost sight of them', Pethick told the inquest. 'I had previously been near enough to see that they were a man and woman. The woman had up an umbrella. The evening was misty. The man was a little man and was lame.[18] I then returned to Fox Hole and came back, still looking for my cattle, by Roughtor Ford'.

'On coming round the hill', said the farmer, 'I saw the man and woman again. They were about a gun shot from Roughtor Ford (70 yds.) and I was about half a mile from them. They were walking on as if going down to the water and not in the direction of the ford. They appeared to see me and immediately stopped and looked at me. I continued going on, nearing the ford, and, just before I got to the ford, I saw the man nearly opposite to me.'

'He was a little in advance of the woman who was nearer Lanlary Rock and was standing still. I was then within about a stone throw of him. The woman was standing a little way up from him. She was a middle size woman. I could not see her face. She was far off, she had an umbrella. The man and the woman were twenty yards asunder. They were the same persons as I had first seen.'

'I spoke to them', Pethick went on, 'and said "be ye afraid of each other?" and, after a bit, I said "have you lost yourselves?". They made me no answer. But the man looked towards me start (straight), standing very upright. I observed that he limped a mite in walking and that he had on a dark short frock coat and that his trousers were rather turned out of the light.'

'I continued on my way, leaving the ford a little to the left, and, in about ten minutes, lost sight of them. But, my curiosity being excited', said the farmer, 'I got off my horse and went back a little to see what they were about. The woman had joined the man. I watched them for about ten minutes as they were so standing together and so they continued when I left looking at them.'

'It was rather misty at times, not always that day', Pethick told the inquest.'It was good light, enough to enable me to see to the top of Roughtor. When I saw them last, it was nearly seven. I mentioned having seen these people when I went home.'

Attention turned from the moorland couple when the next witness gave evidence at the inquest. She was Rebecca Jewell, who was about twenty-three and had been a farm servant for William Hocken at Trevivian and a great friend of Charlotte. Her purpose was to say that Charlotte invariably wore gloves on Sundays.

The girl was known to have possessed two pairs of gloves, a silk pair and a cotton pair with three stripes on the back. Because John Peter was sure that Charlotte had left Penhale in gloves on April 14 and Mrs. Peter was subsequently to say that her silk pair were at home, it was necessary to confirm the existence of the cotton pair and Charlotte's habit of wearing such apparel on the

Sabbath. This, Rebecca Jewell did. But exactly where the cotton gloves were, was unknown. They, like other of Charlotte's garments, were missing from the body.[19]

Then came Thomas Prout to stand witness at the inquest. And, with his evidence, it was at last discovered what had passed between him and Charlotte on the Sunday morning. 'I saw her (on the) 14th April in Mrs. Peter's house, sat in the settle by (the) kitchen (fire)', he said. 'Weeks was there and Mrs. Peter and Stevens. I went out of (the) kitchen; Charlotte came out after me. (She) fetched her bonnet and came after me.'

'She spoke to me', Thomas Prout continued, 'he was inside. An appointment was made to meet that evening at Tremail chapel, (which is) not in (the) road to Roughtor Ford. I went to the chapel. She was not there.'

And so ended the investigation. Elias Bettinson had not told his story, about Weeks's having mentioned that Charlotte's mother had threatened to kill her, although the press gleaned it from someone's evidence that day.[20] Neither were Christopher Arnold and other, un-named, searchers of the moor recorded as having appeared. But it is likely that the twenty-four, including the constables, who had given evidence had produced enough for the jurors to make up their minds, as far as the inquest was concerned.

It was, according to the press, *without a moment's hesitation*[21] that the twelve Davidstow farmers brought in their verdict-

that Matthew Weeks, late of the parish aforesaid in the county aforesaid, labourer, not having the fear of God before his eyes but moved and seduced by the instigation of the Devil, on the 14th day of April in the year aforesaid, with force and arms at the parish of Advent, in the county aforesaid, in and upon the said Charlotte Dymond in the peace of God of our said Lady, the Queen, then and there being feloniously, wilfully, and of his malice aforethought, did make an assault. And that the said Matthew Weeks with a certain instrument, to the jurors unknown, which he, the said Matthew Weeks, then and there had and held in his right hand, the throat or gullet of her, the said Charlotte Dymond, feloniously, wilfully, and of his malice aforethought, did strike and cut. And that the said Matthew Weeks, with the instrument aforesaid, by the striking and cutting aforesaid, did then and there give unto her, the said Charlotte Dymond, one mortal wound of the length of eight inches and depth of two inches and a half, of which said mortal wound she, the said Charlotte Dymond, then and there instantly died..And so the jurors aforesaid, upon their oaths aforesaid, do say that the said Matthew Weeks her, the said Charlotte Dymond, in manner and form aforesaid, feloniously, wilfully, and of his malice aforethought, did kill and murder against the peace of our said Lady, the Queen, her crown and dignity. And the jurors aforesaid, upon their oaths aforesaid, do say that the said Matthew Weeks withdrew and fled from the same. And that the said Matthew Weeks at the time of the doing and committing the said felony and murder aforesaid, had not any goods or chattels, lands or tenements, within the said county, or elsewhere, to the know-

ledge of the jurors aforesaid...." [22]

Matthew Weeks, having been neither present nor represented at the inquest, was thus accused of the capital crime of murder.

It mattered not that, whereas the pathologist had reported Charlotte's neck wound to be eight and a half inches long, the indictment read eight inches only. It was of no concern that, of the three who purported to have seen a couple on the moor, none could identify Charlotte as the woman and one could not say if the man limped. Never asked, let alone answered, were questions as to where Charlotte obtained the umbrella noticed by the three witnesses, when neither she nor Weeks was seen to leave Penhale with one, and as to how Weeks managed to leave no boot prints by the patten marks on the Penhale side of the moor although some were found on the Roughtor Ford side.

The rumour, that Charlotte's mother had threatened to kill her if she went home, apparently came out at the inquest; but the woman was not called to account for herself. The word of Thomas Prout, regarding what had passed between himself and Charlotte, was accepted without question. Were it the truth, he had been the first person to notice that Charlotte was missing that Sunday evening, yet he had joined neither the local concern for her nor the search party, as far as may be ascertained; and no-one was called to stand witness that he had attended chapel as he said.

There *was* a letter. But, search as Mrs. Peter said she did, it was never found. Whatever it contained, Matthew Weeks knew only what Charlotte had told him, he could not read. And whether or not Spear and the Lanxons expected the girl that day, their word was never doubted, in their direction the patten prints suggest that she set off.

That she changed direction upon reaching Lanlary Rock and was joined by a man soon afterwards, is evident from the patten prints and the appearance of boot marks. If Matthew were not that man - and it is difficult to explain how he could have been - then the question remained as to where he was, in view of the Halworthy Westlakes' refusal to corroborate his alibi.

What concerned the inquest was that he left Penhale with Charlotte Dymond, having previously honed a razor, and purchased a knife, according to Stevens who had not yet changed his yarn (yet whose evidence had not been corroborated, Charles Parsons, the alleged vendor, having not been called). He had been seen with three silver fourpenny pieces, suspected to have been Charlotte's and had he stolen that amount (5p) he'd have hanged for larceny only six years before. His limp fitted the description of the man on the moor given by two of the three witnesses. He had returned to Penhale without Charlotte. But, above all, circumstances and hearsay pointed to his having murdered her - they had been levelled at him even before a body had been found.

The law had now to take its course. The suspect was to be arrested and brought before magistrates so that the case against him could be heard and the witnesses professionally examined. The inquest jury had accordingly noted that, in the event of the magistrates' deciding there was a prima facie case upon which he could be sent to the assize court for trial, Matthew Weeks possessed nothing liable to forfeiture upon conviction, as was required up to 1870.[23]

Yet even before Matthew could reach any magistrates, the record would be black against him. Within twenty-four hours of the inquest, Joseph Hamley the coroner would be giving as the cause of death on Charlotte's certificate 'wilfully murdered by Matthew Weeks'. [24]

In the meantime Hamley issued a warrant for his apprehension. And off set Constable John FitzGerald of Camelford in his pursuit. [25]

Across the Tamar to Plymouth

10. Constable FitzGerald of Camelford might have had the warrant for Matthew Weeks's arrest, but it was Constable John Bennett of South Petherwin who was first on his scent. Whether he acted on a hunch, a tip-off, or from local knowledge was never disclosed, but it was probably a bit of all three.

Although Matthew Weeks came from Lezant parish adjoining Bennett's South Petherwin, his grandfather, John Weeks, had lived in the constable's parish for thirty-five years up to his death in February of 1837. Had he been literate, John Weeks could have written 'yeoman' after his name as he was a landowning farmer, a freeholder, one rank below that of 'gentleman'. [1]

He had grown up at Landrake in Lezant where the Weeks family was based and had married a local girl, Jane Congdon, in 1786. Several of their six children were born in Lezant while he was a labourer during the early years of the marriage, including the first son who was named after his father.

In 1802, however, John Weeks senior inherited a holding at Trecrogo in South Petherwin from his father, Richard Weeks, yeoman; and the family thereupon removed itself to the newly acquired estate. But John Weeks junior remained in Lezant and, in 1812 at the age of twenty-four he married Jane Hicks.

The couple had ten children during the next twenty-two years, all of whom survived with the exception of a son, George, who was buried just after his first birthday in April of 1833. But in less than two years, real disaster struck the family for John Weeks died; and his widow, Jane, was left with four or five of the children still to be brought up at Larrick, yet without his labourer's wage.

By 1844, when John Weeks had been dead for nine years, the family had grown away from home except for the youngest, Eliza, who was ten. Constable John Bennett of South Petherwin probably knew that, apart from her, the surviving children were Elizabeth (15), Jane-Hicks (16), Hannah (19), William (21), John (26), Richard (29), Mary (32), and Matthew Weeks who, having been baptized by Thomas Johns the curate in Lezant parish church on November 5, 1820, was approaching twenty-four years of age. [2]

The policeman was possibly sufficiently acquainted with the Weeks family history to know that one of the girls had married and gone to live in Plymouth. It was knowledge that would stand him in good stead; but, meanwhile, he apparently felt his best bet would be to enquire around Larrick in Lezant for Matthew's whereabouts.

Within a mile of reaching Larrick, having left the morning's post mortem examination and inquest at Penhale ten miles away, he would have passed through Coad's Green in the parish of Northill.

There, he must have heard that Matthew had called upon the Stevens family, some six hours after he'd walked out of Penhale, on Sunday, April 21. According to the daughter of the household at Coad's Green, Elizabeth Stevens, he had said that he was on his way to stay with his mother at Larrick for the night and had to be up very early the following morning in order to get back to Penhale.

Matthew apparently stayed talking with Elizabeth Stevens and her friend, Eliza Butler, from three o'clock that afternoon until about nine in the evening; and they must have known that he was courting Charlotte, as they asked after her at least twice but, on both occasions, received no answer. Eliza Butler thought he seemed ill at ease, while Elizabeth Stevens found him sometimes gay and at others rather dour.

During the time Matthew spent with the girls at Coad's Green, Elizabeth Stevens's little sister was present. When the child took a handkerchief out of her bag, Matthew said to her 'I have a bag in my pocket belonging to a young woman' ; and, from his breast pocket, he produced a medium-size, square, black, silk handbag trimmed with black lace and with a black string handle.

Elizabeth Stevens took it from him, presumably for the child to see, and then gave it back to Matthew who replaced it in his breast pocket. [3]

To Constable John Bennett, who had been listening to evidence at the inquest - regarding John Stevens's having noticed Matthew with three silver fourpenny pieces, suspected to have been Charlotte's, and concerning a black silk handbag with which Charlotte was seen to leave Penhale - this story must have had a ring of truth. Whether he ever enquired at Larrick in Lezant or whether Matthew had, in fact, stayed the night there on April 21, is not know.

However, Constable Bennett soon continued on his way from Coad's Green and, sixteen miles further on, at Saltash, he took a boat across the River Tamar to Plymouth in Devonshire. With him, he probably had the description of Matthew Weeks which was issued to the newspapers - *about 22 years old, 5 ft. 4 inches tall, lame in the right knee, teeth missing on top left side, light hair, dark coat, high hat, low boots, dark trousers much rubbed from the knee down.* [4]

It was not long before he was in the vicinity of the Hoe, where Matthew's sister and her husband lived; and, having gained entrance to the house, the constable went in to find Matthew there as he'd somehow suspected he might. There is some discrepancy as to whether Matthew was walking on the Hoe or actually in his sister's house when Bennett caught up with him; but,whatever the situation, the constable shook hands with the brother-in-law and then asked Matthew how he was.

Matthew had apparently, according to the policeman, not met Constable Bennett before but he replied that he was well.

'You must go with me', Bennett said to Matthew.

'Where?' asked Matthew.

'I am going to take you before Mr. John King Lethbridge (one of the Cornish committing magistrates)' the constable replied.

'What for?' Matthew enquired.

Charlotte Dymond

'You know what for', Constable Bennett told him.

At this point Matthew's sister, who was also present during these exchanges, asked the meaning of Bennett's intrusion.

'He knows what for', the constable told her, pointing at Matthew.

'Tell me the sense of it', insisted Matthew's sister.

Constable Bennett noticed that she was large with the child she was expecting and, turning to Matthew, he said 'I don't like to tell anything to your sister, Matthew.'

At this, Matthew replied either 'no' or 'don't', according to Bennett.

Whether or not, by his dress or some other indication, John Bennett was recognisable as a parish constable, is unclear. Whether or not Matthew knew who John King Lethbridge was is just as vague. But evidently Matthew, his sister and her husband accompanied Constable Bennett without a warrant and crossed the River Tamar by boat to Saltash.

Upon arrival on the Cornish side of the river, Matthew asked if he might relieve himself in a stable and the constable agreed. And now that Bennett had succeeded in returning the suspect to the county in which the alleged crime had been committed, as was required, he obviously felt he was justified in interrogating him, although that was, in fact, a magistrate's job in 1844. [5]

'Matthee, you're charged with a very heavy crime of murdering a young woman who had lately been a servant along with you', the constable started. He then said that he did not know the name of the young woman and asked Matthew 'what is she called?'

As only one young woman had lately been a servant with Matthew, it seems only logical that he should have replied 'Dymond'. In fact, had Matthew known that John Bennett's name had been recorded as a witness at the inquest that very morning, in the presence of a body identified as being Charlotte Dymond's, he might have questioned why the constable told him that he did not know the name of the allegedly murdered girl.

However, 'what is she called besides?' persisted the constable.

'*Charlotte* Dymond' Matthew replied.

'Did you cut her throat with a pair of fleams (a blood-letting instrument)?' asked Bennett. [6]

'I did not', Matthew answered, although the constable later swore that he had said 'not with that'.

Bennett then turned his attention to a bundle of clothes which, up to then, had been carried by Matthew's brother-in-law. Noticing that the garments were new, he got Weeks to admit that he had purchased them during his stay in Plymouth. This was significant, as far as the constable was concerned, for, as it had been made clear at the inquest that Matthew had left his clothes at Penhale with the exception of those he wore away, he had not intended to return if he had bought new in Devonshire.

Then, having made a note of the clothes Weeks was wearing - a fancy waistcoat, his best boots, the trousers he'd worn out with Charlotte and away from Penhale - Constable Bennett proceeded to search them. In the side pocket of Matthew's coat he found a right hand cotton glove with stripes on the back. The following day, when he would search Weeks more thoroughly, the policeman would find the left glove in the waistcoat pocket.

Whether or not Matthew's sister and brother-in-law accompanied him and the constable further than Saltash is unknown. But it would seem that Bennett's travels this day had been by means of his own horse-drawn gig for it was in such that he and Matthew rode back, along the turnpike towards David-stow. Generally, constables at this period were known to walk miles with prisoners, the use of such as Bennett's two-wheeled cart only being made were there a risk of the prisoner's escape or rescue. [7]

However, back through Coad's Green rode Bennett with Weeks and, when they reached the next village, there was Constable William Dingle of Northill parish awaiting their arrival, at Congdon's Shop. From there, the three proceeded to Constable Bennett's house at Hicks Mill in South Petherwin parish. [8]

Upon arrival, Matthew was left in the charge of William Dingle, while Bennett saw to his horse and trap. The conversation between them for that quarter of an hour could not have amounted to much because Dingle, the butcher and part-time policeman, was deaf to excess. Nevertheless, by the time that Bennett returned, Dingle had claimed what he considered to be vital evidence regarding the moorland prints, he had taken into his custody Matthew's best boots.

Where Weeks slept that night is not recorded. But as, by the following day, Thursday April 25, Bennett had handed him over to Constable John Fitzgerald of Camelford, who had the warrant to bring him before the magistrates, it is assumed he was taken to Halworthy for the hearing.

Fitzgerald certainly slept with him. And, it was during the time that Weeks was in his charge, that he underwent another unauthorised interrogation.

'How came Bennett to take you?' Fitzgerald asked Matthew.

'Bennett would have had no chance to take me but for my sister', came the reply, 'I had gone down before (he arrived) to take a vessel for Guernsey or Jersey.'

'Have you any friends there?' enquired the constable.

'No', said Matthew.

'What were you going to do there?' Fitzgerald continued.

'I don't know', was the answer.

Fitzgerald had apparently been told the details of the arrest by Constable Bennett and that Matthew had money on him. He thereupon questioned the prisoner as to his stay in Plymouth. He had been told by Bennett, Fitzgerald said, that Matthew had said that he thought 'it was not safe to stop in Plymouth or Devonport' but had altered his mind when he got there.

Matthew was subsequently not to agree with this version of the conversation between himself and Constable Bennett, maintaining that he had told the policeman that he had gone 'to see the place', Plymouth, and meant to return to Cornwall. No doubt, as a countryman whose sister had gone to live in so famous a port, he *had* wanted to see it.

Whatever Weeks had said or intended, however, was not the point. The disturbing aspect was the discrepancy itself, in the terms of what passed between him and the constables. In the first place, they had no business interrogating him at all, that was a magistrate's job in 1844 as the judge was eventually to caution Bennett. But his virtual reprimand was no good to Matthew. The constables' word on oath contributed towards the case against him .

In the second place, had the inquest indictment been lost, we would today believe the word of John Bennett, when he told Matthew that he did not know the name of the allegedly murdered girl. From the inquest record we know that John Bennett was sworn in as a witness. For, although it was not actually recorded as 'Constable' Bennett, as the Davidstow John Bennett was sworn in as a juror and the other policemen connected with the case were recorded without the title 'Constable', the odds against his not having been present at the inquest must be heavy.

If he were at the inquest, he not only heard the name of Charlotte Dymond but he also viewed her body, only hours before arresting Weeks. By requesting her name from the prisoner on the pretext that he himself did not know it, he was deliberately setting a trap. He had charged Weeks with murder, without cautioning him, and then asked him to show guilty knowledge by naming the victim.

In a period when extremes are the accepted standard - good or evil, innocence or guilt, freedom or the death penalty- there can be no discrepancy of this kind. That an officer of the law was permitted licence in this case is surely an indictment on the system itself.

At the same time, it must be admitted that Matthew Weeks did not help himself by seeming to resent interrogation, whether by his employer, workmates or the constables. He had, after all, been the last person seen with Charlotte Dymond.

One explanation could be that, innocent or guilty, he considered himself a cut above his station and therefore beyond question. His superior style of dress might support such a contention and go some way towards explaining his reactions to events.

His apparent calm, when charged with Charlotte's murder by Constable Bennett, is not to be wondered at if he had, indeed, walked out of Penhale away from scandal-mongers. He had been branded as a murderer worthy of being hung in chains, even before a body had been found. Bennett's charge was therefore but a repetition of his friends' accusations.

That he was not without feeling is evident from his behaviour on at least two occasions. His antipathy for Mrs. Peter was obviously because, whereas she expected him to divulge information entrusted to him, she did not respond by believing his word. And a regard for his sister is apparent. He might have resisted arrest, were it not for upsetting her late in pregnancy.

What is not so easy to understand is his seeming disregard for Charlotte once he was told she was dead. Guilty or innocent, he should have reacted.

Yet, had he murdered the girl, surely no-one in his right mind would have given away such disgust for her, when asked to take in her washed bonnet cap, by saying he would 'drag it in'. But that had happened before the body was found; and, if he had had nothing to do with her end, what was the meaning of this attitude?

Although it has been suggested that Constable Bennett's word was not wholly to be relied upon, it is possible that part of his version of the arrest

Charlotte Dymond

contained an explanation. The brief to the prosecuting counsel mentioned 'a further conversation' between Matthew and the constable 'as to the period at which he had left keeping company' with Charlotte.

As the writer of the brief considered this information of little use to the prosecution case, he did not enlarge upon the point. But, later, the press understood the constable himself to say in court that Weeks had told him that he had not 'kept company with Charlotte since Lady Day but some other chaps had'. If this were true, then the courtship had been over and finished three weeks before Charlotte disappeared.

But this situation seems not to have been known, or at any rate not accepted, by other people. And it is possible that it was not advertised by Charlotte or Matthew.

Nevertheless, it could explain the seemingly inexplicable. For a teen-aged farm servant unwanted by her family, Charlotte had a substantial wardrobe. Doubtless, as the couple had been virtually engaged, hence Mrs. Peter's allowing Weeks to keep some of her clothes in his box, he had given her various articles as seal of promise. When, however, the promise was breached by one or other of the parties, they could have been returned, as a ring might be today, such as the handbag, the gloves and the handkerchief that were found in Matthew's possession.

He was hardly going to explain the situation. Had it been her decision, he would feel a fool. Had it been his, and she had vanished, he would be blamed for abandoning her, 'a poor, friendless creature'. So he was off-hand regarding her whereabouts the following week. He really might not have cared. After all, when Thomas Prout had threatened to live at Penhale, Matthew had said he would leave because he disliked him, not because he said he might take away Charlotte.

It might have been the truth he told of Charlotte's intention of going to Blisland. He would not lend her all the money she asked before she left, but he gave her some, for old time's sake, perhaps. Her going might even have given him an idea of making the break.

He would go to his mother's and think. When he got to Coad's Green, he might well have intended to return to Penhale the next morning, as he said. And then he decided to go to Plymouth. His sister was there.

He had probably felt awkward enough, when Elizabeth Stevens and Eliza Butler kept asking after Charlotte and he could not bring himself to say it was over. He might even have toyed with giving that little girl her bag. But then he would have had to divulge the broken romance and it would have been all over his native parish in no time.

His sister was the best bet. She might not have known about Charlotte, whereas his mother would surely ask. And why stop at Plymouth? He might as well buy some new clothes and start a new life in the Channel Isles.

And so he might have, had he not found his sister pregnant and stayed on at her home. Yet he was absconding from his mistress without leave. Charlotte had been given notice, so she told Matthew, but he knew he had not. Any moment, an officer of the law could arrive and take him back.[9]

One did. 'You must go with me', said Bennett.

'Where? asked Matthew, as though he did not know it was back to Penhale.
'I am going to take you before Mr. Lethbridge', the constable told him.
'What for?' Matthew enquired in genuine amazement.......

It would have been then that he stepped into the looking glass and events became 'curiouser and curiouser'.

And, before he came to, he was up in front of the magistrates.

King John, the Doctor, & the master of the hounds

11. The threat of facing just one magistrate had apparently frightened Matthew Weeks into revealing Charlotte's intentions to Phillipa Peter on Tuesday April 16. Now, nine days later, he found himself in the parlour of the Halworthy inn before three justices. And well might he have feared them. They were powerful local figures.

Once information was placed before a magistrate, a summons or warrant of arrest for a suspect to attend a hearing could be issued, and the examination could take place even if the accused were not found in time to attend. Before 1848, the accused need have no legal representative, although his accuser might have a lawyer; and he could be interrogated by a magistrate, without being cautioned that anything he said would be taken down and might be given in evidence at a trial.

The so-called informal hearing was dangerous as far as an accused was concerned for he was virtually powerless. There need be no jury; and just one magistrate could listen to as many witnesses as liked to appear against him, while he was given no opportunity to cross examine them. The object was to establish whether or not there was a prima facie case on which he could be committed for trial.

As the procedure was based upon the principle that the accused was innocent until proved guilty, it was not up to him to defend himself by calling witnesses and engaging counsel but up to the prosecution to substantiate the case against him. And, as the press and public were admitted to the hearing, its outcome was liable to be accepted as a verdict in the popular mind, even although it was not a trial.

So there stood Matthew, reputedly handcuffed to a bar that stretched from the floor to the ceiling of the room, in front of not one but three justices of the peace. And, as non-borough magistrates had to be land-owners until 1906, they were country squires who revolved in a society a galaxy away from the world of Matthew and the goings on in the Davidstow farmsteads.[1]

There was the sixty-three-year old Reverend Samuel Chilcote, Doctor of Divinity and Rector of Otterham. He had been presented to his living by executors of a member of his own family.[2]

There was sixty-six-year old John Braddon, a deputy lieutenant of Cornwall and married to the daughter of a Devonshire magistrate. Having succeeded, through his mother, to the ownership of Downinney manor in the parishes of Treneglos and Warbstow, he resided at Treglith; and, not only did he hunt as a typical landed gentleman of his time, but he kept his own pack of harriers.[3]

Charlotte Dymond

And there was John King Lethbridge, the fifty-five-year old chairman of the bench. Not for nothing was this grandson of a Davidstow vicar known as 'King John'. By the time he was forty-four, he had held office in Launceston as deputy recorder and town clerk, had twice served the borough as mayor, and had fought against Launceston's losing the assize to Bodmin at the Quarter Sessions. When he died in 1861, this deputy lieutenant had chaired the Sessions for twenty years and had been a magistrate for Devonshire as well as for his own county. Having come in to Tregeare in Laneast through his first wife, Elizabeth Baron, he was well placed to stand as Member of Parliament for Launceston; but, when the invitation to do so came in this year, 1844, he chose to decline. [4]

Apart from the imposing gentlemen of the bench, the hearing was apparently attended by another notable. Since Mrs. Phillipa Peter had found herself in the role of prosecutrix, she required a legal representative and evidently chose John Lethbridge Cowlard.

As his middle name suggests, the thirty-two-year old Launceston solicitor was related to the chairman of the bench. His mother was 'King John's' sister; and his father's living, the perpetual curacy of Laneast, was in the magistrate's gift as possessor of Tregeare. The surname, Cowlard, was an anglicisation of the French name Cuillard, forebears of the solicitor having been amongst Protestants who escaped the massacre of St. Bartholomew's Eve in 1572.

At the time of the magistrates' hearing, Cowlard was in partnership with Launceston's town clerk, Gurney, at Madford House. But his practice was later to include his son, Christopher, and another lawyer, Charles Grylls, in Exeter Street. And, apart from the Madford family home, he purchased Ullacombe farm in Devon as a change of air for his eight children. [5]

So, the *Alldrunkard Inn* at Halworthy must now have been the centre of local attention. Matthew Weeks, 'the murderer', was up in front of 'King John', the Doctor, and the master of the hounds in the busy little public house on the 1759 Camelford-Launceston turnpike road. He'd been arrested on Plymouth Hoe 'while trying to escape to the Channel Isles', 'found guilty' by the inquest jury, and the chances were that the magistrates would commit him for trial at Bodmin. A day out in the county town for a public hanging was now a distinct possibility, as far as the locals would have been concerned.

* * * *

But while the first of the twenty-six witnesses,[6] who were to come forward against Matthew, began giving evidence and Cowlard the solicitor compiled depositions, Constable William Dingle of Northill had other things to see to. He had claimed Matthew's best boots at the house of Constable Bennett in South Petherwin. And as, despite his deafness, he apparently heard the boot print evidence at the inquest, he could not reach the moor quickly enough to compare the marks with the footwear.

On his way, he called at the *Brittannia Inn,* at Trevilian's Gate, for Humphrey Vosper to guide him to the scene of the alleged crime. And off set the publican and policeman in the direction of Roughtor Ford.

When they came to within sixty to eighty yards of where the body had been found on Tuesday, April 23, Vosper showed Constable Dingle the toe-to-toe prints of a man's boots and a woman's pattens which the search party had found on the slope there. And the constable judged the boot prints and patten marks to be about eighteen inches apart.[7]

Taking Matthew's right boot, Dingle held it on its side by the right print while Vosper went down on his knees to compare the two. He noted that the nail heads were proud of the metal heel protector on the boot and that their impressions were correspondingly stronger in the print than those of the protector itself and its outer edge. He also noticed that Matthew's boot had a toe plate which corresponded with an impression of one in the print.

Constable Dingle then knelt down and held Matthew's boot directly above the print. He found that both the boot and the print corresponded as far as the heel and the flat part of the sole were concerned, the print being stronger on the outside. But, because Matthew's right boot was the one he wore on his lame leg, its toe turned up and would not have made an impression in the ground had he stood still on the spot. So the constable came to the conclusion that the boot print on the ground was not full length, to him the toe print was not defined, and that way Matthew's boot exactly fitted the impression.

Humphrey Vosper tried to compare Matthew's left boot with the left print but was unable to as the print was, by now, too faint. However, Constable Dingle, having been satisfied that Matthew's best boot fitted the moorland print, as he had been determined he would be, moved further towards Roughtor Ford in search of more prints.

He was not disappointed, he found several which corresponded with Matthew's boots as far as he was concerned. And, when Vosper took him to the river to point out the place where the body had been found, the constable found one print within eighteen paces of the site. Two of the prints he found had impressions of the toe of the boot and they corresponded with Matthew's boots.

Whether or not the prints Dingle found, between the slope some sixty-to-eighty yards away and the site where the body was discovered, were as old as the prints on the slope which Vosper and other searchers had examined, was not stated. Dingle obviously assumed that they were. But the fact that twelve men and the surgeon had been walking around that area on the Tuesday when the body was found - and, although the men might have been in nailed boots, the surgeon would probably have been in 'best boots' - seems not to have been considered.

It is evident that Vosper had been right in thinking the prints had been made by boots with heel protectors and toe plates, the kind that most men at that time and in that area would wear on Sundays. He was also sure that the print included a toe plate impression, although Constable Dingle chose to ignore this in order to prove that the print, although shorter than Matthew's boot, had nevertheless been made by it because his lameness caused the toe to turn up and therefore to leave no mark.

This was to worry Cowlard, the solicitor, who argued that 'from the manner in which the toes of Weeks's boots turned up, the heel and sole only would have been impressed except in very muddy or sticky ground.' Yet, the prints which were to be crucial to the prosecution case had been found where the ground *was* 'moist and clayey'; and it is obvious from Dingle's evidence that they would not fit Matthew's boots unless he swore against the word of Vosper that the toe impression was missing.

An even more important fact was overlooked. Of the two crucial prints, the right one was the more distinct. Yet, as Matthew was lame in his right leg, the left boot would have taken his weight when standing still. [8]

Nonetheless, the two men returned to Trevilian's Gate determined that they had proved the boot print evidence against Matthew. They had convinced themselves for sure by actually pressing his boots on the moorland prints. That had been Constable Dingle's brainwave.

And, having left Humphrey Vosper at his inn, the policeman apparently went down to Penhale farm from Trevilian's Gate. There, he found Phillipa Peter at home and doubtless related his and Vosper's success. She thereupon handed over the dark velvet jacket which Matthew had worn out with Charlotte on Sunday, 14.

With this, Constable Dingle was tickled. He was in the habit of wearing a similar garment when going about his business as a butcher, he said; and, carefully, he went over every inch of it in search of clues. As the cloth was dark, it showed no marks; but Dingle's finger nail found what he was looking for.

From the cuff to the elbow of the left sleeve, a large mark and several small ones could be felt. These could only have been made by Charlotte's blood, according to Con. Dingle, as Matthew had not worn the jacket for the pig kill.

There were no means of telling what the marks actually were. Constable Dingle would not have been interested, anyway. He was hot foot to the magistrates' hearing. He did note, however, that nothing was to be found in the jacket pocket.

* * * *

Mrs. Peter's daughter, Mary Westlake, had obviously pipped him to the post that first day of the magistrates' hearing because, some time during it, she called at Penhale and collected the contents of the pockets. Matthew's red cotton handkerchief from the jacket's outside pocket and Charlotte's green gauze handkerchief from the inside breast pocket were needed to illustrate the evidence regarding her and her mother's search of Matthew's clothes on Sunday, April 21.

And it was while collecting them for this purpose now that Mary Westlake noticed something that had escaped her attention on the Sunday. On Matthew's red cotton handkerchief there were several spots of blood.

As the prosecutrix, Mrs. Phillipa Peter would probably have been the leading witness at the hearing. But, by this time, she was something of a reluctant accuser. Her solicitor came to that conclusion and was later to write *in spite of the certainty of Weeks's guilt which she has, she is evidently kindly disposed towards him and, although a respectable woman, would not probably be sorry if he was acquitted. In giving her evidence, therefore, there will doubtless be bias in the prisoner's favour.*

Mainly because of what the neighbours had been saying and also because, to her mind, Matthew had been incapable of providing satisfactory explanations of Charlotte's disappearance and his own movements on Sunday 14, Phillipa Peter had felt duty bound to lay information before a magistrate. Even had she not, someone else would have ensured that the matter reached the ears of authority.

In any event a body had been found and a pathologist and coroner had had to be notified. Matthew might have been her trusted right-hand man for some six years. But the law had to take its course. She had no alternative but to prosecute.

Accordingly, she outlined events leading up to Charlotte's vanishing; and was apparently required to identify various articles as they were produced during the hearing - Matthew's boots and jacket by Constable Dingle, Charlotte's gloves by Constable Bennett, Matthew's shirt by Constable Brooming, Charlotte's gown and broken necklace by Constable Rickard - and she herself had brought Matthew's stockings from which she had washed the turfy mud.

During her statement, she admitted having given Charlotte notice to leave Penhale on Lady Day, three weeks before Matthew had returned without her on April 14. And, as she also admitted to having seen something like a letter, which Matthew had maintained invited Charlotte to a new position in Blisland, Rebecca and George Lanxon of that parish were required to give evidence.

They repeated the denials they had given to John Stevens on April 21 and at the inquest three days later, however, And Hezekiah Spear, when called, reaffirmed that he had neither expected nor received Charlotte at Brown Willy.

Mrs. Peter's solicitor, John Lethbridge Cowlard, recorded the evidence as it was given. In the event of Matthew's being committed for trial, these notes would be needed when he came to compile the case and brief a barrister.

But listening to his client's son, John Peter, Cowlard reached the conclusion that he was rather soft and desirous of stating more than he really knew. And he noted that the three magistrates seemed of similar opinion for they allowed him but a brief appearance, although they were willing to accept that he spoke the truth when he said that Charlotte left Penhale wearing gloves.

In fact, they had to believe him, if they intended to pin Matthew on this point, because John Peter was the only witness to swear that Charlotte was in gloves on the Sunday she vanished. The girl had apparently possessed two pairs of gloves, a silk pair 'now at home' according to Mrs. Peter and a striped cotton pair similar to those found in Matthew's very best jacket and waistcoat pockets when he was arrested.

Rebecca Jewell was called. Her identification of the gloves found on Weeks as Charlotte's was tentative, however, because she felt the stripes should have been wider. But Mrs. Peter was positive they were the girl's. The cotton gloves were thereupon accepted as having belonged to Charlotte and as having been taken from her body by Matthew Weeks, even although only soft John Peter could swear she had worn them and despite the fact that one of the pair had been found in a coat other than that worn by Matthew on the Sunday in question.

When John Stevens, the servant Phillipa Peter had engaged on Lady Day, came to give evidence, her solicitor's opinion of him was little better than he held of her son. He was a stupid fellow, Cowlard felt, but one who might nevertheless tell the truth.

Unfortunately for Matthew Weeks, John Stevens stuck to his story about having seen him buy a knife from Charles Parsons; and further alleged that he was in possession of two knives before Charlotte's disappearance. He also spoke of watching Matthew hone a razor, although he had never seen him with one until the eve of the supposed murder. And he gave the magistrates to understand that Matthew had absconded because he guessed that he and John Peter would ride to Brown Willy and Blisland and return to Penhale with the news that Charlotte had neither been expected nor arrived at those places.

The prima facie case for committing Matthew Weeks for trial was mounting.

The constable denied it

12. On the second day of the magistrates' hearing, Friday, April 26, the newspapers broke the news of the Charlotte Dymond case to the Cornish public.

The *Royal Cornwall Gazette,* founded in 1803 and with a tory bias, regretted *to announce the commission of a most atrocious crime, by which our county is seldom disgraced,* with the headline *MURDER NEAR CAMELFORD.* This was on page 2 of the paper; and the report went on to say that the excitement, which the discovery of Charlotte Dymond's body had created in the Camelford neighbourhood, was most intense. Policeman Fitzgerald had gone in pursuit of Matthew Weeks, it informed its readers, and every confidence was felt that he would soon be in custody, having last been seen on the road to Plymouth.

Under *LATEST NEWS,* on page 3, the Gazette was able to give particulars of the inquest *received at the moment of going to press.* It outlined the events leading up to Charlotte's disappearance and the locality's subsequent suspicions of Weeks, who had absconded by the time the body was found. Surgeon Good, it said, thought that Charlotte could not have killed herself because the bones of the neck were partially separated, such was the force of the cut, so the jury returned a verdict of wilful murder. A description of Matthew followed.

The *West Briton,* founded in 1810 with a whig bias and, by 1835, with twice the readership of the Gazette, reported much the same on page 3, under the headline *CORONER'S INQUEST — CHARGE OF WILFUL MURDER.* [1] Charlotte's bonnet, shawl, shoes and pattens were still missing, it said, and Weeks appeared to have been jealous of her speaking to others. The coroner had issued a warrant for his arrest and Constable Fitzgerald of Camelford had gone to Devonport on Tuesday, April 23 in pursuit of Weeks.

The case must have been already open and shut, cut and dried, as far as the Cornish were concerned, for those who could not read about it for themselves doubtless soon heard all about it from those who could.

Matthew still had to face two days handcuffed to a bar before the bench of magistrates, however; and this was merely a hearing, to see if a case could be made against him, not a trial. So the witnesses continued to give evidence — Prout that Charlotte had arranged to meet him at Tremail chapel on the day she disappeared, Bettinson that he and Matthew had discussed the rumour that Charlotte's mother had threatened to kill her, Hocken that Matthew had said that no-one could swear anything against him.

Yet, swear against Matthew, many were evidently willing to. Sarah Westlake swore he had not visited her, as he'd said, on Sunday, April 14. Mary Westlake, her daughter-in-law, swore that Matthew had not been near Halworthy, as far as she knew, on that day, that he had suspiciously changed the subject when she'd asked her mother, Phillipa Peter, where Charlotte was the next day at Penhale, and that the green gauze handkerchief she'd found in Matthew's pocket was Charlotte's.

Mary Westlake also told the magistrates that she had gone to the moor, when the body had been found, and collected the broken bead necklace; and Simon Baker explained how the body had been discovered. Humphrey Vosper described the search beforehand and also his and Constable Dingle's trip to the moor, during the first day of the hearing, in order to test Matthew's best boots against the prints.

* * * *

Meanwhile, William Northam of the Halworthy inn, where the justices' investigation was taking place, and his neighbour, John Westlake, Phillipa Peter's son-in-law, had arranged to meet Isaac Cory on the moor before giving evidence. The purpose was to establish exactly where the man and woman were, when Cory first saw them, on Sunday April 14.

On the day of the search, Tuesday, April 23, Northam and Westlake had followed patten marks through Higher Down Field and Gate, over the common, and across the Altarnon-Camelford road to a spot beyond Trevilian's Gate. There, they had lost the marks, apparently because the ground was grassy, and had not found more until they had reached Lanlary Rock. It was therefore important to connect the two sets of prints by means of Cory's evidence.

So Cory showed them where he had stood, at the top of Moor Lane, and watched Matthew Weeks with a woman on the moor; and he pointed out the spot, where they'd been when he'd first seen them, about sixty yards on to the moor from his field at Trevilian's Gate. It was there, Westlake and Northam agreed, that they had lost the patten marks on the day of the search.

The three men were now ready to give their evidence at the magistrates' hearing.

* * * *

Having listened to Surgeon Good's report of the post mortem examination of Charlotte's body and his opinion that, *although the wound was the kind a person might have inflicted upon themselves,* he did not think she had killed herself, the attention of those at the hearing then shifted to the evidence of Pethick and Gard, who had seen the couple in the Roughtor area on the evening of Charlotte's disappearance.

As far as chapel-goers were concerned, William Gard - the Methodist preacher who'd seen the couple walking towards the ford and then turn back - would have been a most reliable witness. It had been said of him in 1822 that 'you might as soon expect to find the pulpit out of place as not to find the preacher in it when William Gard was planned' to preach. Come what may and however remote the preaching place, apparently, William Gard would be there to keep the appointment.[2]

It was therefore a pity for the prosecution that he could not identify the couple on the moor for, with the reputation he had, his word would have been strong.

'The person I saw was as near as can be the height of the prisoner (Weeks)', he told the magistrates, 'it was not foggy then although it had been so and mist was hanging about Roughtor.'

'They were about two gun shots from me', Gard continued, 'I cannot say whether he walked lame, they walked very slow'.

It was now imperative that the other witness on the moor, Richard Pethick, the cattle farmer, positively identify Matthew as the man. And, in the hope that he would do so, he was called.

J.L. Cowlard, the solicitor, noted that the magistrates examined him cautiously, as so much depended upon whether Pethick could or could not swear that Matthew was the man at Roughtor Ford on Sunday, April 14, with Charlotte. When it came to the question of identification, Richard Pethick looked at Matthew as he stood there in front of the magistrates.

'He is like the man (on the moor)', Pethick admitted, 'I believe him to be the man from his size and appearance. I had watched him and he walked like a lame man.'

Further than this, Pethick would not go. For some reason or other, the solicitor thought, he seemed shy of swearing positively that Matthew and the man on the moor were one and the same. The prosecution's case, regarding the couple on the moor, now relied upon Gard's and Pethick's descriptions of their behaviour, tying in with the foot prints in the Roughtor Ford vicinity, and the clothes worn by them. The prints and behaviour might correspond but the clothes were difficult. Neither witness noticed a red shawl on the woman; and, although both said that the man was in a short, dark, frock coat, this was of little use if such as Constable Dingle went around telling people it was just like his own.

However, when Elizabeth Stevens told the magistrates that Matthew had produced a black silk handbag in her father's house at Coad's Green and the bag could be identified as Charlotte's, the possibility of Matthew's guilt grew stronger again. The bag was not produced, as it had not been found amongst Matthew's effects, but its description sufficed to add yet another black mark against him apparently.

Constable Bennett outlined his arrest of Matthew, and Constable Fitzgerald told the hearing about the conversation he had had with Matthew while sleeping with him.

According to the press,[3] Matthew was permitted to ask witnesses questions from time to time throughout the hearing - although there was no formal cross-examination - and one of his queries came at the close of Constable Fitzgerald's evidence. Fitzgerald had mentioned that Matthew had told Constable Bennett he'd originally thought it unsafe to stay in Plymouth or Devonport - hence his considering going to the Channel Isles - but had later changed his

Charlotte Dymond

mind and was therefore arrested.

Matthew turned to Constable Bennett and asked 'did'nt I say I was come to see Plymouth and meant to return (to Cornwall)?'

The constable denied it. The word of two policemen added up to Matthew's having told a lie to save his skin, as far as the hearing was concerned. It had, after all, been convened to establish whether or not a case could be made against him. Thus, anything in his favour, such as the 'further conversation' between Constable Bennett and Matthew regarding the end of his courtship of Charlotte, was passed off. In the solicitor's words, 'it is not apprehended that much use can be made of this' by the prosecution.

Attention turned to the evidence of Cory, Westlake and Northam.

Isaac Cory related how he had watched Matthew walk across the moor in the direction of Lanlary Rock in the company of a young woman on Sunday, April 14. He still would not identify the woman as Charlotte; but it was assumed that they were one and the same. Westlake and Northam then described how they had taken measurements of boot and patten prints on the day of the search; and also told the magistrates of their visit to the moor with Cory this second day of the hearing.

Northam, the inn-keeper, explained that the boot measurement, which was notched on his stick, had been taken from a deep impression near a patten mark (and not from the toe-to-toe prints of a couple standing still on the slope). He said that he and Westlake had taken the dimensions as well as they could, being more interested in the actual length of the print than in any heel-protector or toe-cap impressions.

Northam had only to compare Matthew's boots with the measurement on his stick, it seemed, and the case would be serious enough on the face of it (prima facie) to send the prisoner for trial.

The boots had been brought to the hearing by Constable Dingle, after his and Vosper's experiments with them on the moor the previous day, and they now lay on the table in front of the magistrates.

Northam took his notched stick to the table and tried Matthew's boots against its measurement. The comparison confirmed what Constable Dingle must have discovered but would not admit, hence his swearing that the marks on the moor were not full length.

The boot prints on the moor were shorter than Matthew's boots. [4]

The road to Bodmin gaol

13. The attention of the entire Westcountry was attracted to the Charlotte Dymond case by the headline *HORRID MURDER - CORNWALL* in the *Western Flying Post*. Better known as the *Sherborne Mercury* and general advertiser for Dorset, Somerset, Devon and Cornwall, this paper broke the news on the third day of the magistrates' hearing, Saturday, April 27, with a six inch paragraph, sent in by a correspondent, on page three.

Like the *Royal Cornwall Gazette* and *West Briton*, the *Mercury* outlined events up to and including the wilful murder verdict of the inquest but, unlike the Cornish papers, it rightly reported that it was the South Petherwin (and not the Camelford) constable who effected Matthew's arrest. Then followed some elaborations, such as that Matthew had left Penhale saying he would visit friends in Linkinhorne, and that Charlotte's body had been found with its *face exposed to the sun which had turned it to a ghastly yellow.*

No doubt it had. The gruesome details had not been included in the pathologist's report. But what Surgeon Good had certainly not supposed, as the Mercury told its readers, was that Charlotte *must have struggled hard, as several bruises were apparent on the neck and wrist.*

The correspondent went on to say that *little doubt is entertained of the guilt of Weeks, but what could have induced him to commit such an atrocious deed is rather uncertain. Report says that it was jealousy - that the deceased* (Charlotte) *was coquettish and favoured the advances of other young men - but, whether this was the case, time perhaps will show.*

To the press and its readers, months before any trial took place, the death of Charlotte was 'horrid murder' even although a pathologist admitted the possibility of its having been suicide; a 'verdict of wilful murder' had been returned against Matthew although he had only been indicted or accused of such by an inquest jury; and already there was speculation as to why he had 'committed such an atrocious deed' when there was still one day to go of the magistrates' investigation.

* * * *

This Saturday, Mary Westlake evidently received Charlotte's bonnet cap from her mother who had apparently produced it in evidence of its having been found 'badly washed' on April 16. This, together with the equally badly washed best light waistcoat of Matthew, wound up the evidence given by twenty-six witnesses during the three-day magisterial examination of the case.[1]

The presiding magistrate, John King Lethbridge, then apparently addressed Matthew. He said that the bench had gone through a very long and painful investigation and that Matthew was now at liberty to make any communication he might think proper. With little hesitation, it seemed to the press members present, Matthew stated that he would say nothing.[2]

It was then up to the magistrates to decide whether or not a case could be made against Matthew from what they had heard. It was recognised that there was no apparent motive unless it could be proved that Matthew had acted out of jealousy, that only Cory could positively identify Matthew as the man on the moor and no-one could prove that Charlotte was the woman, and that even although the nine shillings Charlotte was thought to have possessed were nowhere to be found, it could not be proved that Matthew had her money.

Nevertheless, Charlotte's arrangement to meet Thomas Prout at Tremail chapel showed that she had no intention of leaving Mrs. Peter's, John Stevens's saying that Matthew bought another knife and honed a razor showed that he was premeditating Charlotte's murder, and Constable Fitzgerald's statement that Matthew had told Constable Bennett it was not safe to stay in Plymouth proved that he had guilty knowledge.

It was all circumstantial evidence; but it added up to a case against Matthew.

Charlotte Dymond

He was therefore to be imprisoned at Bodmin pending the next assize when the case would be tried. Mrs. Phillipa Peter, as the prosecutrix, was bound over to prefer a bill of indictment against Matthew and the witnesses were bound over to attend the trial. The preliminary hearing was over.

* * * *

Whether Matthew were guilty or innocent, the magistrates' investigation must have been quite an ordeal. He had no legal representative to advise him. His family could not support him because, until 1898, next of kin were unable to give evidence. His employer, workmates and acquaintances had spoken against him. He was out on his own. [3]

It is difficult to imagine just how one might behave in those circumstances. As far as the Mercury reporter was concerned, Matthew *betrayed an almost careless indifference, merely asking two or three of the witnesses a few unimportant questions. We never recollect seeing such obtuseness of conduct displayed before and can only account for it from the fact of his being uneducated, unable to read or write. He ate, drank and slept as if quite unconscious of the serious position in which he is placed. He was dressed in a manner superior to the generality of farm servants and appeared very little concerned.* [4]

If he were guilty, one would have thought that Matthew would have acted differently. He might have blatantly denied the charges, made counter accusations against someone else, cooked up another alibi when his Halworthy one was broken, or even professed guilt to draw sympathy. That is, unless he were so simple-minded that he had no idea what his accusers were saying and where it was all leading.

The Mercury reporter would seem to think that was the case, 'the fact of his being uneducated'. Yet this was not an unusual state of affairs for Matthew's kind, Charlotte Dymond stood out precisely because she could read and write while most of her class could not. Serving people in 1844 tended to be illiterate; but that didn't mean that they had no brain power, merely that they were not as fortunate as those who were literate. [5]

Matthew Weeks was no fool, or J. L. Cowlard, the prosecution solicitor, would have noted the fact. That he 'appeared very little concerned' might point to his being brazen, but this just would not fit what we know of him. He made no flamboyant gesture throughout the case, except to dress 'in a manner superior to the generality of farm servants'.

And, with this, we return to what seems to have been Matthew's chief crime towards the humanity of his time - he thought himself above his station. He would not accept his place. That kind of man, surely, needed no Charlotte Dymond to bolster his ego; she would have needed him. If Matthew could sit talking to two young women for six hours at Coad's Green, and they seemed perfectly happy to enjoy his company, he had no chip on his shoulder that girls rejected him because of his limp; they were more interested in the money he appeared to have, he dressed well.

But how could he afford to? That should have been the question. Yet nobody asked it.

Charlotte Dymond

If the Mercury reporter had, he might have solved the problem that perplexed so many - what made Matthew 'obtuse', not clear-cut, unable to be pigeon-holed as a personality?

Instead, his 'obtuseness' was interpreted by the reporter - and, probably, everybody else - as dim-mindedness. He 'merely' asked two or three of the witnesses 'a few unimportant questions'. We know one of those questions, whether or not he said to Constable Bennett that he 'had gone to see Plymouth and meant to return'. Far from being 'unimportant', it was of vital concern to Matthew for the contable's answer meant the difference of his being said to have guilty knowledge of Charlotte's alleged murder or complete innocence.

The constable's word was accepted in preference to Matthew's when there is reason to believe it should not have been.

These things considered and if Weeks were neither a fool nor guilty, we might expect him to have taken the opportunity of making a statement.

* * * *

In fact, he did take the chance. But, evidently, he did not feel inclined to address the hearing. Instead, about half an hour after the proceedings had ended and one of the magistrates had already left for home, he volunteered to speak.

According to Cowlard, the solicitor, when his statement had been written down and signed (presumably with a cross, as he could neither read nor write), it was 'very carefully' read over to him and the words were 'literally his'. But the lawyer imagined that, as Matthew's statment was looked upon as being continuous to the evidence of his accusers, the heading of the magistrates' examination was not re-read to him.

In other words, as the Indictable Offences Act of 1848, which was regulated by the 1952 Magistrates Courts Act, did not obtain in 1844, obligations to read over accusers' statements to the accused, to explain the nature of the charge against him, and to issue a caution before the statement of an accused person was taken were not binding in Matthew's time. [6]

Consequently, Weeks was to find himself once more at the mercy of the system, particularly as he had as yet no solicitor to safeguard his position. His statement is illustrative of this -

In the morning (of Sunday, April 14), *Charlotte told me that her mistress* (Mrs. Peter) *had given her a week's warning* (notice) *and that she was going to leave; and she asked me to lend her half-a-crown. I let her have 18 pence and asked where she was going. She said she did not know. Then she asked me if I would go along with her a little way in the afternoon. I went along with her a little way the other side of the* (Altarnon-Camelford) *road going to chapel; and then she said she did not want me to go any further. I wished her well and bid her good afternoon, and she left me and I left her. I did not speak to her any more. The blood on the shirt was when the pig was killed.* [7]

Whether or not this was all he said, we cannot know. The original statement seems not to have survived so that we now rely entirely upon the press for its content. If we accept, when he stated that Charlotte said she 'did not know' where she was going, that he meant she had no idea of the position the Lanxons had got for her, his tale is consistent with what he had been saying all along except that he now admitted accompanying her a quarter of a mile further than he had owned up to Mrs. Peter.

He may, of course, have implied as much when he told John Stevens on April 17 that he 'went a little way out along with her'. But, by now saying that he crossed the Altarnon-Camelford road, he had put himself very near the place on the moor where the couple were supposed to have been seen by Isaac Cory on Sunday, April 14.

Had Cory been prepared to swear that the woman on the moor was Charlotte, this seeming admission of Matthew's could have been serious. But, as Cory was only able to say that he saw Weeks with a woman, there is but one possible explanation.

It probably was Charlotte that Cory saw. She was in pattens; and there were patten marks from the direction of Penhale to the place where Cory saw Matthew, and Matthew says he left Charlotte. But the fact that Matthew's boots left no prints on this side of the moor, although there were boot prints on the Roughtor Ford side, suggests that Matthew was not the man seen later that afternoon with Charlotte. And precisely because Charlotte left Matthew at the spot where Cory saw him and went on alone, Cory could not with certainty name her as the woman on the moor.

What is noticeable about Matthew's statement is that, apart from this admission, he had stuck to his story. And it was possibly because of this that Mrs. Peter's solicitor recognised the difficulty of making a case against him stick.

There was no apparent motive. No weapon had been found. The river was an unlikely place for the alleged murder to have been committed. Charlotte's shoes, pattens, shawl and bonnet were missing. And the witnesses left much to be desired, he felt.

John Peter might be caught out if he tried to say more than he knew. Constable Dingle was deaf. Richard Pethick seemed shy of identifying Weeks with the man on the moor. William Gard couldn't identify him any way. William Northam's print measurement would not fit Matthew's boot. And Mrs. Peter would as soon see him get off scot free. The case needed careful management, particularly as Weeks would be defended in the assize court.

* * * *

Meanwhile, Matthew was escorted from the Halworthy inn by two constables and driven in a cart to Camelford, four miles down the road. There, in the ancient borough that had sent two representatives to Parliament until the 1832 Reform Act, large numbers of sight-seers from the surrounding countryside had assembled.

Matthew's arrival in the town caused great excitement. And, after he had taken refreshment, the crowds watched him being led to a gig by the borough's own constable, John Fitzgerald. They lined the route up the narrow street by the town hall and the *Darlington Inn,* and saw him off along the road to Bodmin gaol.[8]

By half past nine on that evening of Saturday, April 27, Matthew Weeks was within the walls of the county prison.

And Constable John Fitzgerald was driving back in his gig to Camelford, the trousers that Matthew had worn, when he had left Penhale with Charlotte on Sunday April 14, now in his custody.

Charlotte Dymond

Something black showing

14. On Sunday, April 14, the area around Roughtor Ford on Bodmin Moor had been little thought of and less used, except by such as the couple of walkers, a local preacher, and a farmer on horseback looking for his cattle. What happened on the evening of that day, however, changed the scene dramatically.

Just two weeks later, on Sunday, April 28, hundreds of sight-seers converged on the area.[1] The Cornish and regional newspapers had, as yet, covered the Charlotte Dymond case only as far as the inquest verdict. But the reports had their effect. The people arrived to view the spot where the body had been found.

Amongst them were Isaac Cory and his wife, Maria, of Trevilian's Gate. And the purpose of their visit was, as Cory subsequently explained, to find Charlotte's clothes.

* * * *

Why he was intent upon this, he did not state. His evidence, regarding his having seen Matthew Weeks with a woman in a red shawl walking from sixty yards beyond Trevilian's Gate in the direction of Lanlary Rock, had been all important. It, alone, connected the patten marks, which petered out around Trevilian's Gate, with those discovered near Lanlary Rock. Yet he did not identify Charlotte as being the woman who wore the pattens on the moor - although it must have been her - seeming only concerned to ensure that everyone believed Matthew to have been the man with her.

Isaac Cory had called at Penhale at sometime after five o'clock on the evening of Sunday, April 14, seemingly to say that he had watched Matthew walk towards Lanlary Rock with a woman, late that afternoon, and that the woman had worn pattens, because he had followed prints of them on his way down to Mrs. Peter's farm. That was the last day that Charlotte was seen alive, her body having been found at the ford nine days later.

The way between Penhale farm and Roughtor Ford could have been more direct than via Lanlary Rock. It was possibly only because Cory had told Mrs. Peter, about seeing Matthew with a woman going towards the rock, that the local men on the day of the search made in that direction and so picked up the patten prints, they had lost at Trevilian's Gate, which led them to Charlotte's body.

It is true, of course, that Matthew had said that Charlotte had told him she intended staying at Hezekiah Spear's for the night, on her way to take up a new position at Blisland; and Lanlary Rock is in the direction of Spear's at Brown Willy. But he had told this tale two days after Cory had spun his yarn about a couple making for the rock; and it seems possible that he could have used Cory's details on the spur of the moment and in the unexpected turn of events.

If we assume for the moment that exactly what Matthew said in his statement actually happened, we are left with the bare bones of a story as follows. Charlotte told Matthew that she had been given notice by Mrs. Peter; and she asked him to accompany her a little way in the afternoon of Sunday April 14. He accordingly did and left her a little beyond the Altarnon-Camelford road.

Leaving Penhale at about four o'clock and reaching the spot sixty yards beyond Trevilian's Gate and the Altarnon-Camelford road, where Cory said the couple were by about twenty to five when he first saw them, Charlotte would have been walking at a pace between 1½ and 1¾ miles per hour.[2] As this seems to have been the speed of Matthew's progress between Penhale and Coad's Green on April 21, it is likely that he accompanied Charlotte as far as the place in question as he stated.

During the next twenty minutes that Cory was watching the couple on the moor, they covered a further quarter of a mile according to him. If the woman were Charlotte, she had slackened her pace from between 1½ and 1¾ miles per hour to ¾ of a mile per hour.

If this suggests that Charlotte changed her pace between the points on the moor where a woman was first and last seen by Cory, the boot print evidence supports Matthew's contention that he was no longer with her at this stage. On the Penhale side of the moor where he was with her, his boots left no marks alongside her patten prints. On the Roughtor Ford side of the moor, where a man was seen to limp beside Charlotte, boot marks and patten prints were found together.

If that man were not Matthew but had assumed a limp to look as though he were, his exaggerated walk left an impression. Where the ground was clayey and anyone would have left an imprint, even by standing still on a spot, the mark of the right boot was heavier than the left and definitely showed a toe plate impression. But, since Matthew was lame in his right leg and the toe of his boot turned up, that print could not have been made by him: even had the upturned boot left a mark, it would have been lighter than the left which carried his weight.

Had Matthew therefore been doing something other than walking across the moor with Charlotte on April 14, it would have come as a shock to him when Mrs. Peter expected her back that night and had obviously not given her notice to leave. And, as he would probably have heard Cory's yarn from a member of the household by the time Mrs. Peter pressed him to reveal Charlotte's whereabouts on the Tuesday, he could have adapted it to fit his Brown Willy and Blisland tale; and given himself the Halworthy alibi.

Alternatively, and even given his Halworthy story doubtful, he might have been telling the truth about Charlotte's intentions. Spear and the Lanxons may have had no idea that Charlotte had decided to call upon them; but, in their direction the evidence suggests she was making, that Sunday April 14. We know that she set off from Penhale farm in Davidstow at about four o-clock; the patten marks indicate that she walked at least as far as sixty yards beyond the Altarnon-Camelford road and Trevilian's Gate; and, if Cory saw her there at about twenty to five, she would have taken forty minutes for the uphill climb so far, which is ample.

But, even allowing for the difficulty of negotiating the moorland humps in pattens, Charlotte would surely have increased, not slackened, her pace across the heath to Lanlary Rock, if she intended reaching Brown Willy before dusk. The patten marks found beneath the rock confirm that she did make for this landmark on the way to Brown Willy, which would not have been aimed for had she taken the shortest route from Penhale farm to Roughtor Ford.

What, then, of Cory's evidence that the couple were 'going on very steady' but 'not very fast' towards Lanlary Rock, while he watched them for twenty minutes until five o'clock?

Had his timing been correct, Charlotte would still have had just under a mile to cover before reaching the rock, when Cory last saw her. And, if she were walking at the pace he said she was - which works out at ¾ of a mile per hour - she could not have reached it until about 6.17 p.m. [3]

Charlotte Dymond

Yet, by half past five, when William Gard saw the couple, they were within three gun shots of Roughtor Ford, which is 1¼ miles from Lanlary Rock. As a gun shot was between sixty and eighty yards, according to Vosper's and Westlake's evidence regarding the search, the couple were between 180 and 240 yards from the ford. This would have meant that Charlotte must have walked from where she was last seen by Cory to the spot where Gard saw her – between 3720 and 3660 yards, well over two miles - in thirty minutes.[4] If so, she would have been walking at a pace of over four miles per hour and one which would not tally with Gard's description of the couple's 'very slow place' or of their stopping and starting which was confirmed by Pethick.

Isaac Cory's evidence, regarding the timing, seems not to fit the possibilities.

The 1¼ miles of moorland between his home at Trevilian's Gate and Lanlary Rock can be crossed in half an hour. The downward stretch from the rock to Roughtor Ford could, in Charlotte's time, be covered in thirty minutes, perhaps less, at a similar pace, as the ground is not quite as hard going. And the distance from Penhale farm to Trevilian's Gate takes about half an hour to cover.[5]

We therefore have three fairly equal parts of Charlotte's walk, which can be - and apparently was - covered in 1½ hours. But, as the last stretch - between Lanary Rock and Roughter Ford - was walked by Charlotte and whoever was with her at a 'very slow pace', the first two - from Penhale to Trevilian's Gate and, from there, to Lanary Rock - must have been covered fairly quickly.

The normal walking pace on a good surface is reckoned to be five miles per hour. This may be cut by half on such as the 1¼ miles of rough moorland between Trevilian's Gate and Lanlary Rock, which takes some thirty minutes to cross.

Accepting the pace of 2½ miles an hour and that Charlotte left Penhale at 4 p.m., she would have reached the spot, where Cory said she was at 4.40 p.m., by 4.28 p.m., and could have got to Lanlary Rock at 4.57 p.m.[6] If she then slackened her pace to just over two miles per hour, she would have reached the place, where Gard said the couple were at 5.30 p.m., at exactly that time.[7]

Should just over two miles per hour seem too fast to match Gard's description of the couple's 'very slow pace', Charlotte would have been required to walk faster on the first two legs of her journey and more slowly on the final stretch. In which case, she must have reached the spot, where Cory said she was at 4.40 p.m., even earlier than 4.28 p.m.

It might be argued that Cory mistook the time. It is assumed that he walked the 2¼ miles to his vantage point, from the Davidstow service that ended at 3.30 p.m., there is no mention of any conveyance. But, as he 'stayed some little time after' at the church, and watched the couple for twenty minutes before reaching his house on the moor at 5 p.m., his timing was probably correct. If it were not and he rode home, he would have watched the moorland couple for longer, and their progress could not have tallied with his version.

Yet, if he *were* watching from 4.40 p.m. as he said, Charlotte could not have been sixty yards beyond Trevilian's Gate when he first saw her. Walking at the the 2½ miles per hour pace, the slowest possible to be seen at the places and times described by Gard, she would have been over half a mile away. [8]

Exactly where Cory was standing, is uncertain. If his field of wheat were at Trevilian's Gate, the only land shown to be occupied by him on the 1841 tithe map, the couple coming from Higher Down Gate must have approached and passed him on their way across the moor. But, then, he would have identified the woman, and described the pair as 'coming' rather than 'going'. In the event of his having done neither, he must have stopped to look at his wheat somewhere near the top of the lane coming on to the moor from the Davidstow churchtown direction, about a quarter of a mile from his house as he said.

In this case, he must have been over ¾ mile from the couple he watched, rather than the 60 yds. the press understood him to say in court or the 500 yds. we have thought up to now. The forty-eight-year old preacher, William Gard, could not say if the man on the moor limped when he was 160 yds., at the most, from him.[9] Yet we are expected to believe that sixty-three-year old Cory knew it was Matthew because of the limp when he was either 953 yds., or 1393 yds., away from him. [10]

The problem was, in fact, investigated by the B.B.C. television *Pebble Mill* company when a documentary on the case was filmed in June of 1977; and, even in good weather, it was judged impossible to identify anything animate on the moor except at close range.

Something is, therefore, wrong with Isaac Cory's evidence.

What he actually saw, if he saw anything, may never by fully established. But, three details of his stand out - a young woman in a red shawl, patten marks, and the lame Matthew Weeks. These were enough to make his listeners assume that the woman was Charlotte, follow the marks and find her body, and believe that Matthew had been present at her death.

From details to hand, events might be reconstructed as follows. Charlotte was up to something that Sunday afternoon and Weeks was not included in her plan. Out of his presence, she told Mrs. Peter that he would be back for milking but she would not.

She and Matthew set off from Penhale together; but, once out of sight of the farmhouse, she moved more quickly than usual and, at Higher Down Gate, had left him behind. He, either suspicious of her intentions or actually knowing them as he said, limped up to the moorland behind her to watch her progress.

At 4.40 p.m., if Cory were looking, he would have seen Matthew sixty yards beyond Trevilian's Gate and, in the distance, a woman hurrying towards Lanlary Rock. At a pace of 1½ to 1¾ miles per hour - his capability between Penhale and Coad's Green - Matthew could have reached the spot Cory mentioned and by the time he was watching. But Charlotte must have been well beyond it, at a pace of 2½ miles per hour, if she were later to be seen by Gard.

What Cory then saw Matthew do, we cannot know. But, what Cory could have done, when Matthew had gone, is to have walked towards his home at Trevilian's Gate still watching Charlotte's progress and wondering what was

Charlotte Dymond

going on between her and her boyfriend, Matthew.

At least, he had seen that the man was Matthew; but he could not have been sure that the woman so far in the distance was Charlotte. And then he spotted patten marks. If he followed these, they would lead to Penhale if the woman had been Charlotte. And, once at the farmhouse, he could mention having seen Matthew with a woman, during casual conversation with Phillipa Peter, and probably learn what had been going on.

His story thus told on the Sunday evening, it could not be withdrawn nor rectified once it was known she had disappeared. Cory was committed to it. But we do not know what time he called at Penhale.

What, however, is probable is that at least two men knew that Charlotte Dymond was on the moor by twenty to five that Sunday afternoon - Matthew Weeks and Isaac Cory.

If neither crossed the moor between Trevilian's Gate and Lanlary Rock with her, both had time to cut across the moorland and catch up with her at the place where the boot prints appeared. One or the other might have shouted to her, as she reached Lanlary Rock and he drew parallel on the lower moorland route, and their paths would have converged beneath Showery Tor had Charlotte changed direction.

That she did change direction is evident from the patten marks. And had she kept up her pace of 2½ m.p.h. until her new path converged with the man's, what William Gard said he saw just before 5.30 p.m., as he rounded the hill and noticed the couple, would have been possible. For then began the slow walking to and fro, stopping and starting, in the Roughtor area until the couple were last seen by Richard Pethick, at about 7 p.m., near the place where Charlotte's body was eventually found.

But, as there was between over half and over three-quarters of a mile between the man - Matthew or Cory, respectively - and Charlotte at 4.40 p.m., whoever wanted to catch up with her must have kept up a pace of at least 2½ m.p.h., despite his taking the more direct route. Were it possible for Matthew to achieve this with his limp, he could have been the man on the moor, although the boot print evidence suggests the opposite.

* * * *

Cory would have it to be that he was. He would have known Matthew, he said, twice as far off on Davidstow moorland. And it seems as though he was determined to prove his point. He had denied quarrelling with Matthew over some lost bullocks. His emphasis on the patten marks had led searchers to Charlotte's body. His description of the man's walk had implicated Matthew in her death. And now, on Sunday, April 28, he 'wanted to look for the clothes' which were still missing.

He did not mention that his wife was with him on that day, but we know that she was from Constable Rickard's evidence. The pair were amongst the hundreds who visited the place where the body was found near Roughtor Ford.

'After looking at the spot and in my way back to Trevilian's Gate', Cory was to explain at the subsequent trial, 'I went into the marsh, which is something less than half a mile from where the body was found, in the direction of Penhale. There were many old turf pits about. I observed in one something black showing. I put down my stick and pulled up a single shoe, then a patten, then another shoe. Then I pulled out a shawl, then a whiff (collar), then a bonnet and a piece of black string.'

In a rough draft of his evidence on the back of the prosecution brief, it was noted that Cory said that the turf pit, where the clothes were found, was three feet deep. His statement proper gave the depth as about two feet, however, and the articles as being almost hidden with moss.

'The pit was in the direction that a person would take returning from the old water place (where the body was found) to Mrs. Peter's', maintained Cory. He might also have added that it was in the direction of his own Trevilian's Gate, or Tremail chapel where Prout was to meet Charlotte, if he were determined to be particular.

'Whilst taking these things out of the pit', Cory continued, 'I was on the Roughtor Ford side of it and I did not go the Lanlary Rock side of it.'

The incident was then taken up by Constable Thomas Rickard of Davidstow, who said that he himself 'was on the moors searching for the remainders of Charlotte's clothes', when he saw 'Isaac Cory in a marsh within half a mile of where the body was found. His wife was with him.'

'I saw them take out something from a pit', the constable explained, 'I went up and took possession of the following articles - pair of shoes, a shawl, a bonnet and a whiff with a piece of string. Cory and his wife stood on the Roughtor Ford side of the pit, as did I, and we did not go on the other side of the pit.'

What Cory and his wife then did, is not known. But Constable Rickard took the patterns and tried them against several prints between Lanlary Rock and Roughtor Ford. As the patterns and prints corresponded in detail and the whiff or collar was of the same material as the gown which had been removed from Charlotte's body in his presence, Rickard was satisfied that the residue of Charlotte's effects had been found.

He then decided to discover from which direction the clothes had been brought to the turf pit in the marsh, within half a mile of where the body had been found. While investigating between the clothes pit and the body site, he came upon a wet, turfy marsh in which there were discernible but indistinct tracks.

In the constable's opinion, a man had passed through the wet, boggy ground. And it crossed his mind, as he considered the marsh, that whoever it was would have been nearly up to his knees in mud. "

Dropped into the grave

15. So Matthew Weeks had been the man on the moor with Charlotte Dymond, after all. His trousers and stockings had been turf muddied up to his knees.

It had to be Matthew. The magistrates had found a prima facie case against him and had committed him to Bodmin gaol awaiting the next assize. Loose ends had to be tied up so that the case for the prosecution was watertight by the time it entered court.

Conveniently forgotten was Phillipa Peter's evidence that, when she had tackled Weeks about his muddied trousers and he had held them up to see what worried her, she had said 'it is not at the back they are dirty but at the knees.' Had anyone, let alone Weeks with a limp, waded through a knee-deep bog on Bodmin Moor, he could not have kept his trousers clean at the back.

While it is true that Mrs. Peter had said she was 'frightened' to find Matthew's stockings 'so muddy and wet, the same as if he had been cutting turfs', she must have known they could have got in that state, with one false move on the cripple's part, between Penhale and Higher Down Gate that Sunday April 14. Not only would the lane have been thick with mud that rainy day but the first field after it, that Matthew had to cross, was part of the former Penminnies Marsh where turfs have been cut for the Penhale fire. [1]

* * * *

Regardless of possible alternative explanations, the search for conclusive proof of Matthew's guilt continued, relentlessly. It mattered not that locals had been to-ing and fro-ing the 'murder area' at the time and since the body had been found, nor that sightseers in hundreds had walked the moor in Sunday boots on Sunday April 28 in response to press reports of the discovery. The following day, three constables took Matthew's footwear there in the hope of finding a print it would fit.

Constable Rickard of Davidstow had apparently noticed more than just the clothes when he investigated the marsh in which they had been found by Cory. Evidently in consequence of this, he sent word to Constable Dingle of Northill to meet him on the site with Matthew's boots this Monday April 29. [2]

As the parish constables, being responsible to the magistrates, were probably under a directive to finalise the details of the case, Rickard took with him his colleague on this occasion. He was Constable Gerrance Hayne of Davidstow. Local tradition has it that he came from Tremail and, as there were three possible persons in the area at the time, he was either the forty-four-year old, or one of two in their late twenties. Whichever he was, he was described by Cowlard, the solicitor, as 'an intelligent man' and was a member of the farming community in which Charlotte had worked before resuming her position at Penhale. [3]

Once the three constables had reached the marsh, within half a mile of where the body had been found, Rickard showed the other two something he seems to have noticed the day before. It was a man's print on the Lanlary Rock side of the turf pit, in which Charlotte's clothes had been found by Cory.

Constable Hayne judged it to be about four feet from the pit itself; and, in his opinion, the impression in the mud was not new. He then watched as Dingle made a print beside it with Matthew's right boot, while Rickard supervised the operation.

The old impression, on the hedge of the clothes pit, was of a boot with a toe cap. But, according to the constables, the toe cap was peculiar in that it left an impression as though an extra half had been added to the point of the boot's sole.

When the new print of Matthew's right boot was compared with the old impression, it corresponded in every detail. And Constable Dingle felt that he could 'speak with great certainty that the print so found (on the moor) was made by Matthew Weeks's boot.'

Such great certainty apparently did not rule out the possibility of the impression's having been made by a boot other than Matthew's however. Constable Rickard subsequently assured the solicitor for the prosecution that he, Cory and Mrs. Cory had not been on the side where the boot print was found. And Cory himself stressed, when giving evidence, that he had stood on the opposite side while taking Charlotte's clothes out of the pit.

What we may gather from this is probably that the so-called peculiar toecap on Matthew's boot was by no means unique. But, whether or not Rickard and Cory took the same size boots as Matthew is impossible to say at this distance from events. What *is* clear is that, even at this juncture, an element of doubt was present and the evidence was not, in fact, conclusive.

But, as far as the constables were concerned, they had nailed their man.

* * * *

Perhaps it was this day, perhaps it was the day before, whichever it was, Constable Rickard seems to have been alone when he discovered something else that had evidently been missed by the searchers. While investigating the vicinity of the river place, where Charlotte's body had been found, he noticed that a clod of earth had been removed from the bank and then replaced.

As this was directly above where the body had been found by the water, he lifted the turf. And, beneath it, in the pit which had been made when the turf had been cut out, he found a good deal of blood. The murder place had probably been discovered, as far as the constable was concerned.

* * * *

What was supposed to have happened there was national news on Tuesday, April 30. *DREADFUL MURDER IN CORNWALL* proclaimed the headline, on page 6 of the *Morning Chronicle,* and over seven inches of tiny print were devoted to the story which had been sent in by the *Falmouth Packet.*

Those who read the story in various parts of the country would have got the gist of the tale. But several of its details were inaccurate by the time it reached their breakfast tables. Charlotte was aged nineteen years, according to the Chronicle, and left Mrs. Peters's house at 4 p.m. on April 14 with Matthew Weeks, the couple having been *seen in the morning going towards Roughtor.*

Matthew mended his shirt on Friday, April 19, not Tuesday 16; and he met a man called Bethson on Saturday 20, who asked him what he had done with the girl, whereas Bettinson had come upon Matthew in the Penhale garden on Tuesday 16 and asked where Charlotte had gone.

Whether or not such details were accurate was, perhaps, immaterial. But, if potential jury members read what followed, they would have got some wrong ideas. On Sunday, April 21, said the Chronicle, Mrs. Peters sent her son and John Stevens to search the moors. They found patten marks; and then, by the time they returned, Weeks had run away.

As Weeks was leaving, the Chronicle continued, *Mrs. Peters said, 'Matthew, how have you got your trousers in that mess? You have brushed them so much that the cloth is almost through'. He said it was very dirty last Sunday. She begged him to come back to dinner, and he said he would, but he has not been heard of since.*

It is true that in the description of Matthew which was carried by the *Royal Cornwall Gazette* on April 26, mention was made of *trousers rubbed from the knee down;* and it seems probable that Matthew did clean them before leaving Penhale and after having had the dirt brought to his notice by Mrs. Peter. But, from her evidence, nothing of the kind was said by her as she merely observed that the trousers were dirty at the knees. Moreover, far from begging him to come back to dinner, she had warned him he'd better be back in time as she would not wait. As for her son and John Stevens, they had gone to Brown Willy and Blisland, not to the moors finding patten marks.

The interpretation put upon these points by the Chronicle, presumably as submitted by the *Falmouth Packet,* would have had readers believing that Matthew had tried to get rid of the dirt on his trousers; and that he, despite Mrs. Peter's pleading, was determined to abscond. Such action and intention would have suggested guilt on his part whereas, had the conversations been properly reported, the opposite might have been suspected.

Similarly, the Chronicle's report of the search was misleading for, apart from getting the day wrong, it stated that a man's and a woman's prints were found *quite close, as if they had had a struggle.* Evidence contained in the prosecution brief stated that there were no signs of a struggle, anywhere. Yet, as the report went on to say that the surgeon felt Charlotte could not have inflicted the wound on herself, as it was *done with such force,* and that Mrs. Peter found Matthew's shirt *under the bed with the collar and all the pleats in front torn off and several spots of blood on the sleeve,* it would have been surprising had readers not assumed Matthew a violent murderer and that Charlotte had attempted to fight him off.

From the report's first paragraph, it would appear that details sent to the Chronicle by the *Falmouth Packet* had been obtained by someone who had attended the inquest. The piece ended with the jury's wilful murder verdict and the news that Weeks had been apprehended at Plymouth and removed to Camelford on the Wednesday (April 24).

It seems a pity that the reporter did not get the facts right or, if he did, that witnesses gave evidence on that occasion inconsistent with their depositions. For, on the following day, Wednesday May 1, readers of the *Morning Post* and of the *Times* were treated to similar stories from the same source. However, the statement regarding the couple's having been seen in the *morning* going towards Roughtor was corrected to their being seen on the *moors* going towards Roughtor in the Wednesday papers, both of which repeated the Chronicle's *DREADFUL MURDER* headline.

Charlotte Dymond

The next day, Thursday May 2, yet another report from the *Falmouth Packet* source appeared, in *Trewman's Exeter Flying Post*. With this, the whole country must have been acquainted with events that had taken place, up to and including an inquest jury's verdict, in a remote area of Bodmin Moor in Cornwall.

* * * *

There were two days to go, however, before news of Charlotte's funeral was released. Strangely, only the *Sherborne Mercury* seems to have covered it. But, as it took place on the afternoon of Thursday April 25, the first day of the magistrates' hearing, the staff of the rest of the newspapers were obviously otherwise engaged. [4]

Yet Charlotte's send-off was one that few Cornish people would have chosen to miss. A certain F. W. Scott of Davidstow parish had especially composed three hymns for the occasion; and these had been printed on broadsheets by another, T. Pearce of Penryn.

As the cortège prepared to move off from Penhale, the farm where Charlotte had lived and worked and where her body had rested for three days, one hymn was sung. Then, the procession moved along the lane, across the fields and out on to the road until Trevivian was reached. There, where John Chapman the butcher and William Hocken lived, another hymn was sung.

Off, in the direction of Davidstow churchtown, the cortège progressed until it reached Tremail. And there, where Thomas Prout was supposed to have met Charlotte on the evening she disappeared, the last hymn was sung.

Most of the words, and all of the music, of the hymns seem nowhere to be found. But, if the words of one verse that is extant are illustrative of the rest, the hymns told the story of Charlotte Dymond as the locals understood it -

Dear friends, behold a helpless child
Left thoughtless, giddy, young and wild.
In childhood banished from her home,
Nor near her parents durst she come. [5]

According to the *Sherborne Mercury* reporter, the burial of Charlotte's body in the churchyard at Davidstow was a *heart-rending sight*. She, *being the fruit of an illicit love and spurned from the door of her who was in nature bound to protect her, was dropped into the grave unwept of by parents or kind friends to sympathise with each other, the last tribute of respect paid by strangers.*

There was no mention of any church service. But John Gillard, the curate, must have officiated at the interment for it was he who made the entry in the burial register 'Charlotte Dymond, Penhale, April 25 1844, aged 19 years'.

Who paid for her grave seems unknown. The plot, south of the church and of the path between the two gates into the yard, was unmarked at the time of her burial.[6] But local people knew its position.

And on occasion, rumour had it, a streak of blood could be seen on the churchyard wall near the place where Charlotte lay.[7]

79

This fire of iniquity

16. By May, 1844, the Charlotte Dymond case had truly caught the imagination of the press; and, presumably, Cornish, regional and national readers eagerly awaited the details as they became available. To all intents and purposes, here was the typical passion murder, which early Victorians would have revelled in, with the jilted lover destroying his sweetheart rather than she should go to chapel with another suitor.

And so the *Royal Cornwall Gazette* sallied forth on Friday, May 3, with details of Matthew's arrest, appearance before the magistrates, and committal to Bodmin gaol. Journalistic licence came to the fore with the mention of his having been *just about to leave for Jersey* and then *conveyed to Camelford where investigation took place before the justices.*

Nevertheless, the Gazette maintained a certain propriety at this stage, with a rather subdued headline of merely *CAMELFORD*. And the reason is apparent from its statement to the effect that *the motive is understood to have been jealousy; but, as he is now in the hands of justice, we think it right to abstain from publishing any matters which may lead those to pre-judge him who will hereafter be required, as his jury, to determine the nature and extent of his crime.*

Would that such sentiments had obtained from the evening that Charlotte Dymond had disappeared; and, even now, the correct expression would have been *alleged* crime.

On the same day, the *West Briton* carried a somewhat more forthcoming article under the heading *THE MURDER NEAR CAMELFORD*. This outlined the Plymouth arrest and Halworthy hearing, then detailed the Bodmin gaol committal and discovery of Charlotte's clothes in the marsh the following day. Weeks was a native of Lezant, it stated, and Charlotte of Boscastle. Then came the punch line which ensured future sales - *since the prisoner's commital, a rumour has prevailed that he has confessed, but we have not been able to verify its truth.*

The following day, Saturday, May 4, the *Plymouth, Devonport & Stonehouse Herald* devoted some seven column inches to the story under the headline *DREADFUL MURDER IN CORNWALL*. After outlining events upto the inquest jury's verdict *without a moment's hesitation,* it went on to say that Matthew had been *apprehended on Wednesday 24th ult. on the Hoe and immediately removed to Camelford....It appears that he was about to leave Plymouth for Jersey, but the police officer arrived just in time to prevent his escaping.*

Also on the Saturday, the *Sherborne Mercury* continued its coverage of events. Its main article on page 3, headed *THE MURDER NEAR CAMELFORD*, dealt with Matthew's demeanour during the magistrates' hearing, his reception in Camelford en route to Bodmin gaol, the burial of Charlotte's body, and the subsequent discovery of the clothes and a print in the turf pit.

As several of these details appear to have been exclusive to the Mercury, it is likely that the Somerset-based paper had an on-the-spot observer. His standard of accuracy was fair, apart from reporting the one boot print as several and saying that they were Matthew's because there was *one heel longer than the other.*

But a small insert, at the bottom of page 4 in the same issue of the Mercury, failed to achieve the main article's standard. It stated that Matthew had been arrested on May 1, whereas it had been April 24, and immediately removed to Camelford. As this conflicted with the paper's accurate details of the arrest and the location of the hearing in its April 27 issue, we may take it that the insert was part of a general press release, whereas the main articles were the work of an eye witness correspondent.

On Sunday, May 5, *The Bell's New Weekly Messenger* carried a report. And, so close in detail was it, to reports in other national newspapers which acknowledged the *Falmouth Packet* as the source - even as far as saying that the couple were seen on the *morning* going towards Roughtor - that the Cornish paper was obviously at the bottom of it. But the source of the *Times's* five column inches on Friday, May 10, was acknowledged as being the *Devonport Independent.*

In fact, the report in the *Times* was, in practically every detail, the one which had appeared in the *West Briton* on the previous Friday. *The only cause that can be assigned for the murder is that of jealousy, as it was thought the young woman preferred another young man,* they informed their readers, *Weeks is a little man, of very decent appearance, 22 years of age, and his victim was in her 19th year.*

So said the papers. And so believed their readers, including those who were eventually to decide his fate as members of the assize jury.

* * * *

The result of all this publicity for the Davidstow-Camelford area turned out to be an extraordinary interest in the temperance movement. On Tuesday, July 4, in 1843 - the year before the Charlotte Dymond case - the teetotallers of East Cornwall had held a festival at Roughtor. And, although it had been thick mist in the morning and the entire day had been damp, long lines of passengers had arrived on foot and horseback, and in carriages, waggons and carts so that there was an attendance on that occasion of some 3,000 persons.

A temporary platform of waggons had been set up below Roughtor, upon which sat Lieutenant Dunstan, R.N., who chaired the mass meeting. Singing and prayers opened the event, banners flew, bands played, and at least five speakers addressed the meeting before it ended at 5 p.m. The one cloud on the temperance horizon had been that, although the permitted coffee and refreshment booths were in evidence, there were also *some few spots where other beverages, than those used by the teetotallers, might be procured.* [1]

If this augured ill for the 1844 rally, the Charlotte Dymond affair set a seal on its good reputation. Not 3,000 this time, but upwards of 10,000 persons were present. The *West Briton* put this down to many having been *attracted by the announcement by the enemies of temperance that there would be donkey racing and other amusements.* And it went on to say that while *speakers addressed the rally for about three hours....others were at the donkey race, wrestling ring, or listening to two cheap jack orators.*

Charlotte Dymond

Unless the sale of intoxicating drinks can be stopped on such occasions, a meeting had better not be held again thought the whig-minded *West Briton, many remained dancing and singing until a late hour.*[2] And, the following week, the paper carried a letter from *a well wisher to mankind,* who complained that *such scenes of drunkeness and rioting were exhibited (together with the midnight dance and festive song) as could not fail to shock the feelings of all;* then the writer added that it was *sincerely to be hoped that one and all* would *quench this fire of iniquity.*[3]

As the Roughtor area was several miles removed from small settlements, let alone the town of Camelford, it may only be imagined that those who complained were, in fact, present at the late hour to witness such goings on, on that Tuesday, June 25, 1844. However, in a letter to the editor of the *West Briton* in its July 12 issue, W. K. Norway, the secretary of the Roughtor Meetings, assured readers that the teetotallers had left Roughtor by 6 p.m. on June 25 and that the protection of the law would in future be sought against persons who misused the meetings.

In its issue of July 5, the *Royal Cornwall Gazette* had placed the onus of the trouble fairly and squarely on the shoulders of local publicans. They, it seemed, had been responsible for the sports; and, the Gazette had heard, the teetotallers were about to lay information against some of the publicans for selling liquors without licence. *The controversy causes no little excitement in the neighbourhood,* added the paper.

The suggestion could be ventured that it was not really the publicans, who had achieved the notoriety of what came to be known as the Roughtor Revels, but Charlotte Dymond. For, while it is true that local publicans did set up booths and might well have advertised their sports and pastimes, it was the location of the event that probably effected the change of headline from TEETOTAL FESTIVAL ON ROUGHTOR in 1843 to THE ROUGHTOR MONSTER MEETING in 1844.

For there, before the very eyes of teetotallers and enemies of temperance alike, was the place where Charlotte Dymond's body had been found just two months before. And, as the trial of the murder suspect was a month in the future, the case was still uppermost in the public mind.

This is evident from the *West Briton's* report of the rally for it stated that *a pole with a black flag was fixed on the spot, where the murdered body of Charlotte Dymond was found, about half-a-mile from the mountain* (Roughtor). *This attracted much attention and penny subscriptions were received to defray the expense of erecting some monument to mark the spot.* [4]

A memorial *was* eventually erected. A solid, granite upright by the little river. Upon it, were Inscribed the words - *monument erected by public subscription in memory of Charlotte Dymond who was murdered by Matthew Weeks, Sunday, April 14th, 1844.*

And, ever since, it has been wondered why a monument should have been set up on a remote moorland site to keep an alleged murder in mind.

There could have been many reasons - a regard and sympathy for Charlotte, a 'hung-in-chains' substitute punishment of Matthew's memory, a collective guilt that such a thing should have happened on a Sunday in a church-minded community, a tourist attraction which could yield tips for local youngsters acting as guides, or a spur-of-the-occasion prank by drunkern revellers - there is no knowing.

But, when it is remembered that the publicans were blamed for the sidelines of the teetotal festival and that no fewer than three local licensees were prime witnesses in the Charlotte Dymond case, one explanation stands out. If William Northam of the Halworthy inn, Humphrey Vosper of the *Britannia Inn* at Trevilian's Gate, and Simon Baker of the Trevalga churchtown beer shop were amongst the publicans who had booths at the rally, it is more than likely that their chief topic of conversation was the impending trial.

If that were so, theirs must have been the black flag on the spot where the body was found and theirs the idea of erecting a permanent monument in its place - for one, several, or all of the reasons suggested above. With upwards of 10,000 persons at the event, some £100 could have been forthcoming from penny subscriptions to defray the cost.

The names of Charlotte Dymond and Matthew Weeks would be carved in stone.

The case requires management

17. Meanwhile, since the magistrates' hearing at the Halworthy inn had ended on Saturday April 27, with Matthew Weeks's being committed to Bodmin Gaol to await trial, Phillipa Peter's lawyer, J. L. Cowlard, had been preparing the case against him.

As the prosecutrix, Mrs. Peter had to prefer the bill of indictment in the name of the queen - Regina versus Weeks - so that the case became an issue between the Crown and Matthew.[1] And it had been arranged that the prosecution should be led by Alexander James Edmund Cockburn, Queen's Counsel.

Destined to attain the second highest legal position in the country, that of Lord Chief Justice of the Queen's Bench, Cockburn was in his late 30s or early 40s in 1844. But his reputation was already as formidable as his having been said to have 'excelled all the eloquent advocates' of his time. Heir to the baronetcy of Nova Scotia, he had graduated from Cambridge and been called to the bar by the society of the Middle Temple in 1829. He had then joined the western circuit and attended the Devonshire sessions, taking silk in 1841.[2]

Assisting him was to be William Carpenter Rowe of Launceston, who had been called to the bar by the society of the Inner Temple in 1830; and who, within six years of the Dymond case, would become the first county court judge in his home town. As a contemporary of Cockburn, he was probably the Mr. Rowe who collaborated with the Q.C. in publishing reports of decisions arising out of the 1832 Reform Act. These assisted Cockburn's advancement in the political world so that he eventually became Liberal M.P. for Southampton, in 1847. [3]

The third member of the team for the Crown was another Cornishman, forty-five-year old George Nutcombe Oxenham of Paul near Penzance. He had graduated from Oxford in 1820 and been called to the bar by the society of Lincoln's Inn in 1825.[+]

In order that these barristers should be conversant with the facts of the case and the points of law concerning it, Cowlard, the solicitor, wrote them a brief. With the exception of the pages before number one and after number 56, the document is extant at the time of writing this book. Originally comprising some 65 foolscap pages, it contained three parts - preliminary observations; depositions of witnesses for the prosecution; and, on the back of pages, rough notes of their evidence which, as there are details not included in the depositions, were probably taken down at the magistrates' hearing.

If we may assume that the brief was compiled by Cowlard in his Madford office at Launceston, we enter his thoughts upon the terms of the bill of indictment. He explained that the murder would 'be laid as having taken place in Cornwall'. But he recognised the difficulty, were the prosecution 'required to prove with certainty that such was the case', as the body had been found in an unlikely place and close to the boundaries of another parish. If it were in Cornwall, it could not be said with certainty whether it had been in St. Breward or Advent parish.

He then reviewed the possibilities of Charlotte's having first been drowned or strangled, thinking it prudent 'for precaution's sake' to add these counts. It seemed to him, he wrote, 'hardly probable that she would have tacitly submitted to having her throat cut or that Weeks could have done it without previously throwing her down'. The murder weapon had not been found and 'there were no marks on the (body's) hands or any evidence of a struggle other than Weeks's torn shirt.'

Beginning his observations, Cowlard wrote that 'it was of course doubtful what fresh evidence bearing against Weeks would be elicited previously to the trial. At the time (of the magistrates' hearing) the residue of Charlotte's clothes had not been found. Many facts are therefore stated in such examinations which, as they do not bear materially upon the case, are omitted in the present proofs (the witnesses' depositions).... it was important to let witnesses say what they knew in their own words with a view to guard against the omission of any important fact. As the case is to be presented to the jury, however, it will stand thus and it is apprehended that a careful consideration of all the circumstances of the case will not leave a doubt as to Weeks's guilt.'

Cowlard went on to write that 'Mrs. Peter's house is about a mile only from very extensive and barren moors known as the Davidstow moors, the whole neighbourhood is very thinly populated and it is hardly possible to select a spot in which an offence might be planned and executed with less chance of immediate detection'.

'It was at a distance of 4 miles from Mrs. Peter's house and 3 miles from Higher Down Gate that the murder was supposed to have been committed', Cowlard explained, 'and as this 3 miles is entirely on the moor, we are prepared with a plan showing the several points to which the several witnesses will depose.'

The plan referred to by the solicitor had been drawn up by John Fowler, a forty-three-year old Launceston surveyor,[5] with the help of witnesses such as Pethick, Baker and Cory. The various places they pointed out to Fowler, such as where the couple on the moor were seen and where foot prints and the body were found, were marked by letters of the alphabet on the plan. Fowler also, evidently, measured the distances between places of importance to the case and gave them as follows - 'Penhale farm to Roughtor Ford, about 4 miles; Penhale to Higher Down Gate, ¾ mile 220 yds; Higher Down Gate to Lanlary Rock, 1½ miles; Lanlary Rock to Roughtor Ford, 1¼ miles.'

Phillipa Peter's Launceston solicitor, J. L. Cowland, then went on to outline in his brief to the barristers the events up to the time that Matthew had walked out of Penhale. And 'at this point', he wrote, 'it is worth considering what prisoner's (Weeks's) motives were in murdering the deceased. It is known [though we do not see how this can be proved] that he was a person of a very jealous temperament and the fact of his being lame, thereby probably constituting a defect in a woman's eye, might lead him to be suspicious as to anything of a slight to him and a preference for another. That prosecutrix (Mrs. Peter) believed him to be jealous, there is no doubt, as she expressly told him that jealousy had made him do it.. It appears also that the present cause of jealousy had been a person called Thomas Prout of Helset.'

Regarding Phillipa Peter and her being 'kindly disposed towards' Matthew, Cowland felt that she, 'in giving her evidence', might show 'a bias in prisoner's favour.' He then went on to say that her servant, John Stevens, was 'a stupid fellow but will probably tell the truth..... In his examination before the magistrates, you (the barristers) will observe that he speaks of prisoner's having bought a knife of a person by the name of Parsons. Some doubt however about this and it is probably inexpedient to encumber the case with it.'

In fact, John Stevens seems to have had second thoughts about the evidence he had given, probably at the inquest and certainly before the magistrates, because a further statement was taken from him, to which Cowland obviously referred - 'In my examination before the magistrates,' ran the addition, 'I stated that prisoner had bought a knife of Charles Parsons. I believe that I was mistaken in this and that prisoner only looked at the knife and did not buy. I saw some money pass and prisoner take something to his box, but I find since that it was a pair of braces.'

'I also spoke of finding two knives', went on John Stevens in his new statement, 'this was after the murder, however, and was to kill the pig with. By "the Friday before", I meant "Friday before the justices' meeting".'

John Stevens had come clean, at least as far as the knife evidence was concerned. But it was too late for Matthew Weeks. It had helped secure an inquest jury's indictment against him and to persuade the magistrates to commit him for trial.

Cowland was obviously unimpressed by Stevens, as he advised the barristers to use 'more intelligent witnesses' for all but the identification of the body, regarding details of the search. He also warned counsel about Mrs. Peter's son, John, saying 'he is rather soft and it is probable that he may be desirous of stating more than he really knows. His weakness [if it may be so termed] will probably be got from his mother on her cross examination (by the defence). At the (magistrates') hearing, his evidence was therefore taken briefly..At the trial, it will easily be seen how far this witness's examination..can prudently be carried.'

Cowlard certainly had problems, as far as his witnesses were concerned. For, apart from John Stevens's change of heart and John Peter's unreliability, there was Richard Pethick to worry about. Cowlard felt that the cattle farmer 'may be shaken as to the identification of the prisoner as being the person seen just by Roughtor Ford.'

'In Pethick's evidence before the justices', Cowlard explained to the barristers, 'in reference to prisoner he says "the man appeared to look towards me start (straight) he stood very upright looking at me, he dipped a mite in walking and was lame, the man I now point out (meaning Matthew before the justices) is like the man. I had watched him for many minutes walking and he walked like a lame man". It appears that Pethick will now swear to the man.'

Pethick, like John Stevens, had added to the statement he made at the magistrates' hearing, by the time Cowlard wrote his brief, as follows - 'In my examination before the magistrates, I said that I believed prisoner to be the man from his size and appearance. I had not the least doubt in the matter. I should know him (Matthew) among five hundred. I swear positively to him and, if I had then been asked if I could swear to him, I should have done so. I was near enough to distinguish his features and I was 39 paces [3 feet][6] only from him. It was good light, enough to enable me to see to top of Roughtor.' And, roughly noted on the back of the brief, was his further explanation: 'Weeks was not asked to walk across the room (at the hearing) for me to see him, nor did he.'

Cowlard was uneasy, however, and determined to be prepared for a repeat performance of Pethick's seeming 'shy of' identifying Matthew with the man on the moor. 'Should he break down in this,' he wrote, 'it will be necessary to back up the case with the evidence [slight, we allow, but still, coupled with other circumstances, effective] with which we are prepared, in expectation that Pethick would not speak more strongly than he did before the justices. The case upon this point requires management for, on the one hand it will not do for us, in anticipation of Pethick's evidence being quite to the point, to throw aside the little circumstances which, if his evidence is satisfactory, will be - it is true - useless, but which, should he not go beyond his statement before the magistrates, would be most important. And, in arranging the evidence, it is an object to let his examination be taken so as, even in the case of his not going beyond his statement before the justices, to let him appear as if used in confirmation of the weaker case and not as a break-down of the stronger.'

'Should, however, his evidence go to the point which we anticipate [and Pethick is a very respectable and plain spoken man]', the solicitor assured his barristers, 'much future trouble in examination may be saved, as his evidence will probably be conclusive of the prisoner's guilt.'

But, 'feeling, as we do, upon Pethick's evidence', Cowlard continued, 'it seems desirable to connect deceased (Charlotte) with, and as being, the person seen on the moor by Cory, traced from thence in the direction of Lanlary Rock, and from thence onwards towards Roughtor Ford.' He then outlined the patten print evidence, as having been pointed out by Cory, followed by the searchers, confirmed by Constable Rickard as Charlotte's trail when he tested her pattens against the marks, and as corresponding with the behaviour of the couple seen by Pethick and Gard.

There was, according to the solicitor, every likelihood of its being accepted that Charlotte and the woman on the moor were one and the same, even although no-one could positively identify the two.

Similarly, regarding Pethick's performance, Cowlard opined that 'it becomes necessary to enter into, and connect Weeks with, the footmarks found on the moor between Roughtor Ford and Lanlary Rock, at a space about 18 paces from where the body was found, and on the edge of the pit in which some (of Charlotte's) clothes were afterwards found.'

The evidence of Cory was as important in this respect as it was with regard to the patten prints, thought the solicitor; but, when it came to William Northam's measurements, there were more problems for the prosecution. 'In his examination before the magistrates, it was anticipated that the impression of the man's foot found by Northam would have exactly corresponded with Weeks's boots in length', explained Cowlard. 'On comparing them, however, it was found that Weeks's boot was the longer of the two. The comparison was between the boot and a stick in which the length of the impression found was marked; but it was evident, from the manner in which the toes of Weeks's boots turned up, that the heel and sole only would have been impressed, except in very muddy or sticky ground.'

'There is no doubt',continued the solicitor, 'that this discrepancy, unimportant as it is when explained and when exemplified by the boots themselves, will be much relied on by Weeks's counsel (for the defence). As we before stated, however, the examinations before the magistrates were taken to elicit all that the witnesses [previously unexamined professionally] knew and not with a view to make out [the prisoner, Weeks, then being undefended] an exparte (one sided) statement.'

The boot print evidence was one of the weakest parts of the prosecution case. Cowlard fully recognised this. Yet, at the same time, he knew that his case could hinge upon it in the event of Pethick's refusing to identify positively Matthew with the man on the moor. Pethick worried Cowlard; and he returned to discussing him again. 'He was cautiously examined (by the magistrates)' he wrote to the barrister,' on the uncertainty of his answer as to whether he could or could not swear to the man; and, evidently, at that time, for some reason or other, he seemed shy of doing so. He might certainly have confined himself to answering the questions put; but he then stated in effect that, judging from his size and appearance, from his lameness, and he having watched them for some time, he believed Weeks to be the man he saw. We now find, however [and it would almost seem that he thought he did at the hearing] that he will swear positively; and, if he does so, it will probably be considered that much of the collateral evidence may be dispensed with.'

If Pethick would not swear positively in the assize court, the prosecution faced the prospect of having to use such as Constable Dingle's boot print evidence. This was bound, in Cowlard's view to bring an objection from the defence that,'in testing the impression and (Matthew's) boot, Dingle pressed one in the other. He may have done so in the end', the solicitor admitted, 'but previously, by kneeling down, both by himself and Vosper, he satisfied himself, by close comparison of the two, that they corresponded. He further speaks to the foot print on the brink of the turf pit corresponding with Week's boot. And, here, he adopts a different course and, by making an impression of the boot by the side of the impression found [the ground being muddy] he can speak [and in this he is corroborated by (Constables) Rickard and Gerrance Hayne] with certainty to the impression, rendered more peculiar from the toe plate being thicker at the point.'

Nevertheless, Cowlard thought, 'Dingle is excessively deaf; and, to guard against anything like a misapprehension by him of questions asked, which might prejudice the jury, we propose to call (Constable) Gerrance Hayne, who is an intelligent man and can speak with certainty to this comparison of the foot print at the turf pit'.

The Launceston solicitor was taking no chances on the flimsiness of his prosecution case showing up in court. Uppermost in his mind was the fact that Matthew would be defended this time and the witnesses for the prosecution would be cross-examined.

Not only the witnesses, but the whole case for the prosecution could be questioned. More particularly, Cowlard felt, the fact that Surgeon Good 'could not take upon himself to say that there had been no connexion (sexual intercourse) may possibly be commented on for the defence; and it may be said that the motive for the alleged crime is not in the least apparent but that, had he violated her, his motive to avoid discovery might have been clear.'

'It is possible that he might have desired connexion with her but had been repelled', Cowlard speculated, 'or that a sudden impulse of jealousy might have prompted him to the act. Looking, however, at the honing the razor the night before and the distance on the moor to which he had inveigled her, it is probable that the crime was premeditated; and this is rather borne out by the fact [although it only appears in the magistrates' examination] that Charlotte had no money in her box at home and that she neither had there or on her person her pocket (purse), although she had, at Lady Day, received some four shillings and had not been known to have spent them. Weeks had money about him but it could not be identified as having been hers.'

'It is possible, however,' the solicitor thought, 'that Weeks, with a view to disarm suspicion, may have taken the money so as to create an impression of robbery; and that, as an inducement to her to take her money, he may have deceived her as to Mrs. Lanxon's having got her a place. And, taking the interest, which he did, in her, she may have trusted to him to pacify her mistress for her leaving and to bring or send her clothes.'

Turning to the evidence of Constables Bennett and Fitzgerald, the Launceston solicitor accepted that Bennett did not know the name of the allegedly murdered girl when he charged Matthew upon arresting him. This, and the fact that Matthew 'allowed himself to be taken quietly without a warrant' added up to his having 'guilty knowledge'. And he passed off Matthew's 'further conversation with Constable Bennett, as to the period at which he had left keeping company with Charlotte' as immaterial because it was 'not apprehended that much use can be made of this' as far as the case for the prosecution

Matthew Weeks's pay sheet

showing that, 9 years before the murder case, when he was 14 and 15 years of age, he put in a 6-day week at the rate of 10d per day. Entry one would have been for 15 days at this rate; and, although entry two shows that he could receive 1/- per day for perhaps extra time, other entries show that he lost time and pay, probably when bad weather stopped work. It is noted, at the bottom, that he received 7/- cash-in-advance for a shirt.

[photo: C. R. Clemens, Bodmin; by courtesy: Mr. F. W. Weeks]

Charlotte Dymond

Top - a will made in 1826 by Matthew's grandfather which nominated his father, John, joint heir and executor of the family estate.
Bottom - Matthew's receipt of a ninth part of an inheritance under his grandfather's later will, dated 1836, which read: '....unto the children of my late son, John Weeks deceased, Lezant; to be equally divided between them, nine, as they survive the age of 21 years or be married....'
[photo: C. R. Clemens, Bodmin; by courtesy: Messrs. F. W. Weeks and G. S. Congdon]

Penhale Farm - Davidstow

From left: the lean-to porch entrance to the house; the barn; the stable. The trees on the right are in the mowhay at the rear of the buildings.

[photo: Pat Munn, 1974; by courtesy: Mrs. and Mr. Waldron; and permission: Mr. P. Cornelius]

Penhale Farm House

The tiny window above the porch is of the 'middle chamber' between the 2 front bedrooms; the lower window on the right is of the small parlour, from which there was once a door into the barn; the trees line the path to Higher Down Gate.

[photo: Pat Munn, 1974; by courtesy: Mrs. and Mr. Waldron; and permission Mr. P. Cornelius]

Penhale Farmhouse Kitchen

Showing the window seat inside the table; and, on the right, a window in place of the door which originally led into the mowhay, with a view across the lane to the site of the thorn, shute and trough.

[photo: Pat Munn, 1974; by courtesy: Mrs. and Mr. Waldron; and permission: Mr P. Cornelius]

The site of the thorn, shute and trough

Although the original thorn has been cut down, the hedge altered, and the shute stopped, the trough is still in situ on the lane to Higher Down Gate and within sight of the kitchen side door.

[photo: Pat Munn, 1976; by courtesy : Mrs. and Mr. Waldron; and permission: Mr. P. Cornelius]

Penhale Farm Out-houses

Across the yard from the dwelling house, barn, and stable. On the right, in the shadow of the tree and adjoining the hedge, is a doorway to the pig sty.

[photo: Pat Munn, 1974; by courtesy: Mrs. and Mr. Waldron; and permission: Mr. P. Cornelius]

The Mowhay

At the rear of the farmhouse (right) and barn (left). The doorway, reached by steps, is probably the entrance used for the inquest in the upper room of the barn.

[photo: Pat Munn, 1974; by courtesy: Mrs. and Mr. Waldron; and permission: Mr. P. Cornelius]

Charlotte Dymond

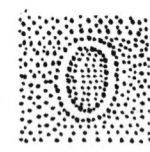

The patten evidence
top left: patten worn as an undershoe
bottom left: print left by the iron oval
above: underside of a patten

© PAT MUNN, 1977

The boot print evidence
Fig. 1: nailed & skuted working boot underside
Fig. 2: dress boot with toe-plate & skute
bottom left: dress boot print

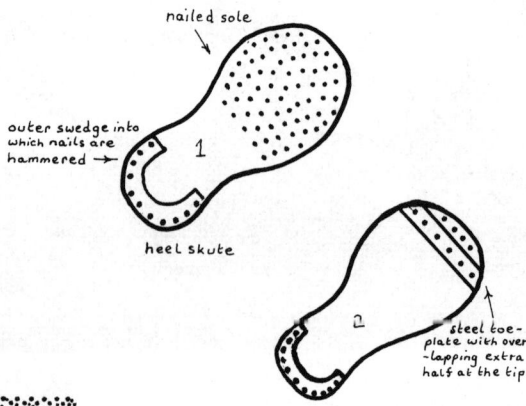

nailed sole

outer swedge into which nails are hammered

heel skute

steel toe-plate with over-lapping extra half at the tip

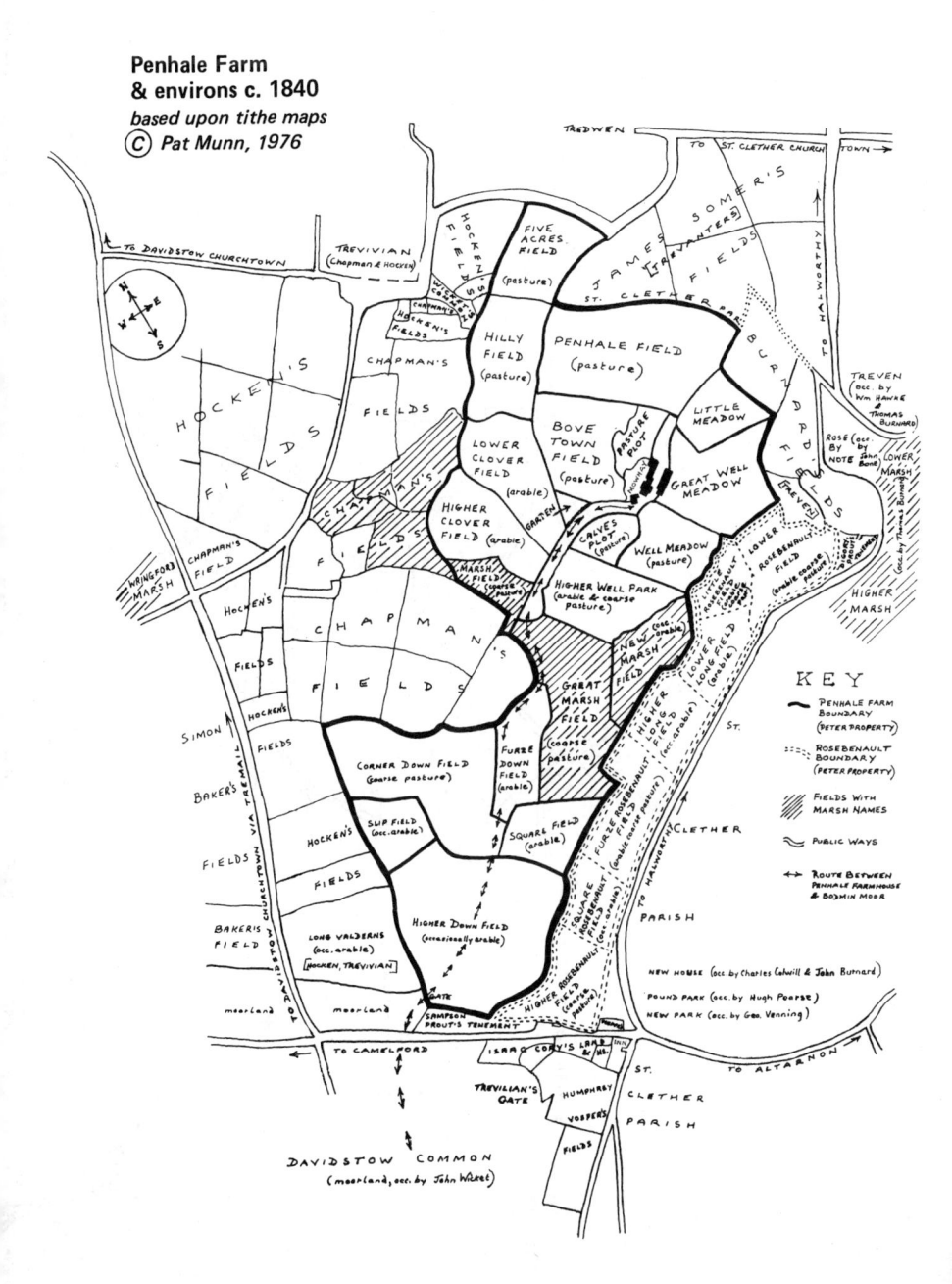

Charlotte Dymond

**Penhale Farm
& environs c. 1840**
based upon tithe maps
© *Pat Munn, 1976*

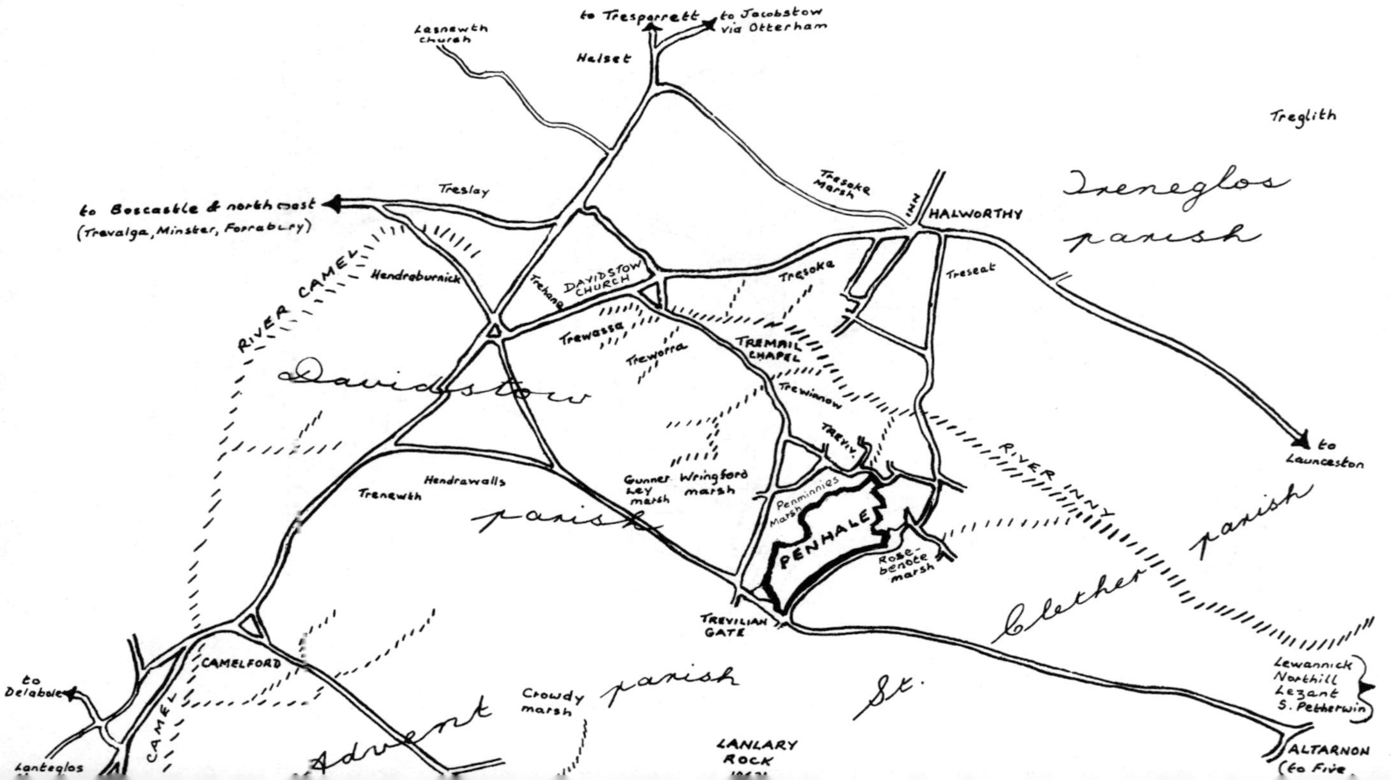
to Tresparrett
to Jacobstow via Otterham
Lesnewth church
Helset
Treglith
Treslay
to Boscastle & north coast
(Trevalga, Minster, Forrabury)
Tresoke Marsh
INN
HALWORTHY
Treneglos parish
RIVER CAMEL
Hendraburnick
Trehane
DAVIDSTOW CHURCH
Tresoke
Treseat
Trewassa
Treworra
TREMAIL CHAPEL
Davidstow
Trewinnow
TREVIV.
RIVER INNY
to Launceston
Hendrawalls
Trenewth
Gunner Ley marsh
Wringford marsh
Penminnies Marsh
PENHALE
Rose-benote marsh
parish
Clether parish
TREVILIAN GATE
CAMELFORD
to Delabole
CAMEL
Crowdy marsh
parish
St.
Lewannick
Northill
Lezant
S. Petherwin
Advent
LANLARY ROCK
Lanteglos
ALTARNON
(to Five

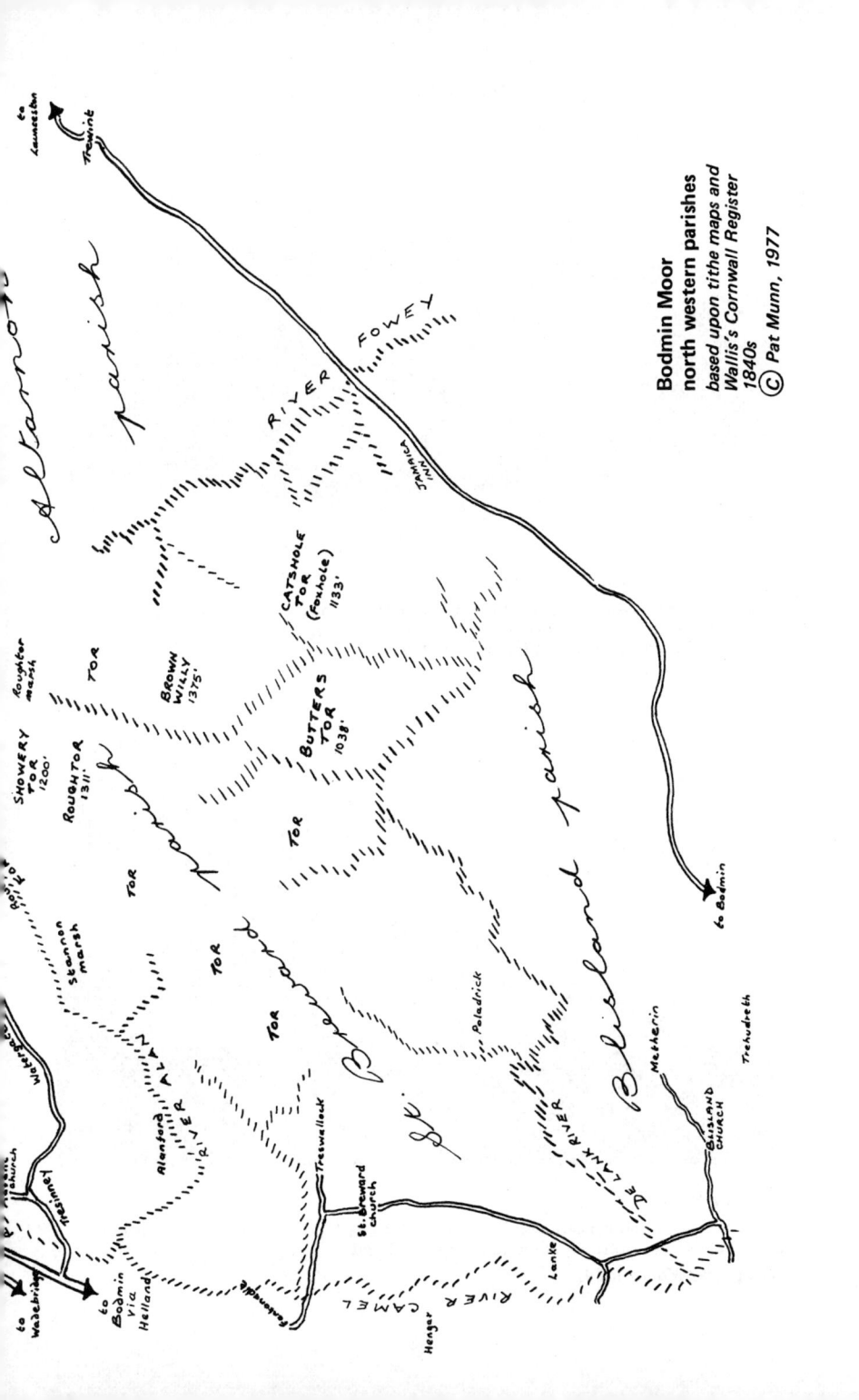

**Bodmin Moor
north western parishes**
*based upon tithe maps and
Wallis's Cornwall Register
1840s*
© *Pat Munn, 1977*

Brittannia Inn, Trevilian's Gate
Now a private residence, this was the former turnpike house rebuilt in 1836 by Vosper, who set the Roughtor chapel arch over the doorway. Right, is the farmstead occupied by Cory in 1844, on the Altarnon-Camelford road.
[photo: Pat Munn, 1976; by courtesy: Mr. C. T. Dowton]

Lanlary Rock
in the boggy ground beneath which moorland landmark prints of a woman's pattens and a man's boots were supposed to have been found.
[photo: Pat Munn, 1974]

Charlotte Dymond

The Roughtor monument
erected by public subscription in memory of Charlotte Dymond who was murdered by Matthew Weeks, Sunday, April 14, 1844 according to the inscription.
[photo: Pat Munn, 1971.]
A property of the National Trust.

The site of the alleged murder
The bank in the foreground is in Advent parish and was presumed to have been the place where Charlotte met with death. Her body was found in the water course below the bank. The monument is now on the St. Breward parish side of the River Alan as the moor slopes up to Roughtor.
[photo: Pat Munn, 1976]

Tremail Chapel

where Charlotte was supposed to meet Thomas Prout on Sunday, April 14, 1844; and where one of the hymns was sung as her funeral cortège passed on its way to Davidstow churchyard.

[photo: Pat Munn, 1974; by courtesy: the Camelford circuit superintendent minister]

Charlotte's grave

in Davidstow parish church-yard, marked by the broken cross which was removed from the eastern gable end of the church during renovations in 1875.

[photo: Pat Munn, 1976; by courtesy: the vicar]

Charlotte Dymond

The scene of Matthew Weeks's arrest
on Plymouth Hoe in Devonshire, showing the citadel (foreground), the hoe (mid-right), and Drake's Island (mid-left); with Mount Edgecumbe and the Cornish hills in the background. The couple in the foreground are in clothes similar to those described as being worn by Weeks and Charlotte.
[photo: Tom Molland Ltd; from a lithograph by courtesy: Plymouth Central Library]

The handcuffs
handed down through the family of Gerrance Hayne, one of the 1844 Davidstow parish constables and believed to have manacled Weeks.
[photo: C. R. Clemens, Bodmin; by courtesy: Mr. D. J. Brookham]

Charlotte Dymond

All Drunkard Inn, Halworthy
Now a private residence, the licence having transferred to a nearby hotel, this was where the magistrates' hearing took place in 1844 and where Weeks was committed to Bodmin gaol; lower left, the courtroom window; lower right, the upping stock.

[photo: Pat Munn, 1974; by courtesy: Mr. & Mrs. J.H. Parsons]

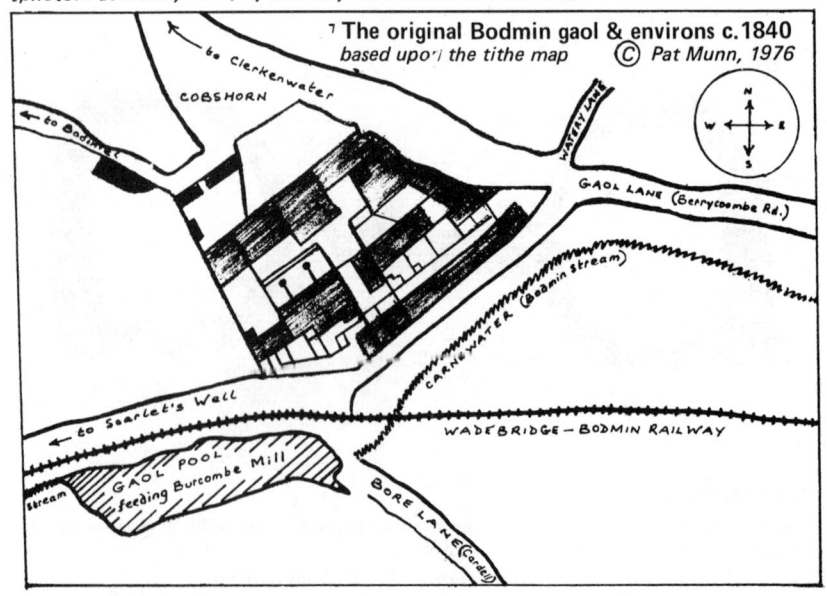

7 The original Bodmin gaol & environs c.1840 based upon the tithe map © Pat Munn, 1976

Richard Peter
Solicitor for the defence, some 30 years after the case.

[photo: C. R. Clemens, Bodmin; from an original in the office, and by courtesy of, Mr. C. G. Peter, Launceston]

Bodmin Assize Court
where Weeks was tried on Friday, August 2, 1844, and condemned to death.
[photo: Pat Munn, 1975]

Charlotte Dymond

[Printed by Authority of the Registrar General.]

CERTIFIED COPY of an ENTRY OF DEATH
Pursuant to the Births and Deaths Registration Act 1953

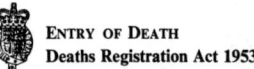

HB 880557

Registration District Bodmin

1844. Death in the Sub-district of Camelford in the County of Cornwall

No.	When and where died	Name and surname	Sex	Age	Occupation	Cause of death	Signature, description, and residence of informant	When registered	Signature of registrar
84	Fourteenth April 1844. Rough Tor Ford Advent	Charlotte Dymond	Female	18 years	Single woman	Wilfully murdered by Matthew Weeks	Joseph Hamley Coroner Bodmin	Twenty fifth April 1844	John Jennings Registrar.

Certified to be a true copy of an entry in a register in my custody.

.... D. M. Thomas ....Dep:....Superintendent Registrar.
.... 20.8. 1974 .... Date.

CAUTION:—Any person who (1) falsifies any of the particulars on this certificate, or (2) uses a falsified certificate as true, knowing it to be false, is liable to prosecution.

Death certificate of Charlotte Dymond
showing the cause of death as wilful murder by Weeks 3½ months before his trial.
[photo: C. R. Clemens, Bodmin; by courtesy: the Registrar General]

CERTIFIED COPY OF AN ENTRY OF DEATH

Given at the GENERAL REGISTER OFFICE, SOMERSET HOUSE, LONDON.

Application Number PAS 59201/1/14

REGISTRATION DISTRICT Bodmin

1844. DEATH in the Sub-district of Bodmin in the County of Cornwall

No.	When and where died	Name and surname	Sex	Age	Occupation	Cause of death	Signature, description, and residence of informant	When registered	Signature of registrar
439	Twelfth August 1844 at the Gaol in the Borough of Bodmin	Matthew Weeks	Male	22 years	Farm Servant	Executed for Murder	Thomas Dungey Present at the Death. Gaol in the Borough of Bodmin	Fifteenth August 1844	Jacob Thomas Registrar

CERTIFIED to be a true copy of an entry in the certified copy of a Register of Deaths in the District above mentioned.
Given at the GENERAL REGISTER OFFICE, SOMERSET HOUSE, LONDON, under the Seal of the said Office, the 1st day of August 1974

DA 614061

Death certificate of Matthew Weeks
showing his age as 22 when he was really almost 24. Dungey, the informant, was a warder at Bodmin gaol.
[photo: C. R. Clemens, Bodmin; by courtesy: the Registrar General]

was concerned.

The one worrying aspect was the 'little discrepancy in the terms' of the conversation between Matthew and Constable Fitzgerald, regarding whether Matthew had told Constable Bennett it was 'not safe to stop in Plymouth' or that 'he was come to see Plymouth and meant to return' (to Cornwall). 'We refer to this', Cowlard told the barristers, 'to guard against any confusion, as the question and answer is put at the end of Fitzgerald's deposition.'

Yet another problem for the prosecution, as far as Cowlard was concerned was 'whether it would be admissable to give in evidence what is stated by Thomas Prout.' It was important that, what had purportedly passed between Prout and Charlotte outside the kitchen door on Sunday, April 14, came out in court for it showed that Charlotte had no intention of leaving Mrs. Peter's service if she were going to chapel in the evening, according to the solicitor. He therefore thought that 'although we may be prevented from giving in evidence what passed in conversation, Prout may be asked as to facts. The questions and answers as to which will, of themselves, convey to the jury the conversation wished to be elicited.'

Amongst his final remarks to the barristers, Cowlard mentioned Matthew's having made a statement before 'two of the committing magistrates' who were 'still on the spot' about half an hour after the hearing had ended.

He also referred to Matthew's having said that he had intended going to the Channel islands. 'Enquiries have been made at the packet stations at Plymouth and Devonport', the solicitor reported, 'but without any clue to Weeks'.

Cowlard's brief thus came to a close. But we might wonder if, in fact, Matthew had 'gone down before (Constable Bennett's arrival) to take a vessel for Guernsey or Jersey', as he had told Constable Fitzgerald.

It could, of course, have been bravado on Matthew's part in answer to Fitzgerald's question as to how he allowed himself to be taken by Bennett, yet another example of his unwittingly playing into the hands of the prosecution. On the other side, he might have gone down to the docks with such a trip in mind but, as he made no booking, those at the packet office did not notice him.

Whatever, he was evidently considered capable of affording the journey. Additionally, the case was the more exciting if the newspapers could advise readers that he had been *arrested on the point of escape* from the mainland.

It was now up to Alex. Cockburn, Q. C., William Rowe and George Oxenham to present the Crown's case to the judge and jury in such a way that Matthew Weeks would be convicted of the murder of Charlotte Dymond and pay the penalty. That case was shaky, the solicitor realised this. But he was confident that, with careful management, the circumstantial evidence would leave no doubt as to Weeks's guilt.

In the final analysis, however, it all depended upon Matthew's defence.[7]

A strong opinion

18. Who paid for Matthew Weeks's defence is not known. The courts had power to assign counsel to a pauper litigant but whether or not Matthew would have qualified for such aid, when it was thought that he could afford a passage to the Channel Isles, is uncertain. The engaging of a lawyer who, in turn, would brief a barrister, would probably have been beyond the means that he did seem capable of mustering.[1]

It therefore appears that his mistress's family came to the rescue. Phillipa Peter had found herself with a murder on the doorstep, in which two of her servants were involved. It is possible that she had already taken responsibility for Charlotte's funeral and grave and, even although the law required that she prosecute Matthew, it is as likely that she also provided for him.

She was certainly in a position to help, were she so inclined, There was in Launceston a namesake cousin of her late husband, Richard Peter, who ran a legal practice. And he, it was, who took up Matthew's case. [2]

Even were he not instructed by Mrs. Peter, few at the time would have been surprised at his accepting what might turn out as a lost cause. The thirty-four-year old then batchelor, Richard Peter, was known as 'the Liberal attorney' who had been determined to maintain the practice he had founded in the borough in 1838, despite having been hounded from address to address by Launceston's powerful patron and landowner, the Duke of Northumberland.

Yet, although his branch of the Peter family had been based in Northill parish since the 17th century, no-one of that surname could really be considered an upstart in Launceston. He and Mrs. Peter's late husband were descendants of John Peter, the borough's mayor in 1553, and of Thomas Peter the elder and younger who were prominent burgesses in Elizabeth's reign.

By the time he defended Matthew, Richard Peter had succeeded in establishing an office in Church Street, the practice eventually removing to Westgate where it still exists. In time, he became town clerk of the borough; and, like his forebear, he served as Launceston's mayor in 1864. [3]

Upon accepting Matthew's case, Peter must have compiled the details, just as Cowlard had for the prosecution. The man who received them, to act on Matthew's behalf in the Bodmin assize court, was Frederick William Slade, the third son, the elder of twins, of Sir John Slade of Maunsel House near Bridgwater in Somerset. [4]

The forty-three-year old barrister, an Oxford graduate called to the bar by the Middle Temple in 1830, had become Sir John's heir by the time he took Matthew's case, his two elder brothers having died. This was something to live up to because his father had been given a baronetcy and had twice been honoured with the thanks of the Commons for distinguished military service in the Peninsula wars. Many members of his family subsequently took army commissions but the law was Slade's chosen profession.

Having been called to the bar by the inn of court which had called Queen's Counsel for the prosecution, and being of similar age and social standing, Slade might have enjoyed a legal career similar to that of Cockburn. But he never achieved the bench and it was not until 1851, a decade after the Q. C., that he took silk. Now, in 1844, while Cockburn had two at his side for the big case, Slade was to be Matthew's sole representative in court. [5]

Nevertheless, with the trial imminent, a case for the defence had been prepared, although the brief Slade accepted from Richard Peter seems not to have survived.[6] And Bodmin braced itself for one of the most exciting assizes ever held in the town.

In fact, being the only place of assize in Cornwall was still something of a novelty for the borough. The courts had been held there at various times during the middle ages but their usual venue had been in Launceston, the county town. Gradually, however, and because Bodmin was situated at almost the geographical centre of the county, successive petitions of Cornish representatives had brought about their entire removal to Bodmin despite the protestations of such as 'King John' Lethbridge on Launceston's behalf. So, in July of 1838, the Queen's justices of assize had held court in the new county town complete with purpose-built Shire Hall courthouse and Shire House judges' lodgings.

Between the beginning of the 19th century and Weeks's trial, Bodmin's population had doubled so that there were, by then, some four and three quarter thousand residents. The increase was mainly attributable to a revival of mining speculation in the area, as in the county generally, although there was now apprehension lest a deteriorating economic climate should spoil things. Local industries for which the town was noted, such as shoemaking, blanket production, clock making and milling, served both the indigenous and incoming populations.

In turn, the population rise and resultant flourishing trades attracted service industries like banks and other offices and also meant that there was considerable building of churches, schools and villas in the area. Improvements in public sectors were possible, such as additions to the county lunatic asylum and county gaol, the opening of the East Cornwall Hospital and the erection of a market house and Union workhouse. Inns abounded. Cornwall's first locomotive railway had been opened between Wadebridge and Bodmin in 1834. And, incidental to but indicative of this expansion, a new cemetery had been opened at the Bery because the churchyard could not cope.[7]

So it was into a thriving Bodmin that a coach-and-six was escorted by a splendidly uniformed sheriff's troop on Tuesday, July 30, 1844. Mr. Justice Wightman and Mr. Justice Patteson had journeyed from Exeter and across Bodmin Moor for the Cornish civil and criminal courts, respectively.

It was about five in the afternoon and, as usual, the route would have been lined by townsfolk who were accustomed to greet the judges' arrival in the Cornish capital. Down over the new Barn Park road from the moor would have come the procession and through Brewery Lane past the parish church.

As the present-day through way, Turf Street, meant negotiating an awkward bend in 1844, the judges would probably have been escorted up Honey Street - Lady Huntingdon's chapel on the right and the Globe and London inns on the left - and around the corner, where the old butter market was giving way to a new turret clock, into the Mount Folly square.

With trumpets sounding and javelin men on guard, the justices apparently immediately crossed the square from their Shire House lodgings and entered the Shire Hall courthouse to open the commission. There, in the new granite-faced building on the site of the Franciscan friary,[8] the royal Letters Patent was read by the judge's clerk. And 'Mr. High Sheriff of this county', H. L. Stevens of Tregenna Castle at St. Ives, was requested to 'be pleased to produce the several writs and precepts to you directed and delivered and returnable this day so that my lords, the Queen's Justices, may proceed thereon'. [9]

The following day, Wednesday July 31, the customary assize service took place at ten in the morning at the parish church. The procession to St. Petroc's, which was to feature in Lord Russell's bill before Parliament three years later as the most suitable foundation for the proposed Cornish cathedral, was also a crowd-pulling spectacle. Accompanied by the High Sheriff and his chaplain, the judges were escorted to church by John Ward the mayor, Richard Bray the town clerk, the four aldermen, twelve councillors, town crier and sergeants-at-mace.

During the service, it was traditional for the Bidding Prayer to be said by a standing congregation, the judges to be reminded of the account they must give of themselves before the Almighty and, after the ringing of the assize bell, for a sermon to be preached by the sheriff's chaplain.

On this occasion, the text chosen by the Reverend Edward Fursdon, whose mother and wife were members of the Rodd family of Trebartha Hall in Northill, was from the last verse of Job, 28: *Behold, the fear of the Lord, that is wisdom; and to depart from evil is understanding.*

The service over, public attention turned to the courthouse which was due to open at noon. Apart from the ceremonial, there was interest in the presiding judge, as this was fifty-four-year old Sir John Patteson's first appearance on the western circuit for ten or twelve years. [10]

The Norwich-born son of a clergyman had been called to the bar by the society of the Middle Temple - like Cockburn and Slade - in 1821. But his rise had been swifter than members of his own, or any other, inn of court. *No other instance ever occurred of one who, after only nine years' practice at the bar, had been raised to the bench,* according to Edward Foss, his biographer. And *so unreservedly were his merits acknowledged* that he had become a judge in 1830 *without a murmur among his colleagues.*

But Sir John's promising career was impeded, and was to be curtailed, by deafness. Even although he used *ingenious instruments* in an effort to overcome his increasing infirmity, he would be prematurely retired within eight years of Matthew's trial. [11]

Nevertheless, when the grand jurors, magistrates, mayors and coroners had answered to their names and the Queen's Proclamation Against Vice had been read, something of the *lucid reasonings* for which Sir John was noted was discernible in his charge to the grand jury.

As the twenty-three county freeholders (who, before 1933, were selected by the sheriff to consider accusations against prisoners and to decide whether or not there were cases for trial by a petty jury) listened to the judge, he told them that he had noticed quite a few of the prisoners had had a fair education. But he did not want people to think that that education had failed, he said, because even the best education was no protection against temptation.

Then, obviously alluding to the Charlotte Dymond affair, he drew the grand jurors' attention to 'the murder case of circumstantial evidence'. He would not enter into the details, he told them, but he did feel that they would be presenting this case to a petty jury.

And, had Matthew Weeks run his eye along the benches of the grand jury, he might have reached a similar conclusion. There was John King Lethbridge, the chairman of the magistrates who had committed him for trial. It was hardly likely that he would have changed his opinion since the Halworthy hearing three months before.

And the rest had little in common with Matthew's kind. There were Thomas Agar, in his early thirties, who had assumed the surname of Robartes when succeeding to Lanhydrock near Bodmin in 1822; forty-six-year old Deeble Peter of Colquite in St. Mabyn, who had assumed the surname Hoblyn in 1836; Charles and Sir Joseph Sawle of Penrice in St. Austell; Edward Pendarves of Pendarves in Camborne; John Tremayne of Heligan in St. Ewe; William Gregor of Trewarthenick in Cornelly; William Arundell of Kenegie in Gulval; and Humphrey Williams of Carnanton in Mawgan-in-Pyder.

There, also, were the half cousins sixty-two-year old Edward Collins of Truthan in St. Erme and sixty-five-year old Captain Edward Collins of Trewardale in Blisland; two others sporting rank, sixty-four-year old Captain William Hext of Tredethy in Helland and fifty-year old Captain Frederick Rogers of Penrose in St. Tudy; and Richard Spry of Cuddra in St. Austell; Edward Archer of Trelaske in Lewannick; William Horndon of Pencrebar in Southill; Charles Rashleigh of Menabilly in Tywardreath; and the Hon. George Fortescue who was to come into Boconnoc near Lostwithiel.

Foreman of the grand jury was sixty-three-year old Sir William Trelawney of Trelawne in Pelynt. And the remaining members were Francis Rodd of Trebartha Hall in Northill, relative of the sheriff's chaplain; forty-four-year old Nicholas Kendall of Pelyn in Lostwithiel; and John Enys of Enys in Mylor, the forty-eight-year old son-in-law of Davies Gilbert the historian.

These, then, were the men who would decide the fate of Matthew Weeks. There was no provision for the case in his defence to be considered. The case for the prosecution was set out in the bill of indictment; and, if the grand jurors felt it was strong enough for a petty jury to try, they would send their foreman back to the courtroom with it marked *true*. Only in the event of their returning it marked *ignoramus,* would the trial be off because no case had been found against him.

As the grand jurors retired to make their decision and a petty jury was sworn in so that the first cases on the calendar could proceed, those who had answered their names as magistrates, as tradition had it at the beginning of assize, must have reflected on the judge's comments. R.G. Bennett, J. Carpenter, W. B. Clements, S. Davey, J. Lyne and William Braddon, mayor-elect of Camelford, J. B. Messenger, W. W. Morshead, J. Paynter, T. Pearse, H. P. Rawlings, W. Sandys and H. Thompson might well have thought upon them as they took their leave for home. There seemed every likelihood, if the grand jurors took the judge's hint, that Matthew Weeks would stand trial for his life on the morrow.[12]

That following day, Thursday August 1, found Bodmin teeming with people in the hope that he would. The town was usually crowded for the judges' arrival and opening of commission. But now, as the *Morning Herald* reporter noted for the August 5 issue of his paper, *it having been expected that two cases for murder in the calendar of this county would come on for trial* this day *a vast concourse of people* had assembled early in the morning before the courts, *the access to which was rendered difficult from the crowd.*

He was not the only press-man there. The *Royal Cornwall Gazette* representative was obviously on the spot to despatch the news that *the bill against Weeks has not yet been returned* but *the learned judge in his charge* (to the grand jury) *expressed a strong opinion on the evidence.* Yet the *Morning Herald* reporter, probably because he was an outsider, had an eye for detail. *A strong feeling against the punishment of death seems to exist in many parts of Cornwall,* he wrote.

He had noticed that handbills - headed *TO JURYMEN,* dated July 30, and signed *A LOVER OF THE HUMAN RACE* - were being *circulated amongst all the persons in the place who were supposed to belong to the jury, with the hope that a perusal of them would affect their verdicts in the cases of murder.*

In a well-reasoned and a surprisingly 'modern' way, the handbills argued that *since a man has no right over his own life, he cannot invest others with that of which he is not previously possessed, neither can any number of persons be possessed of a power collectively which neither of them possesses individually.*

The writer went on to point out that, although the death penalty had been abolished for crimes such as animal stealing and house-breaking, their number had fallen rather than risen; and that, while murderers escaped *the pale of society* by the rope, their kinsfolk who were left had to bear the stigma of their sentence.

Maintaining that *all punishments should be corrective,* the handbill author urged jurymen to return verdicts of *guilty while labouring under temporary bouts of insanity* against convicted murderers, since no-one in his right mind would kill. And he ended with a reminder that the old testament 'eye for an eye' philosophy had been reversed by Christ's 'love your enemies' commandment.

In the criminal court, a case concerning a Peter Body had been going on; but few seemed interested enough to record its details.

Then, at twelve noon, Sir William Trelawney returned to the courtroom with the bill of indictment against Matthew Weeks. And everyone was intensely anxious to learn the grand jurors' decision. Would he, or would he not, be tried for the murder of Charlotte Dymond ?

That day, Charlotte Johns was being tried for the murder of her bastard child; and the case was going well for the defence which was being led by F. W. Slade, who was to appear for Matthew in the event of his standing trial. In the civil court, meanwhile, Alexander Cockburn, who would appear against Matthew, was not enjoying such success while acting for the defendant in a seduction case.

If this boded well for Matthew Weeks, he needed all the encouragement he could get.

For a true bill had been brought in against him. [13] The trial was on.

His wretched position

19. To all intents and purposes, the trial was on.

In the public mind it had been on ever since Charlotte Dymond had failed to return to Penhale farm that Sunday April 14. As far as three people in the farmhouse kitchen that night had been concerned, Matthew Weeks was the cause of her disappearance. And the number of his accusers had grown so that, by the morning of Friday August 2, 1844, there was a larger crowd at the Bodmin assize court than the *West Briton* reporter could remember having witnessed since the trial of the Lightfoot brothers in 1840. [1]

Yet, until and unless Matthew Weeks pleaded 'not guilty' when arraigned at the bar, the trial the crowds had come to see and hear might not take place. A true bill of indictment had been returned to the courtroom by the grand jury; and Matthew would have to plead to that accusation. But, in the event of his pleading 'guilty', judgement would be passed immediately and all the expected gruesome details of the case would not come out in a courtroom drama. [2]

This probably never crossed the minds of those who started queueing outside Shire Hall at seven o'clock on the morning of that Friday. To the *Times* reporter they seemed to have come from all parts of Cornwall and he found it impossible to describe their excitement. The area around the courthouse and every avenue to it was so densely crowded by eight o'clock, that it was obvious that most of the people would be turned away once the court was opened. In fact, the place had been packed all the previous day, even although it had been known from noon that the Dymond case would not be heard until this morning.

While they waited, many probably read the new editions of the *Royal Cornwall Gazette* and of the *West Briton* which had just reached the streets. Under identical headlines, CORNWALL LAMMAS ASSIZES and BODMIN, THURSDAY, 12 NOON, they carried the details of the judges' arrival and opening of the commission, the assize service and charge to the grand jury, and of the return of a true bill against Weeks.

Meanwhile, members of a special jury were answering to their names in the civil courtroom. And, this over, it was announced that the parties in the previous day's seduction case had agreed to compromise so that a verdict could thereupon be taken for the plaintiff. Now Alexander Cockburn, who had appeared for the defendant, was free to lead the expected prosecution against Matthew Weeks. And, so that the crown courtroom was available for that long awaited murder trial, Wightman the civil judge took the remaining criminal cases.

When the doors of the crown court accordingly opened, so many people rushed to get in that, had she not screamed, a woman who fell would have been trampled to death. Police constables came to her rescue; and then they entered the courtroom to clear it of the large number of people, for whom there could be no accommodation, so that some sort of order was called by the time the judge arrived. [3]

As soon as Sir John Patteson had taken his seat, the star of the macabre show was led in; and members of the press recorded their impressions of Matthew Weeks. The reporter for the *Morning Chronicle, Sherborne Mercury, Morning Herald* and *Falmouth Packet* considered him to be twenty-two years of age, short and rather lame, and of a countenance so dogged and sullen that it was certainly not calculated to prepossess anyone in his favour.

The *West Briton* and *Royal Cornwall Gazette* observers described him as being *about 5 ft. 4 ins. high, and lame; dressed in a blue cloth shooting jacket, a black stock ornamented with a pin, a fancy waistcoat with three rows of glass buttons and a pair of greyish trousers.* And, contrary to their colleague's opinion, they thought that *on the whole* Matthew *would not be called ill-looking, although he has rather an insignificant appearance. He looks not more than eighteen although he is four years older. He has a good head of hair of a brownish colour and curly; his eyes are what are commonly called down-looking, the eyebrows overhang and he is slightly marked with small pox.*

Once in the dock, Matthew was arraigned by the clerk of assize. He stood charged on the coroner's inquisition and also on the indictment preferred by the prosecutrix, Mrs. Peter, which was read over to him. [4]

The indictment was straight to the point and did not include the counts of strangling and drowning which Cowlard, Mrs. Peter's solicitor, had suggested in his brief to the barristers might be made 'for precaution's sake'. But there were discrepancies between the indictment and the inquest accusation. Matthew was 'late of the parish of Advent' according to the indictment but 'of Davidstow' in the inquest charge. 'With a certain knife of the value of 6d (2½p)' he was supposed to have cut 'the left side of the neck and throat' of Charlotte, according to the indictment, whereas it was 'with a certain instrument to the jurors unknown' that he cut 'the throat or gullet' in the inquest charge. And, although the description of the wound in the inquest accusation almost tallied with that of the pathologist's report - 8½ inches long and 2½ inches deep - the indictment stated that it was 'of the length of 6 inches and of a depth of 4 inches.' [5]

It did not seem to matter. Matthew's surname was sometimes spelt 'Weeks' and at others 'Weekes'. Most thought him twenty-two years of age. Few appeared to know or to bother where he came from. It was too early for birth registration when he was born in 1820, admittedly, but the baptismal register in Lezant parish church was available for those requiring authentic detail. Evidently, anything went. [6]

Thus indicted, Matthew was called upon to plead. *He stood with his head a little on one side hanging down, one hand firmly clenched, the other holding a pocket handkerchief,* the *West Briton* reporter noticed. And he and the *Royal Cornwall Gazette* observer found it almost impossible to say whether the appearance of a smirk or smile on Matthew's face arose from the peculiar conformation of his mouth or from indifference to his wretched position.

The tone of Matthew's reply might have suggested that his expression was merely an unfortunate quirk of fate. Almost inaudibly he answered 'not guilty.'

The trial was on. A petty jury could be empanelled and sworn in. But, before it was, Matthew's counsel, Frederick Slade, requested the removal of all witnesses from the courtroom; and his wish was complied with.

Presumably to give an appearance of disinterest, the twelve good men and true of the petty jury had been drawn from West Cornwall for this case concerning the eastern part of the county. But, as they must have been well acquainted with the so-called facts from reading their newspapers, it would be too much to believe that they were not already biassed as they answered to their names.

John Thomas White, yeoman, of St. Just-in-Penwith (foreman)
Richard Brush, farmer, of Gulval
Isaac Butson, yeoman, of St. Agnes
Matthew Cardew, farmer, of Paul
William Davey, farmer, of Illogan
John Fox, farmer, of Illogan
Thomas Hitchens, farmer, of Crowan
Henry Ivey, miller, of Ludgvan
Charles Jacka, farmer, of St. Buryan
Henry John, farmer, of Paul
Thomas Mitchell, farmer, of Uny Lelant
John Mitchell, farmer, of St. Levan

Alexander Cockburn, Q.C., counsel for the Crown, then rose to make the opening statement for the prosecution. He had lost the seduction case in the civil court by compromise that very morning. But the defence could draw no comfort from this, Although noted for being *indisposed to bend his mind to the daily work* of his profession, Cockburn was making a name for *extraordinary exertion* on *any great occasion*. He flew better than he walked.

And apparently Cockburn did rise to this occasion. As Matthew listened in the dock, the hand in which he held a handkerchief resting on the bar of the court, Queen's Counsel gave *one of those luminous and eloquent addresses for which he is so justly celebrated, carefully abstaining from pressing any part of his statement more heavily upon the prisoner than the evidence in the case would warrant*, thought the *West Briton* man. And a newspaper colleague agreed that counsel's manner was *most masterly* as he dealt with *all the minute circumstances on which the prosecution was founded in the most forcible and concatenated style.*

Describing Mrs. Phillipa Peter as a 'remarkably kind person, whose conduct to all her servants appeared to have been marked with the most exemplary kindness', Cockburn told the court about the members of her household and how 'Charlotte Dymond, an 18-year old illegitimate child with but few friends, had for some time kept company, as it is called in this county', with Matthew Weeks. 'The girl, however, it would seem, was pleased with admiration', he continued, 'and was not insensible to the attentions of others, and a person of the name of Prout had been favoured by her.' [7]

He then began the story of Charlotte's disappearance. But, in saying that, although Weeks probably did not know about her appointment with Prout, the girl told Mrs. Peter she would not be back for milking 'in the hearing of the prisoner', Cockburn led the jury to believe something more than the brief advised him.

And, in fact, when Mrs. Peter was called to give evidence, the details as the press understood them did not always tally with her former statement. She also gave the impression that Matthew had heard Charlotte tell her she'd not be back for milking. Further, she said that Charlotte had been at Penhale for one year and four months up to her death and had kept company with Matthew only during that last 16 months, that she had noticed; yet, in her deposition, she had stated that Charlotte had been her servant 'for about 18 months before her death' and had kept company with Matthew 'for some time both before and since' returning to Penhale for that period.

The press also understood her to say that, when she gave Charlotte's clothes to Matthew, there was 'a white skirt' amongst them; whereas, in her former statement, the article had been 'a (bonnet) cap'. Even if we allow for a little lapse of memory in this respect, the discrepancy does undermine her maintaining in her deposition that 'there was not amongst the articles I gave him any gloves or green gauze handkerchief'; Mrs. Peter's memory was not wholly to be trusted.

Whether or not, when she said that the trousers Matthew was wearing in court were the ones he had on when last seen with Charlotte, she was right, cannot now be known. Her son was later to corroborate this evidence. But we do know that those trousers were taken from Matthew by Constable Fitzgerald on the evening of his imprisonment.

It was when she reached the point in her story, about having 'threatened' Matthew with a magistrate, that Frederick Slade objected on Matthew's behalf. What had been said in consequence of that threat was not admissible evidence, he thought. But he was over-ruled and Mrs. Peter continued. **8**

When, at the end of her witness, she was cross-examined by Slade, she described the weather on Sunday April 14 as having been 'dirty and rainy' and the moors as having been particularly wet as 'the springs were all full then'. She also said that almost every week she had occasion to send Matthew to a Mr. Langridge who sold butter, pork and so on, and that he wore his two-year-old second best velvet jacket on these errands.

Slade was obviously seeking to show that Matthew's muddy trousers and stockings could have been the result of walking anywhere in the Penhale area that day and not necessarily through a moorland marsh on criminal activity; and that the marks on the quite old jacket could have been other than Charlotte's blood. At the same time he made her admit that she did not actually see Matthew sew the button on his shirt, although she overheard him ask Stevens for a needle and thread. Slade's efforts were in vain, however, when Mrs. Peter said the shirt was 'torn by the wrist', as well as 'out of the collar' and unpleated as she had formerly stated.

She also maintained in court that Matthew had told her that *he* had received a letter from Blisland; whereas, in her deposition, she had stated that she searched Charlotte's 'things to see if there was any letter directed to her' as Matthew had told her that the *girl* 'had had a letter for her to go from Rebecca Lanxon'.

If Cowlard, Mrs. Peter's solicitor, had been afraid that his client would be biassed in Matthew's favour when he wrote his brief, he must have been satisfied now that she was, indeed, on the side of the prosecution.

As her cross-examination drew to a close, Matthew requested to retire from the court for a few minutes, and permission was granted.

John Stevens, the servant Mrs. Peter had taken on on Lady Day, then took the stand; and he was examined for the prosecution by one of Cockburn's assistants, William Rowe of Launceston. On Cowlard's suggestion that it was 'probably inexpedient to encumber the case' with Stevens's doubtful knife evidence, Rowe evidently steered clear of it and kept the witness to details of Charlotte's body. 'I saw no blood about the place nor on the body', Stevens told the court, 'no knife nor hatchet, no marks of any person struggling'.

The next to be called was Thomas Good, the surgeon, who was examined by Cockburn. 'The wound was deeper at the back part than on the right side (of Charlotte's neck)', he said, 'therefore I think it commenced there'. And, if the pathologist were correct in his analysis, Charlotte's assailant must have attacked from the front with his right hand, as the wound was deeper on the left side than the right. In which case, the so-called blood on Matthew's left sleeve would take some explaining, it must have occurred to counsel for his defence.

However, 'the wound was inflicted with great force', the surgeon was saying to Cockburn, 'probably with a knife, though not very sharp because the ends were somewhat jagged. I found blood on the clothes, the appearance was that of pale blood, nothing like coagulation. The quantity of water (in the river place) would be sufficient to account for its pallid appearance.'

Slade then cross-examined Dr. Good and was told 'the clothes were not in the water, the undergarments were wet, the head and trunk of the body were in the water course. Such a wound would have emptied nearly all the veins of the body. It was the sort of wound a person might inflict on himself. I should not expect the wound to commence on the other side unless the party had been left handed.'

If Slade were satisfied with this, Cockburn evidently was not. He re-examined the pathologist, who explained 'it was the sort of wound a person might inflict on himself. I mean a cut wound that a person might be likely to inflict upon himself with a cutting instrument. I think it possible, but not likely, that the wound would commence at the back of the neck.'

'The depth of the wound was not too much for a person to inflict upon himself because the space from the surface to the bone is not considerable', the surgeon continued. He seemed not to relish the position in which he found himself, however. 'I am not prepared to say, with reference to the extent, how much of such a wound a person could inflict upon himself', he told Cockburn. 'It would depend on the instrument. It was two cuts. I could see two cuts distinctly on the carotid artery, a complete one and a partial one, the partial one being a little above the complete division.'

'The instrument would have come into contact with about the end of the first third of the whole length of the cut, when it came into contact with the carotid', the doctor explained, 'and then it was that there was an incomplete cut. There was nothing to lead me to think that the wound might not have been inflicted at a short distance and the body carried to that place.'

Thomas Good had been examined by Cockburn for the prosecution, cross-examined by Slade for the defence, and re-examined by Cockburn; but he was not yet to escape from the witness box. Frederick Slade wished to question him again.

When he did, the pathologist replied that 'it would depend on the position of a murderer as to whether or not he had blood on him. Most likely some on his arm and some on his body if he carried her.'

Because Charlotte's wound had been deeper on the left side of her neck than the right, her assailant must have been right handed and attacked from the front, or the girl must have committed suicide with her right hand, the surgeon had implied in his evidence. If the jury had got that message, the lack of blood on Matthew's clothes, with the exception of a few spots and a suspected mark on his left sleeve, just did not add up to his having been the assailant.

Dr. Good gave way to John Fowler in the witness box, and Cockburn to Rowe, who examined the surveyor. Then, the plan of the murder area explained and distances between places confirmed, Fowler stood down, his place being taken by Simon Baker who described the discovery of the body to Cockburn's other assistant, George Oxenham of Paul.

Next to step up was Isaac Cory, one of the most important witnesses for the prosecution as far as the solicitor, Cowlard, had been concerned. But, what the press understood him to say, when examined by Rowe, conflicted with certain of his statements beforehand.

He had left Davidstow church at half past four on Sunday, April 14, he told the court, whereas he had previously given the time as half past three. Matthew Weeks had been about sixty yards from him when *he* saw Cory first, said the farmer, whereas he had stated that, from a place a quarter of a mile from his home at Trevilian's Gate, he had first seen Weeks 'about sixty yards from the corner' of his field 'adjoining the moor...on the moor side of the road and that by a good bit.'

Then, the *Morning Herald* and *Falmouth Packet* observer understood him to say that he did not see the face of the woman on the moor but she had on a brown bonnet; yet, he had said in his deposition that, as her umbrella was open, he 'could not see her bonnet'. And finally, the court was given to understand that Cory had found the rest of Charlotte's clothes on the day her body was found, whereas it had been five days later according to his own and Constable Rickard's previous statements.

Under cross-examination by Slade, Cory admitted that the weather on Sunday April 14 had been foggy; but he insisted, nevertheless, that he had seen all that he had described as it had cleared off in the afternoon. He had mentioned having seen the couple to Mrs. Peter that evening, he said. And he again denied that he had quarrelled with Matthew Weeks.

Then into the witness box came Richard Pethick, the cattle farmer. The man the prosecution depended upon to identify Matthew Weeks with the man on the moor near Roughtor Ford. If he repeated his shy performance at the magistrates' hearing in court, the case for the crown could be in trouble.

The couple were within three hundred yards of him, Pethick explained to the court, when he could see that they were a man and a woman; but 'I did not observe the man's gait' he admitted. At this, Cowlard the solicitor must have held his breath. If Pethick, being only three hundred yards away, did not notice a limp, how would the court then believe that Cory, despite failing to recognise Charlotte, could identify Matthew by his lameness?

Pethick went on to describe his riding on to Deptford and then between Fox Hole and Roughtor. 'When I came round by the Fox Hole', the cattle farmer said, 'I was about half a mile from Roughtor Ford, I saw the persons again . That time I came within 39 yards of the man, I have measured the distance since. I observed that he was lame. I believe the prisoner was the man'.

Cowlard must have remembered the magistrates' hearing, where all that Pethick would say was that he only 'believed' that Weeks was the man on the moor. That had not been good enough. And now here was Pethick repeating that inadequate performance.

Frederick Slade cross-examined Pethick for the defence. Then, as all seemed lost and this evidence drew to a close, Pethick said 'I swear that the prisoner was the man beyond belief.'

The cattle farmer had at last committed himself. Cory had insisted that Matthew Weeks was on the moor with a woman who could only have been Charlotte. Pethick had now identified Weeks as the man seen with the woman, at almost seven in the evening on Sunday April 14, a hundred yards from the place where the body was later found. It was all over bar the shouting.

It hardly mattered that William Gard, the local preacher, who had replaced Pethick in the witness box, was saying that he could not identify the man on the moor and had not noticed that he limped. Nor need there be too much anxiety, as he stepped down from Oxenham's examination, about soft John Peter's evidence. He did let out that the butcher had had to provide Matthew with a suitable knife, because his own was inadequate to kill the pig, and also that Matthew suffered from occasional nose bleeds. But, as Rebecca Lanxon denied having sent a letter, she and Hezekiah Spear swore they had neither expected nor received Charlotte on April 14 or 15, and Sarah Westlake undermined Matthew's Halworthy alibi, the case for the prosecution hardened.

When Mrs. Peter's daughter, Mary Westlake, took the stand, she drew some sympathy as she was still recovering from having been crushed in the crowds around the court the previous day. She was followed by Elias Bettinson who recounted his conversation with Matthew, regarding Charlotte's mother having allegedly threatened to kill her.

With the case seeming to slip from his grasp, Matthew's counsel managed to push William Hocken into an important admission under cross-examination. The farmer had been telling the court that Matthew had said that no-one could swear to his having done anything which might have contributed to Charlotte's disappearance. And, when Slade asked if an innocent man might have said the same, Hocken had to admit to that possibility.

Thomas Prout was then called as a witness for the prosecution; and those in court showed great interest as he appeared. He related his visit to Penhale farm, his arrangement with Charlotte to meet at chapel, and her subsequent non-appearance on the evening of April 14. Then came Elizabeth Stevens with her story about Matthew's having produced a handbag at Coad's Green; and it was corroborated by her friend, Eliza Butler. While the first girl said that she knew Charlotte only by hearsay, the second said she'd known Weeks 'a good while'.

There was little doubt about it, it was the prosecution's day by the time Constable John Bennett of South Petherwin took the stand to describe the arrest of Matthew. 'I knew his brother-in-law and had heard Weeks was lame', he said, 'I told him "what you say I'll have to use against you". He said nothing more than "if I tell you, you will have to tell of it?".' He named the new clothes, that had apparently been purchased in Plymouth, as a pair of drawers, a shirt, trousers and stockings and said that there was an umbrella with the bundle. And he was just telling the jury that, when he had asked Matthew if he had cut Charlotte's throat with a pair of fleams, the reply had been 'not with that', when Frederick Slade challenged him. [9]

'Look at your depositions, sir!' counsel for Matthew's defence cried out. 'You said before the magistrates that Weeks said "I did not".'

Constable Bennett insisted that what he had said in court that day was accurate, despite Slade's being right about its incompatibility with his deposition. He also said Weeks had told him he hadn't 'kept company with Charlotte since Lady Day but some other chaps had'. At this, the judge himself broke in and cautioned Bennett saying that, as a constable, he must never again question prisoners while they were in his custody.

Thus reprimanded, Bennett stepped down and Constable Fitzgerald of Camelford was called. And well might Cowlard the solicitor have feared how he would get on in the witness box for, when he stated that Weeks had said he thought he would be safe in Plymouth or Devonport, his word was challenged also. Slade cross-examined him in connection with what he had previously stated before the magistrates; and Fitzgerald was forced to admit that he had 'no doubt now, after looking at the depositions, that Weeks said he was *not* safe in going to Plymouth or Devonport.'

And there was more trouble for the crown side. When Rebecca Jewell was called to identify the gloves which had been found on Weeks as Charlotte's, she felt that the stripes might have been wider. So Mrs. Phillipa Peter had to be re-called to identify them positively as having belonged to the dead girl.

As for evidence given by William Northam and John Westlake regarding the boot prints, the *West Briton* reporter felt it *not worth while to give.* The court seems to have been given to understand that Weeks's boots left no impression of the toe, his lameness apparently making him use the centre of the foot. According to the reporter, *Westlake said that Constable Dingle told him he swore to having seen an impression of the skute*(heel guard) *of Weeks's boot on the moor;* upon which witness *(*Westlake) *said that he had sworn grievously false. Subsequently, when Constable Dingle was called, he flatly denied that any such conversation had occurred at all and stated distinctly that he saw the impression of the skute, in which he was confirmed by Constables Rickard and Hayne who were present when he made the comparison between the boots and impressions.*

What should the court have made of this?

Charlotte Dymond

It, not having the details we have to hand, could make little. What *we* know is that the prosecution had to rely upon the boot print evidence, in the event of Richard Pethick's refusing to say that the man on the moor was Weeks. And as, in front of the magistrates, Northam's measurement of the moorland print had fallen short of Weeks's boots, it had probably been decided to tell the court that either the heel or toe left no impression because of the lameness. That the heel was to be eliminated, explains why emphasis was placed upon the so-called 'peculiar' toe plate impression when the independent observer, Constable Hayne, was taken to witness a comparison at the clothes pit.

Northam and Westlake, however, speaking first, seem to have given the court to understand that there was no toe impression, although their intention had been to say that Constable Dingle was mistaken in swearing he had seen a heel print. To add to confusion, other speakers to the print evidence could not hear this and adjust their own stories, because witnesses had been removed from court at the request of Matthew's counsel. Consequently, when Dingle stepped up, what the solicitor feared really happened. The deaf constable would not budge and the other two policemen had to back him, although they had before made no mention of seeing a heel impression at the clothes pit.

But the prosecution got away with it. The subject in court was changed. Constable Rickard produced the clothing Cory had found in the turf pit. And Mrs. Peter, re-called, identified it as having been Charlotte's. Constable Brooming produced Weeks's shirt; and Mary Westlake produced the green handkerchief.

Cockburn, Q. C., even performed one of the tricks of his trade by pointing out to the court that the blood on Charlotte's green gauze handkerchief was only a spot upon which he placed no reliance. Yet it might have been noticed that this was the first mention of blood on that article, as Mary Westlake had stated that the blood was on Matthew's red handkerchief.

However, the case continued. And the statement that Matthew had made before the magistrates was read to the court and proved. Then, as the trial had been going on for some 9½ hours when the prosecution closed at twenty to seven, the jury was allowed to retire a short while for refreshment.

Yet there was still great interest in court, particularly in the prisoner. 'From first to last', it seemed to the press men, he appeared 'to regard everything with indifference', the enigmatic smile on his face continuing 'nearly all the day'.

There is no hope

20. At some time before seven o'clock on that evening of Friday August 2, 1844, Frederick Slade arose in the Bodmin assize court to defend Matthew Weeks.

Matthew himself could not speak as, prior to 1898, prisoners were unable to give evidence. Yet he was lucky compared with those accused of felony before 1836 because he was at least allowed the assistance of counsel to examine witnesses and sum up on his behalf.[1] And, judging from Slade's objection to Constable Bennett's evidence, he had had access to the proofs of the magistrates' hearing.

The calendar for this commission of assize had contained two murder cases; and Slade was acting for the defendant in both. The previous day, he had appeared for a Charlotte Johns, who had been accused of murdering her new-born bastard child. A surgeon had maintained that the child was born alive; but, with skilful cross-examination, Slade had broken his evidence and with 'a very feeling and powerful appeal to the jury', he had saved the woman from the rope. [2]

If there was now, as he rose for Matthew, some hope that he could pull it off again, Cowlard, the solicitor for the prosecution, must have taken heart from one fact. It had been William Rowe who had acted for the prosecution in the Johns trial, whereas the more celebrated Cockburn had laid the charge against Matthew. Slade might have shown himself a match for Rowe but Cockburn was quite a different proposition.

In his brief to counsel for the prosecution, Cowlard had expressed concern for certain aspects that Slade might take up. John Peter's softness and the discrepancy in the conversations between Matthew and the constables had, indeed, come out in court; and the foot print evidence had fallen short. Yet Thomas Prout's evidence had been allowed and Pethick had committed himself. So the only points left to the defence, as far as Cowlard might have been concerned, would seem to be those regarding the absence of apparent motive and evidence of a struggle, the non-production of a murder weapon, and doubt as to where the alleged murder actually took place.

Frederick Slade's opening remarks in Matthew's defence concerned the publicity the case had received, however. He feared that the rumours that had circulated about Weeks would influence the jury's decision, he said, the prisoner's guilt having been assumed as a foregone conclusion by the Cornish. [3]

He then turned, as Cowlard had expected, to the question of motive. It had been stressed that Charlotte Dymond and Matthew Weeks had been courting. It had been proved that Weeks had been on intimate terms with the dead girl yet, at the same time, the jury was expected to believe that he had murdered her, he said.

Slade went on to point out that it had been accepted that Matthew had cut Charlotte's throat; but he wanted to know by what means and for what reason. As the prosecution had alleged that the only possible motive could have been jealousy, proof of that jealousy should have been forthcoming. But, in the absence of it, this murder - if it were indeed murder - was completely without motive, he maintained.

It had also not been proven that Weeks had possessed a capable weapon, Slade continued. In any case, the body had been without marks of violence or of violation other than the neck wound and Weeks's clothes had not been covered in blood as the murderer's must have been. [4]

It was quite clear, he said, that Charlotte Dymond had had no intention of returning early, on that evening of Sunday April 14, to Penhale farm. She had said as much to Mrs. Peter before leaving the place and had shown that she intended to part company with Weeks. The court had heard that, unbeknown

Charlotte Dymond

to Weeks, she had an appointment with another man, Thomas Prout.

Charlotte Dymond, if she were the woman on the moor, had had an umbrella, Slade reminded the jury; yet Matthew Weeks had not been seen to return with one to the farm that night, although he was seen with his when he left Penhale on the following Sunday. And there had been a letter, despite the Lanxons' denial, which must have been read by Charlotte because, of the two who were seen with it, only she was capable of reading. From whomsoever it was and to whomsoever it was addressed, Weeks could have known only what Charlotte chose to tell him regarding it.

Slade doubted that what Isaac Cory had said, concerning having seen Weeks on the moor with a woman, was in fact the truth. Then he turned to what he termed 'the unsuspicious conduct' of Weeks. He had returned home at a normal time, eaten his supper, slept as usual, and left his clothes around. And it was hardly the act of a murderer to draw attention to a shirt, mend it in front of others, and continue wearing it for a week if it were prime evidence against him, he suggested.

As for his so-called absconding on April 21, Slade told the jury that there could have been only one reason for Matthew's walking out of Penhale farm. It was obviously because he was the chief suspect in the eyes of the locals.

Matthew's defence lasted barely an hour, whereas the prosecution had taken some 9½ hours. Yet, whereas so much of the case against him was - or should have been seen to be - doubtful, the points in his defence were incontestable. As far as the circumstances of the case and the period allowed, Slade had done a good job.

So good, in fact, that, as he sat down, Surgeon Good asked the judge if he might explain a portion of the evidence he had given earlier that day. Though Charlotte's wound was the *kind* of wound a person might inflict on herself, the doctor explained, he thought it impossible that she *could* inflict such a wound as that.

Sir John Patteson, the judge, replied that he understood the surgeon to have said as much before. And then, at four minutes to eight that evening, he began summing up.

It was only human nature that anxiety should be felt for the result of such as this very important case, he told the petty jurors, but he hoped they were capable of throwing out of their minds anything they might have heard before that day and of entirely confining their attention to the evidence they had heard during the trial.

It was the judge's duty, Patteson went on, to lay down the law and to apply the punishment when a verdict was reached. The duty of jurors was to decide whether a person was guilty or innocent irrespective of the likely punishment. If there was reasonable doubt, a prisoner was entitled to it.

He then proceeded to read and to comment upon the evidence. It was next to impossible that Charlotte Dymond could have inflicted the wound herself, he felt. The evidence was clear that she was murdered; and the jury had to decide by whom. There was an absence of motive, jealousy had not been proven, and no-one seems to have quarrelled with her that might have done it, the judge admitted; but Weeks was the last to be identified with her.

Slade had made the point that Charlotte Dymond was not returning for milking and was going to part from Weeks who had not heard Prout book her for the evening; but, maintained Patteson, it made no difference because Weeks was seen with the girl at Roughtor Ford. Similarly, the judge could not see much in Slade's point about the umbrella, as Weeks certainly had his when he left for Plymouth and it was raining when he went out with Charlotte Dymond.

'It is doubted whether Cory has come to speak the truth', Patteson continued, 'but I have heard nothing against him. If he is telling the truth, he knew Weeks well, it certainly negatives the account which the prisoner gives of himself.' On his own admission, Weeks had gone beyond Higher Down Gate; and it was hardly likely that Charlotte Dymond met another person near Lanlary Rock. Three persons had sworn that they had seen a couple on the moor beyond Higher Down Gate that Sunday 'and two of the three say that Weeks was the man.'

'It is a case of circumstances entirely', the judge admitted. 'Nobody saw him commit the act, if he did to it. Circumstantial evidence is always to be very carefully and cautiously examined because there is nothing so apt to deceive one for, when any preconceived notion is taken up, how easy it is to dovetail a number of circumstances together and fancy that a very clear case is made out when, in truth, it is not so.'

'Nevertheless', the judge went on, ' it has often been said that circumstantial evidence, if well weighed and examined and if it does bring the matter home to the mind, is often more satisfactory than direct testimony because, in direct testimony, a motive may be suspected whereas, in circumstances, there is often no doubt at all. When they are put together and compared and examined, they tell a story which cannot lead to direct falsehood.'

The duration of the judge's sum-up was to be seven minutes short of two hours. As the hands of the clock crept towards ten, he was saying that 'a jury may come to a wrong conclusion (from circumstances); but that is not like reaching one by some wrong motive and/or false testimony.' The verdict in the present case would be a conscientious one, he felt sure, and one that would do justice between the prisoner and the public. [5]

At eleven minutes before ten o'clock and with these thoughts in their minds, the petty jurors filed out of the courtroom. They had been empanelled and sworn in over twelve hours before. And they were to undergo a further thirty-five minutes of consideration before returning with their verdict.

Although it had been a long trial, containing a voluminous mass of evidence, those who crammed the courtroom nevertheless awaited the jury's deliberation with the most breathless anxiety, according to reporters. And, as far as they were concerned, it had not been proved that the green gauze handkerchief found in Weeks's pocket had been worn away from Penhale by Charlotte, there had been no direct evidence of his alleged jealousy, and there had been no certainty that Matthew had overheard Mrs. Peter's discussing with her son and Stevens their visits to Brown Willy and Blisland and had therefore absconded.

The *Morning Herald* representative thought that Slade had made a very able address to the jury, commenting on all the facts with much ingenuity and skill, and forcibly appealing to them on behalf of the prisoner. It now remained to be seen whether or not it had been successful, as the petty jurors filed back to their places at twenty-four minutes past ten. **6**

The few minutes of suspense that ensued, while their names were being called, were most painful as far as the *West Briton* reporter was concerned; but he noted that, when Matthew stood up to await the verdict, he did so calmly.

An intense silence fell upon the court as John White, the St. Just yeoman and foreman of the jury, rose to his feet to deliver the verdict. 'We are of the opinion', he said, 'that the prisoner is guilty.'

The black cap was reached for and placed upon the judge's head. And Sir John Patteson looked across to where Matthew stood, his demeanour as calm as it had been throughout the gruelling day.

'Matthew Weeks', the judge addressed him, 'the jury, after a very full and patient investigation of this case, have come to the conclusion that you are guilty of the offence with which you are charged, having murdered the poor girl, Charlotte Dymond, though it appears that you were keeping company with her and were on the best of terms with her.'

'The circumstances of this case do not disclose to the jury or to me the motive which induced you to commit this offence', Patteson continued, 'some jealousy may have activated you. But it is my duty to explain why the jury have come to their verdict.'

'The time you pass in this world will now be very short, your age is very young', he told Matthew, 'still, that does not justify me in holding out the slightest hope that the extreme sentence of the law will not be carried out in your case, that there will be any mercy shown to you.'

Evidently Patteson felt that the trial had been satisfactory and that no writ of error could be issued, as was possible from 1705 although there was no court of criminal appeal until 1907. 'There is no hope for you in this world', he therefore assured Matthew, 'and my earnest entreaty is for you to endeavour to obtain that mercy from the Almighty which man cannot grant. If you do choose to avail yourself of the assistance of the gaol chaplain, you may obtain that pardon through the merits of the Redeemer.' **7**

Patteson was passing the buck to his maker. But doubtless Cockburn felt that he was displaying that 'unflinching integrity of purpose and benevolent kindness of nature' that he was to attribute to him upon his retirement. Nevertheless, the reporters thought that the judge was genuinely 'much affected' by what he had to say. **8**

'You shall be taken from hence to the place from whence you came and be hung by the neck until you are dead', he told Matthew.

Weeks stood motionless. But the judge had not finished.

'Your body shall be buried within the precincts of the prison', Patteson started; but, before he could conclude with 'may the Lord have mercy on your soul', Matthew had fallen backwards on to the bench, where he had been sitting since just after nine that morning. **9**

The scene was both painful and distressing, as far as the *Royal Cornwall Gazette* reporter was concerned, for he felt that Matthew had bolstered himself with hope until that very last minute. In fact, Matthew had been shocked into the realisation that his sentence brought ultimate disgrace to a family of the Cornish yeomanry.

It was twenty to eleven when the court rose. And the ghouls cramming the square outside were rewarded with the spectacle of the limp body of Matthew Weeks being carried out by two turnkeys.

Then, as he was still in a state of collapse, two more helped to load him into the prison van. And back it went with him to Bodmin gaol.

All but cut off

21. A girl had gone missing from a remote Cornish farmhouse. Her body had been found on Bodmin Moor. She must have been murdered. Circumstantial evidence had therefore been collected and sufficiently well arranged to secure the conviction of a little lame serving man. Society was safe once again; and could relax in that knowledge to read all about it.

First off the presses with the details were the national morning newspapers of Monday August 5. The *Morning Herald* devoted almost three of its 20-inch long, 2½-inch wide columns to the *WESTERN CIRCUIT* under its *ASSIZE INTELLIGENCE* heading. In tightly-packed, tiny print, it detailed the excited crowds awaiting the Weeks trial, the content of the anti-hanging handbills, the Johns murder trial, the seduction case, and the Charlotte Dymond affair. The last was so long and involved, it said, that *we have deemed it best to present to our readers the facts upon which the case turned rather than giving the evidence in detail.*

Other papers thought likewise. The *Morning Chronicle* of the same day, the *Morning Post* of August 6, the *Illustrated London News, Sherborne Mercury* and *Falmouth Packet* of August 10, and *Bell's New Weekly Messenger* of Sunday August 11, all carried reports very similar to that of the Herald. Some had shortened versions, all had inaccuracies, and the Chronicle inadvertently missed out some forty-two lines so that the sense of its article was ruined. Yet their readers probably felt that they had their money's worth of the latest sensation.

The London *Times* of August 5 carried a slightly shorter but hardly more subdued report of the trial under the headline *MURDER - EXTRAORDIN— ARY CASE*. This quoted several of the witnesses verbatim, showing up the Cornish way of saying things, and spiced its account with detail such as *the head was all but cut off* the body. As the *Exeter Post*'s report on August 8 was very similar in content and headline, it was probably based upon the *Times'* source material.

In fact, if the *Morning Herald* had sent its own observer, the *Times* almost certainly had a man-on-the-spot. On Thursday August 8, it carried what must have been a scoop in just over a column inch at the bottom of page seven. Headlined *THE BODMIN MURDER - BODMIN, TUESDAY* (August 6), it announced that Matthew Weeks had made a full confession of his guilt. Outlining its content, the reporter assured readers that *he acknowledges the*

Charlotte Dymond

justice of his sentence and conducts himself in a very becoming manner.

Weeks was obviously behaving in the way Victorians expected of those condemned to die, having doubtless and at the judge's earnest entreaty availed himself of the prison chaplain's assistance.

But the *Times* reporter had jumped the gun by revealing the content of Matthew's purported confession. The *West Briton,* which had been unable to verify the truth of a rumoured confession as long before as May 3, confided to its readers on Friday August 9 - when, in common with the *Royal Cornwall Gazette,* it arrived on the streets with the trial details - that it was 'reported about Bodmin' that the 'unhappy man' had confessed and the content had 'been forwarded to the judge' although it was not to 'be made public until after his execution.' And that had been fixed for Monday August 12.

Yet the *Times* had got hold of the content by Tuesday August 6 and publicised it two days later, before the Cornish papers had even appeared. Moreover the *Illustrated London News* followed its lead on August 10, including the words *Weeks subsequently admitted that he was guilty, but says it was not a premeditated act* in its report which otherwise resembled that of the Herald on August 5.

Whether the *Times* reporter knew the judge, the prison chaplain, or the governor of the gaol is unknown. Perhaps it was felt that, by the time the so-called confession was printed, it would be permissible anyway. For there were fears that Weeks would not live long enough to be hanged.

He was *so much affected by, and deeply sensible of, his awful situation* according to the *West Briton,* that he was *constantly fainting* and it was thought that he could *scarcely be kept alive till the appointed time.* Several times since his collapse upon being sentenced, it had been rumoured that he had expired. [1]

The black farce was to be played out, however. And, despite his frequent glidings away into states of unconsciousness, he was to be kept alive to die. [2]

On Saturday August 10, friends visited Matthew in Bodmin gaol. It is not known who these were; but they went to take leave of him. At their parting, *the anguish felt by all parties was very great,* according to the *West Briton* and *the scene was most affecting, as may be conceived.* [3]

The gaol in which Matthew had spent the past 104 days had been built in accordance with the enlightened proposals of the prison reformer, Howard, and had first been occupied in 1779. It had been envisaged as a gaol for the whole county and, when the notorious Launceston prison had closed in 1829, Bodmin's had become the Cornish penitentiary.

By 1844 when Matthew was there, John Bentham Everest had been its governor for 17 years. Only the second to have held the post, he had been appointed by the magistrates at the age of forty-five in 1827, having previously been purser of the convict hulks at Sheerness and Chatham.

Soon after taking up the position, he had supervised what turned out to be a five-year repair and alteration project. And, as this was achieved without additional cost to the county ratepayers, he was voted £100 reward by the magistrates. Yet, even although the gaol was then acknowledged as being one of the best conducted in the kingdom, further extensions and improvements took place during the period 1842-1847. Eventually, under this governor, the original gaol was entirely removed by degrees and completely rebuilt on an extended site from the mid-1850s. [4]

Thus, the gaol from which J. B. Everest retired in 1859 looked very different from that to which he had been appointed thirty-two years previously, the one in which Matthew Weeks was imprisoned.

Nevertheless, just months before Matthew's arrival, it had been said that prisoners at Bodmin gaol received better soup three times a day than law-abiding labourers managed to get once a month. It was also suggested that short-term prisoners such as vagrants should not receive such nourishment; and this was reiterated towards the end of 1847. There was always the danger that crimes would be committed for the grub in Bodmin gaol because, after a fortnight on bread-and-water, all prisoners received soup. [5]

But, if some wished to get in for the food, many already within the walls desired to escape. Apart from the obvious deterrents to staying, the rope and transportation, the treadmills were dreaded; and the prospect of being schooled by a literate prisoner or of enduring a tepid bath every three months was enough to discourage some. So there were occasional break-out attempts and escapes between court and the gaol. [6]

Besides the severity of punishments meted out by magistrates and judges and the discipline imposed by the governor, the gaol's success relied upon the prisoners' states of mind. And in charge of the spiritual welfare of inmates was the chaplain, the thirty-nine-year old Reverend Francis John Hext Kendall. Brother of Nicholas Kendall of Pelyn, one of the grand jurors, cousin of Capt. Hext of Tredethy, another juror, and destined to marry the daughter of yet another juror, Edward Archer of Trelaske, the parson was well connected. [7]

It was to him that Matthew had been advised by the judge to turn, if he wished to 'obtain that mercy from the Almighty which man cannot grant'. And he had apparently *paid the greatest attentions to the instructions* of Kendall, who had been *unremitting in his exertions to lead him to the throne of mercy.* In reporting this, the *West Briton* hoped *that these instructions were not in vain.*

On Sunday August 11, his last full day on earth, Matthew attended the service in the prison church where, as a condemned man, he would have sat in a special pew. Afterwards, the *West Briton* told its readers, *he partook of the holy sacrament, when he appeared truly penitent.*

It was also on this day that Matthew dictated two letters. Both were witnessed by a William Peter; and they were marked with a cross by Matthew as he could neither read nor write. One was to his family -

My dear father and mother, and dear brothers and sisters, and uncles and aunts, and I hope my dear brothers and sisters will now take a warning by me. My brothers will not place too much confidence in young maidens; and my sisters not in young men. And I hope that my brother John that he will make a great alteration upon this; and I hope he will seek the Lord because he might be cut off to a minute's notice, and he will not have time to, I hope that he will knock up drinking and attend to a place of worship, and not break the sabbath so much as he has; and William too, and pray think on this when you don't see me.

You may ask the blacksmith, John Doney, what I owe him and I wish you to pay it little or much. I give my love to Maria Doney and Susan, Maria and Thomasine Hayne, and bid them all farewell. If my brother Richard will call at the gaol any time, he will have my hat, braces and stock and half-shirt; and he must please to give the £5 to mother. The clothes box at Mrs. Peter's, I give to mother. There are two watch ribbons in my box; give the one with a seal to it to William and the other to John, to keep for my sake. Mother must have the shirts and stockings. There are two hats. Give one to William and the other to John; and two pairs of trousers and a pair of leggings which mother can do as she please with; also a fustian jacket, three waistcoats and two handkerchiefs.

Bennett, the constable, has an umbrella, a pair of trousers, drawers and a round jacket, and a black silk handkerchief for mother to do as she please with. He has got a watch, which please to give to brother John. There is a horn cable to a threshell at Mrs. Peter's which I should like mother to have again. Mr. Everest (the governor) has been a very kind friend to me since I have been here, and Mr. Kendall (the chaplain) too. Dingle, the constable, have got my velvet jacket and a pair of boots which mother must have and do as she please with. I wish all my brothers and sisters all farewell and all my friends.

I am your unfortunate son,
X (the sign of Matthew Weeks)   [8]

This letter was, in effect if not in actuality, Matthew's will. For, although a condemned man had no power under the law to make a formal bequest because his body was forfeit to the crown, he could give power of attorney to a legal adviser. And, as the surname of the witness was also that of Matthew's solicitor, Peter, it is possible that he was part of the Launceston practice. But whoever took down Matthew's dictation slipped up when addressing this family letter for he included the condemned man's father who had been dead for nine years.   [9]

Matthew's mother, fifty-three-year old Jane Weeks, had been described as a charwoman in the 1841 census returns, so she could doubtless have done with the articles Matthew left her; the money they could realise would not have been inconsiderable. The £5, however, must have been a windfall. If the price of potatoes, for instance, in the 1840s and at the time of writing this book, when farming depression and potato famine were features common to both periods, is compared - 1200 lb. could be purchased then for £5 as against only 50 lb. latterly.   [10]

If the inclusion of Matthew's dead father, in the letter's address, illustrated ignorance of his circumstances on the part of those in whose charge he was, the reference to girls in the text is surely an indication that Charlotte Dymond was not his only contact with the opposite sex. It has already been noticed

Charlotte Dymond

that two young women put up with his company for some six hours at Coad's Green, on the day he walked out of Penhale; and now he was sending his love to Maria and Susan Doney, the blacksmith's daughters, and to Maria and Thomasine Hayne, daughter-in-law and daughter of the Tremail farmer for whom Charlotte was working when the 1841 census was taken. "

The other letter dictated by Matthew was addressed to Mrs. Phillipa Peter of Penhale farm in Davidstow -

My dear mistress, I bid you farewell, and master (John Peter, her son) too. You have been a very kind mistress to me, and I hope you will remember this when you don't see me. For all you have been a witness against me, I forgive you all you have done and said, and forgive master, too. Now, my dear mistress, I have found your words come true, what you have told me have come to pass, that I should see my error after some time, but not thinking to come to this unhappy end; and every word you told me I find comes true.

My dear mistress, I hope this will find you better than when I last saw you, for then you was most heart-broken. I hope young men will take a warning by me and not put too much confidence in young women, the same as I did; and I hope young females will take the same by young men. I loved that girl as dear as I loved my life; and after all the kind treatment I have showed her, and then she said she would have nothing more to do with me. And after this was done, then bitterly I did lament, thinking what would be my end. And I thank the judge and jury, too, for they have given me no more than what was due.

Now, I have the sentence of death passed on me. Since that, I have passed the time in reading and prayer. Now, my dear mistress, I hope you will keep the things I gave to you in remembrance of me. Now, my dear mistress, I bid you farewell, mistress and master, too, and all young men and maidens think on this when you don't see me. See what a wretched end I have come to by loving too true.

Remember me with kind love to Mr. and Mrs. Chapman for they were were always very kind to me. Now then all enquiring friends, I bid you farewell. Now I am a sinner quite undone. Now I must away and bid you all farewell. I shall never see your face no more before we meet in heaven together. Mr. and Mrs. Westlake please to give my kind love to. I conclude this dying speech and have nothing more to say.

My dear mistress and master, I bid you all farewell, and all enquiring friends, and when we meet again I hope we shall meet in heaven. Now I am a sinner quite undone. And now I must away.

I am your unfortunate servant,
X (the sign of Matthew Weeks)

P.S. I bless the day I ever saw Mr. Kendall (the chaplain) in Bodmin gaol and I believe he has been the means of saving my soul.

If the first letter were Matthew's will, the letter to Mrs. Peter was the 'last dying speech', which was expected of a condemned man in Victorian times; and might well have been the one which was run off presses in Devonport and Penryn in time to be sold on the day of the execution.[12] It was important that the judge, jury and those who had spoken against the prisoner, were seen to have been forgiven by him. Consciences were salved and the hanging could be witnessed with less qualm.

In fact, it seems to have been part of the chaplain's duty to ensure that the condemned man lived up to expectations in this respect and also to see that the public had ready access to details. The clergyman in 1820 was actually commissioned by religious tractarians to write an account of a sheep-thief's execution for publication.[13] And the fact that Kendall was mentioned in both of Matthew's letters, whereas there was but one reference to the governor, points to his having taken down the so-called dictation. The moral platitudes and chorus of 'I am a sinner quite undone' ring truer of a man of the cloth than of the eminently practical Governor Everest. As for Matthew's having been 'reading' in gaol, this must have referred to his having been read to because he himself was illiterate.

Matthew's hope that his letter would find Mrs. Peter better than when he last saw her, 'heart-broken', may indicate that she was one of the 'friends' who took their leave of him at the gaol on Saturday the 10th. Whenever it was, he had given her some keep-sakes. The Mr. and Mrs. Chapman he mentioned were probably the butcher and his wife from the farm adjoining Penhale; and the Westlakes were Mrs. Peter's daughter and son-in-law.

Whether or not the two letters were dictated at one sitting by Matthew and read back to him before he marked them with his sign, we cannot tell. He apparently spent 'considerable time in prayer' after they had been written and then fell 'into a daze'.

Even more important than a last dying speech and a will was a confession, however. It was imperative that a condemned man should acknowledge the justice of his sentence by confessing his guilt. So, according to the newspapers, Matthew requested that the following be taken down in the presence of Governor Everest and Kendall, the chaplain -

On Sunday afternoon, the 14th April, Charlotte Dymond went out of Mrs. Peter's house, at Penhale in the parish of Davidstow, about half-past four. I saw her go and very shortly afterwards followed her. When I overtook her, I asked her where she was going; she said for a walk. We then strolled on together towards the moors. Our conversation for a long time was on indifferent subjects. Towards dusk, we had some words together about her giving her company to some other young men, and our words became more high when I told her that I had seen her in a situation with some young man that was disgraceful to her.

She then said 'I shall do as I like, I shall have nothing more to say to you'. This expression aroused my anger so much that I took out my knife and went towards her to commit the bloody deed. Something came across me and I shut the knife and put it into my pocket. On her repeating the words 'I shall do as I like, I shall have nothing more to say to you', I again took my knife out of my pocket, approached behind her and made a cut at her throat while she was standing. She never saw me take the knife out, nor was she aware of what I was going to do.

She immediately fell backwards, the blood gushing out in a large stream and exclaimed whilst falling 'Lord have mercy upon me'. When she was on the ground, I made a second and much larger cut, though she was almost dead at the time. The only way I can account for so little blood being on the spot is that it must have run into the little stream that lay close by the spot where I committed the awful deed.

After standing over her body about four or five minutes, I lifted up one of her arms and it fell to the ground as if she was dead. I then pushed her body a little further down the bank. I afterwards took her bonnet, shawl, shoes and pattens and covered them up in a turf pit. Her gloves and bag, I put into my pocket and then went towards home, and in my road I threw away the knife, which I hope no-one will ever find, as I never wish the instrument to be seen with which I committed the deed.

The bag I also threw away in my road to Plymouth. I never thought of murdering Charlotte Dymond till a few minutes before I cut her throat.[14]

This so-called confession raises two important points. Matthew Weeks could neither write it himself, nor read what someone else wrote down on his behalf; if he did put his mark to it, it was in trust that what he had said was accurately recorded and read over to him. But, secondly, if it *were* accurately recorded, Weeks could not have been the cause of Charlotte's death.

Weeks did not see Charlotte leave Penhale at about half-past four, then follow and overtake her. Witnesses for the prosecution alleged that the two left the farm together at 4 p.m.

They could not have 'strolled' towards the moors if they were seen at the places and times described by Gard and Pethick.

The knife described in the confession could open and shut. It was, therefore, a common pocket knife, quite unsuited to murder premeditated or spontaneous. As the butcher remarked, it was unfit to kill a pig; but it was the only kind of knife that Matthew apparently possessed.

Weeks could not have made the first cut on Charlotte's neck in the manner described, although as far as the confession writer was concerned it may have accounted for the alleged blood mark on his left sleeve. In the first place the bonnet and collar would have got in the way of the knife; this was apparent when the B.B.C. television *Pebble Mill* company attempted to reconstruct the murder as described in the confession during June of 1977, the garments had to be removed before the assault was possible.

In the second place, the assailant's attack from behind would not tally with the pathologist's opinion that 'as the wound was deeper at the back, I think it commenced there'. And, in the third place, as the initial thrust made 'a partial cut on the carotid artery', it would be difficult to explain how Matthew kept himself so clean as Charlotte 'immediately fell backwards, the blood gushing out in a large stream'. It would have been against him that she fell.

Similarly, had he made the second 'and much larger cut, when she was on the ground', he must have been covered with blood. He would have been required to bend over her, raise her partially severed head with his left hand, insert his knife into the back of her neck with his right hand and, drawing it around the front of her throat to her right ear, he would have completely divided the carotid artery.

Yet he, who was supposed to have dictated this confession, had to 'account for so little blood being on the spot' and, doubtless, on himself by saying that 'it must have run into the little stream that lay close by'.

If Charlotte's body had to be 'pushed a little further down the bank', it must have been somewhat removed from the river when she fell. The bank must therefore have been saturated as the blood ran into the water, the 'good deal' reputedly found under a clod of earth by Constable Rickard being too little and too tidy.

Moreover, although Charlotte might have fallen backwards were she unexpectedly attacked from behind, she would hardly have 'tacitly submitted to having her throat cut' a second time, as the prosecution solicitor pointed out. She could have put up a fight. That is why Cowlard suggested that drowning or strangulation might be added to the indictment 'for precaution's sake'. Charlotte appeared to have given up and died too quickly, almost willingly, were the confession to be believed.

Then, the body and broken necklace having been left for all to find, the murderer took Charlotte's bonnet, shawl, shoes and pattens and hid them in a turf pit, pocketed her gloves and bag, and threw away his knife on the way home. And, for good measure, the confession accounted for the complete absence of the bag as material evidence by stating that he threw that away on the road to Plymouth.

We are therefore asked to believe that this crime of passion was committed by someone stupid enough to hide some items but not others, to incriminate himself by carrying articles on his person - and, in the case of the bag, advertising his possession of it - and to throw his weapon where anyone could find it. After all, if Cory could discover 'something black' in a turf pit, surely the knife was as easily found. Yet we do not know for certain to this day exactly what cut Charlotte's throat. No instrument was ever produced.

Whoever killed Charlotte Dymond committed the act after seven in the evening when Pethick said he last saw him near the ford. Were it Matthew Weeks, he had to murder the girl, bury the articles, and limp back over four miles of moorland and fields on a dark and foggy evening in the space of two-and-a-half hours. If he were capable of all this and of arriving in the kitchen of Penhale farmhouse his normal calm self, he was not as lame as people made him out to be.

But why would Matthew confess to a murder he had not committed? **15**

Consider his position. Whether or not he cared where Charlotte was by the time he was charged with her murder, the anxiety, the suspense, and awareness of being avoided by the household, during the week following her disappearance, must have given him a feeling of guilt which could only focus when he was formally charged. His evident fear of magistrates, the uncertainty of what they might do to him, and a bewilderment at hearing his friends' accusations, must have increasingly depressed his spirit. On top of all this, there was fatigue as a result of the journey from Plymouth, the three-day hearing, and the journey to Bodmin; and, finally, came despair when the gaol gates clanged behind him.

Fatigue and despair obviously worsened after he was sentenced, hence there having been fear that he would die before being hanged. As he needed to talk to someone before he was executed, the gaol chaplain who befriended him found Matthew utterly dependent upon his approval. The newspapers of the time made this quite clear.

From then onwards, it was easy for the authorities. They wanted a confession to justify the sentence. And the statement that Matthew gave could only have been the result of a question and answer session. He was an illiterate, incapable of dictating such high-flown expressions as 'our conversation was on indifferent subjects', 'nor was she aware', and 'aroused my anger'.

But the one who took them down, the one doing the interrogating, was clever enough to piece together what people had heard in court or had seen reported as having been said by Matthew in different contexts; for example, the keeping company with others. This, with the reconstruction of how the murder was supposed to have been committed, served the two-fold purpose of increasing Matthew's suggestibility and of convincing readers of the confession that it was authentic. Nevertheless, the reconstructor was hard pressed to 'account for so little blood being on the spot'

The fact that the *West Briton* could,on May 3, say that a rumour prevailed that Weeks had confessed although it could not be verified, suggests that a confession was sought even before he had been tried, so strong was the determination that he was guilty. Yet, because the same paper of August 8 still could not publish the confession, despite its having been 'reported about Bodmin' that the judge had copy, the chances are that it was not extracted from, or at least not signed by, Matthew until his last day on earth.

The so-called promise, that it would not be made public until after Matthew's execution, was a very good excuse for its non-appearance beforehand. Moreover, if the version carried by the *Times* on August 8, when it jumped the gun in revelation, is compared with the eventually published confession, it is more than clear that it was the authorities, rather than Matthew, who made the statement.

He declares, said the *Times, that it was not a premeditated act, but that when on the moors she stated to him that she was fonder of Prout than of him, and he then says that upon her telling him this he was seized with a sudden impulse that he would never allow her to have any other than himself, and he then cut her throat.* The gist was similar to the main confession but the details were obviously still being worked out when this was released to the *Times* for nowhere in the eventual statement was Prout mentioned.

However, it is apparent from Matthew's letters that, once he had pleased his friend the chaplain by putting his mark to the so-called confession, he believed in it himself. The relief he felt was profound.

'I bless the day I ever saw Mr. Kendall', he post scripted.

He was never given chance to wake up from that daze. Within hours of 'dictating' the confession and two letters, he was hanged by the neck until he was dead.

Firmly grasped in death

22. There is little reason to suppose that the scene in Bodmin on the day of Matthew Weeks's execution, Monday, August 12, 1844, was very different from one remembered of the early 1850s by John Burton, whose Falmouth curiosity shop later became well known. There were, in his childhood, twelve turnpike gates in and around Bodmin where all traffic, with the exception of mail coaches, go-carts and dog carts, had to stop while drivers paid their tolls for the use of the roads.

An execution day was the toll-collectors' harvest, Burton recollected. 'Conveyances with passengers from all parts of Cornwall poured into Bodmin to see the morbid sight, some of them three days before the execution. This naturally swelled the coffers of the old gatekeepers', who lived in the nearby tollhouses which bore the collectors' names over the door. [1]

But the train on the ten-year-old Wadebridge-Bodmin railway, which had conveyed excursionists to the execution of the Lightfoot brothers four years previously, was not running on the day that Matthew was hanged. For this was a Monday and, whether or not it meant forgoing the profits of a special attraction, the manager's book read 'not out' as this was engine-cleaning day.[2]

So any wishing to come from the Wadebridge area would have had to find other means of transport, or walk. At least one lady is known to have walked the eleven miles from Liskeard to Bodmin for the occasion, and Wadebridge to Bodmin was but a little over half that distance. [3]

Whatever the difficulties, the people turned up. Matthew's being *sacrificed to the laws of his country*[4] pulled a crowd of some 20,000 men, women and children. The crowd was probably greater than it would otherwise have been, the *Royal Cornwall Gazette* reporter reckoned, in consequence of the weather being damp and unfavourable to the harvesting in the neighbourhood.

Many had been arriving during the previous day. And, on this Monday, the town began to fill at an early hour in the morning, passengers from as far west as Penzance and as far east as fifty miles away being seen to enter the borough. By eleven o'clock, the streets were quite full. [5]

If it were a toll-collector's harvest, it was also an inn-keeper's bonanza. Of some twenty-two taverns in the borough, the *Railway Inn,* a westward-facing beer house at the bottom of Pool Street, was nearest the gaol and consequently the soonest full immediately after the sombre event. And, apart from the taverns, there were places of dubious repute such as *Pretty Billy's* lodging house.

Here, according to Burton, a tramp specialised in producing 'an exact sketch of the execution' for each occasion. This, no more resembling the actual execution than it did the River Camel on fire, in Burton's opinion, was painted on one side of a board - while a sketch of the murder was on the other side - and was carried on a pole about five feet high by a street ballad singer.

In the 1850s, the singer was Jack Perry, a short man with one eye, who attended local fairs and special events.[6] And it was he, or his like, who wandered the Bodmin streets this Monday, August 12, selling 'large numbers of spurious confessions' and the last dying speeches which had been printed in Devonport and Penryn the day before. *Reams of this trash were sold to the disappointment of thousands foolish enough to buy,* in the *Royal Cornwall Gazette* reporter's opinion. His paper, however, he was to write, would publish the real confession which, he understood, Weeks had been promised would not be published until after the execution.

Shortly before twelve noon, the immense crowd had congregated in front of the gaol and on the sloping ground which commanded a view of the drop.[7] The latter comprised iron gratings, with rails around to prevent the man about to be hanged from jumping off, which was approached by a door in the wall above the huge, arched entrance to the gaol. This abutted the Wadebridge - Bodmin railway and faced south, above the entrance being a turret clock;[8] and the space between the railway and entrance had been barricaded for the duration of the execution so that it was kept clear of all but those officially employed.[9]

Inside the gaol that morning, Matthew had risen between five and six o'clock and sent for Everest, the governor. Reverend Kendall, the chaplain, was also present during their meeting. Later, he attended the prison church service and knelt throughout its duration. When it had ended and the other prisoners had left, Matthew took communion; and then requested to be sung the first five verses of Psalm 51.[10]

Up until October of 1844, the psalm singing was a popular part of the prison service and was performed by members of the turnkeys' families assisted by female inmates.[11] So, if the prisoners had gone, it must have been the warders' relatives who sang for Matthew - *have mercy upon me, O God, according to thy loving kindness...*

As the hands of the gaol clock moved towards noon, Matthew was led to the press room where his arms were pinioned. The clock struck twelve; and, as it finished, the tolling of the chapel bell announced to the immense multitude outside the gaol the commencement of the melancholy procession within.

On passing along, the *West Briton* reporter noticed that Matthew's step faltered, as he reached the place where the other prisoners were arranged, procumably to see him off, and he had to be supported by the officers. But, from there, *he walked with tolerable firmness* although *the little strength that yet remained was fast waning.*

The Gazette reporter, who seems to have covered the event from ouside the gaol, then saw the executioner appear on the drop. He was George Mitchell, of Langmaid in Somerset, *a venerable-looking, grey-haired old man of about seventy* and *just the reverse of what the public generally imagine such persons to be,* according to the *West Briton.*

That he was still working at his advanced age was probably because, if he lived on the proceeds of execution, Mitchell could not have been well off. In the old days, when capital punishment was meted out for lesser crimes as well as for murder and the hangman was more frequently required, he received what seems to have been an annual retainer of £20 from the Cornish sheriff. But, since 1840, when Mitchell did receive £6 over the odds for the double execution of the Lightfoot brothers, he appears to have been paid no more until now when the price for Matthew's neck was £26.[12]

Then, followed by the Reverend Kendall, Matthew appeared on the drop.

According to the Gazette man, he looked very wretched and was scarcely able to support himself. In fact, as far as the *West Briton* reporter was concerned, he had seemed almost unconscious of anything - as he walked from the press room to the drop - but the overpowering fear of immediate death.

Mitchell, the hangman, had to assist and sustain him as he adjusted the rope around Matthew's neck and pulled the cap down over his face. For the crowd, which always hoped that a 'last dying speech' would be forthcoming from the scaffold, there was nothing from Matthew; indeed, he appeared to faint, as Kendall read a short prayer.

The formalities over, Mitchell and Kendall withdrew from the drop.

The bolts were withdrawn, the trap fell with an awful sound, breaking the deadly silence maintained by the 20,000 onlookers; and Matthew hung lifeless before them, the handkerchief he had carried from the press room to the drop still firmly grasped in death.

A considerable proportion of the crowd was made up by women. And now several fainted while others screamed. There was jostling, then the multitude began to disperse - to the streets and the public houses.

Matthew's body remained, suspended up over the gaol entrance outside the south wall, for the usual time - an hour and a minute.[13]

It was generally held that a murderer should be hanged in his own clothes.[14] Whether or not Matthew was, is unknown. But his body was taken down to be buried, as it was, within the precincts of the gaol. And, as this was before the Capital Punishment Amendment Act of 1868, no post mortem examination nor inquest was necessary.[15]

The place of interment for the executed at Bodmin was in the coal yard[16] adjoining the gaol. The *West Briton* reporter noticed that the grave that had been prepared to receive Matthew's body was about four feet deep and, for some reason, contained about 1½ ft. of water.

When Matthew Weeks's remains were laid to rest, the coffin floated.

Strange to say

23. So ended the Charlotte Dymond affair.

Or so it might have ended, had not the story caught the imagination of the public and lived on to this day.

Until 1875, when the Davidstow church underwent restoration, Charlotte's grave in the churchyard remained unmarked. During the renovations, a broken stone cross was removed from the eastern gable of the church and, as at this time Michael Williams, the lay rector, was putting the churchyard in order, it was probably he who placed the cross on Charlotte's grave. [1]

Thirteen years later, the Reverend A. H. Malan, vicar of Altarnon, drew attention to the plight of the Roughtor memorial, and to the events it commemorated, in an article. Entitled *NOTES ON THE NEIGHBOURHOOD OF BROWN WILLY,* this was carried in the journal of the Royal Institution of Cornwall, 1888.

It appears that the memorial had been undermined by winter torrents and had fallen down. According to the vicar, he had a site meeting with a Mr. Bastard, who was at the time steward to the landowner, Sir William Onslow of Hengar in St. Tudy. And it was thereupon agreed that the memorial should be re-erected, the cost being underwritten by Malan and two friends, and that a granite mason called Nankivell should be instructed to undertake the task and to retrace the inscription.

The Reverend Malan was eventually able to inspect the completed work and to report that the stone had been re-erected 'on solid ground a few yards from the water where it could not again be undermined.'

If an appurtenance of the Charlotte Dymond affair had gained respectibility with these attentions of an antiquary, his account in the journal was not altogether accurate, however. He wrote -

A girl set off to visit friends across the moor and was followed by Weeks who decoyed her off from the trackway and, having cut her throat by the side of the stream, threw her body into the water where the banks were high. Having relieved his mind by murdering his sweetheart, he returned to Penheal and proceeded to go on with his work.
A week later, nothing having been heard of Charlotte Dymond, her master organised a search party, when Weeks took the opportunity to steal away, halting very leisurely at Altarnon; he was eventually caught and hanged. Nine days after the murder, three men on search followed certain clear tracks along the moor by Crowdy marsh until they came to the place where the body was found, lying in shallow water. The ravens, strange to say, had left it untouched; but the cattle had torn up the ground in a ring round the turf on which the victim had bled to death. [2]

What is obvious about this account is that, unlike this book, it was not based upon the brief to the prosecution but relied almost entirely upon details carried by the newspapers of 1844. Yet at least two observations are worthy of notice, if only because they appear to have come from local hearsay. The first, regarding Weeks's stop at Altarnon, is in error because it was actually Coad's Green; but the second, the tearing up of ground by cattle, is possibly of significance and will be mentioned later, in the final chapter.

Whatever the finer details of the journal article, the fact remains that the Roughtor stone was, and still is, the focal point of interest in the Charlotte Dymond story.[3] It was the most popular of sights prior to World War 1, when local youngsters earned threepenny and sixpenny pieces (1¼p and 2½p) guiding charabanc trippers around Bodmin Moor. The monument was even kept clean for these occasions.

Unfortunately, many members of the generation who had continued the custom did not return from the war; and, in any case, it became less fashionable to visit the moor. The late Mr. W. H. Cornelius of Trevivian told me that he and a Mr. Rickard had been amongst the last to observe the tradition of cleaning 'Charlotte's stone'.

The Mr. Rickard obviously had connections with Constable Thomas Rickard who investigated the case in 1844. It will be remembered that it was he who identified Charlotte's body, received her clothes from the pathologist and Cory, and who noticed tracks through the marsh and a pit of blood on the river bank.

I was told by Mr. W. H. Bragg of Wadebridge that, as a boy, he had worked with an elderly gentleman who was a descendant of Constable Rickard and who remembered having visited a cousin, Mr. Erwin Rickard, at Kestle Mill in Sladesbridge in about 1885. While there, he had been shown a rusty old bill hook that was reputedly the weapon that had killed Charlotte Dymond.

What credence may be attached to this tradition is debatable; nevertheless, it is one too closely connected with someone we know was associated with the events of 1844 to be ignored. It has also been brought to my notice that some of Charlotte's clothes are still in the possession of a member of the Rickard family. I have followed this up; but, as the elderly owner has seemed reluctant to admit possession, that person's obvious desire for privacy and anonymity is respected without further divulgence.

The handcuffs, which are said to have manacled Matthew Weeks and are pictured in this book, are in the possession of a Devonshire farmer. He is a descendant of Constable Gerrance Hayne, the other Davidstow parish policeman concerned with the case in 1844.

So, as far as North Cornwall was concerned, the Charlotte Dymond story lived on mainly because of the interest taken in preserving tangible remains associated with it. For, while it is true that the story itself was mentioned from time to time by writers - such as Malan in 1888 and Murray in 1865 - it was not until the 1930s that the late William H. Paynter began popularising the tale.

Originally from Callington, Bill Paynter became well known as the Liskeard archivist and for his Cornish museum at Looe. And, over many years, he related the Charlotte Dymond story to local organisations and featured it in articles. It was apparently through him that the poet, Charles Causley, heard of the tale and wrote *THE BALLAD OF CHARLOTTE DYMOND.* [4]

Once popularised by Bill Paynter and immortalised by Charles Causley, the affair captured the imagination of the authors Colin Wilson and the late James Turner, the former unwittingly being responsible for drawing my attention to it. So began the long quest for information which culminated in this publication. [5]

It was after working on the case for only a few months, that I felt there should be conducted in the North Cornwall area a survey designed to establish just how much was remembered about it today. And the problem, as to how such a survey might be carried out, was solved by one of the coincidences I mentioned in my introduction.

Out of the blue, arrived an invitation for me to open the November Fair at the Sir James Smith's School in Camelford, a comprehensive establishment serving a wide area of the North Cornwall district. And, naturally, while I talked with the headmaster, Mr. D.G.E. Haynes, in his study overlooking the Roughtor scenery on that autumn day in 1973, the subject was broached.

But it was he who sprang the real surprise. By the end of November, I had received forty-two essays written by his first, second and fourth form students under the direction of the history master, Mr. R. A. Kitching; and, in mid-December, thirty-five more arrived from the fifth form. My survey had been conducted.

In order of distance from the scene of the crime, the students came from what I considered to be the 'conversation catchment areas' (many of the 1844 parishes now having a common incumbent) of Davidstow, Camelford, Delabole, Tintagel, St. Breward, St. Tudy, St. Teath, Blisland, St. Kew, Port Isaac, St. Minver and Bodmin. And, accepting a local criterion that one has to live in Cornwall for twenty years before being considered Cornish, I divided students into two categories - traditional and new - the students having been asked to state their surnames, places of residence, and approximately how long their families had lived in North Cornwall.

The first and second form essays had been set for homework, their writers having been given the task of discovering how much their own families knew about the case but barred from interrogating neighbours. Out of the total of thirteen, nine were from families traditional to the area (over twenty years' residence) and four were comparative newcomers.

All of these students were able to provide some detail of the case, even if it were not always entirely accurate. A reason why the newcomers could, must be that they were resident in the Davidstow, Camelford, Delabole and Tintagel areas near the scene of the crime. But allowance must also be made for the fact that the chapter dealing with the Charlotte Dymond case in James Turner's newly published *GHOSTS IN THE SOUTH WEST* was featured in the *Western Sunday Independent* on November 4, 1973, just weeks before the essays were written, and its influence was perceptible.

To a lesser degree it was discernible in the fourth form essays. These were written during the same week; but, as they were produced in class rather than at home, they are probably more indicative of the impromptu memory of the community.

Eight out of the total of twenty-nine were by newcomers, four of whom were unable to supply any detail of the case. This was understandable, as three had been resident at Halworthy, Camelford and St. Teath for a matter of months and the fourth lived at Port Isaac some miles from the scene.

More puzzling were six members of traditional families, who appeared ignorant of the case. As residents of Tintagel, Delabole and St. Teath, they were near enough to areas connected with the events of 1844 for us to expect them to have heard something.

Perhaps the fairest indication of the impact of the case on North Cornwall, and the extent of present-day knowledge of it, came from a snap survey in the fifth form. This was conducted in class without warning; and, as the resultant essays were written several weeks after those I had received from the other forms, the influence of the Independent article would by then have been minimal.

Out of a total of thirty-five answers to the questions, as to what the students knew about the case, twenty blanks were drawn. Thirteen were comparative newcomers and two, although members of traditional families, lived at Port Isaac away from the crime area. But, as in the case of the fourth form, five members of traditional families, who appeared to know nothing, posed a problem because, living at Camelford, Tintagel, St. Breward and St. Tudy, they were not too far removed from the scene to have had some knowledge.

In all, out of seventy-seven students who participated in the survey, forty-seven had heard something about Charlotte Dymond. And, of the remaining thirty who had not, seventeen were comparatively new to the North Cornwall district.

If a tentative conclusion may be drawn, it is that approximately 61% of the North Cornwall community would admit some knowledge of the case, almost 130 years after the event. And, of that percentage, almost a third was new to the area.

It is therefore evident that the story is being passed on to newcomers, as well as to new generations of traditional families. But, while the survey seemed to indicate that it was necessary to spend years rather than months in the area before a newcomer was acquainted with the details - and, even then, it is possible to live in Camelford for eleven years, or Delabole for twenty, and not hear of the case - the history master who directed it told me that he had been in Camelford for less then thirty-six hours when he was given a full account. I then remembered that I had first heard the story from my father, a Londoner, who had picked it up while working in the Camelford-Davidstow area for a matter of months in the 1930s.

Interestingly, the story according to local people contains three elements which, although at first hearing seem fantastic and are not to be found in original records, actually do tie in with details of the case and are illustrative of hearsay, albeit inaccurate, handed down from the time. The first, that Weeks was incriminated because buttons of his were found by the body, obviously points to the sewing-on of the button incident being jumbled with the discovery of beads by the body. The second, that Weeks was caught up with by means of blood hounds, is probably a mixture of the huntsman story mentioned below with the fact that one of the magistrates was master of the hounds. And the third, that the body was found by the search party because a flock of crows dispersed from the site as it approached, ties in with Malan's comment that ravens *had left it untouched.* [6]

Because newcomers depend upon the readiness of local people to impart the story, we return again to the problem posed by members of traditional families who, although living near enough to the scene of the crime to have heard something, seem not to have. Including the Port Isaac essayists, there were thirteen in this category.

Three could be said to be border-line cases, in that their families had been resident in the Delabole, Tintagel and Port Issac areas for only the twenty years that classified them as traditional. Of the remaining ten, two were from Delabole, one from St. Breward, one from Port Isaac, one from St. Teath and five from the Tintagel district.

For reasons that may be apparent in the next chapter, the last five caught my attention and I cite two of them to postulate what seems to me to be a valid theory, namely that the Charlotte Dymond affair is a taboo subject.

Just five miles as the crow flies from Penhale farm is Tresparrett in St. Juliot parish which, for the sake of the survey, came within my Tintagel district. As St. Juliot adjoins the parishes of Forrabury and Minster and Charlotte, as 'a native of Boscastle', would have come from one or the other, traditional families of that area might have been expected to demonstrate some handed-down remembrance of the case. [7]

However, one of the fifth form 'don't knows' from my Tintagel district gave Tresparrett as his home village and a fourth former of the same surname and category stated St. Juiot to be his native parish. I therefore reached the conclusion that at least one family of that locality genuinely knew nothing or was unwilling to divulge its knowledge.

My suspicion, that the latter obtained, hardened upon noticing that a second former, of a different surname but also from Tresparrett, could not name the murderer although his essay had obviously been based upon the Independent article, in which it was mentioned. But this did connect with a couple of things that had puzzled me.

Although I was contacted by a member of the Weeks family, when it was known that I was researching the case, I have found no-one with the surname Dymond who will admit to having heard of the affair as a family hand-down. There was one exception, a young woman who had wondered why it had been mentioned by her mother just before her death, when she had never before spoken of it; but her story seems to have been the popular version picked up from articles.

Moreover, the member of the Weeks family, who contacted me, himself only learned of his connection with Matthew upon investigating his background after a cousin had been told in Launceston that he must be 'the murderer's descendant'. He also said that he had met an elderly Camelford gentleman, in the mid-1960s, who recollected having been warned as a youngster in the 1880s/1890s that there were two names that should never be mentioned at school - Dymond and Weeks. [8]

It would therefore appear that neither the Weeks nor the Dymond families have handed the story down to new generations, and that other North Cornwall families have forbidden the mentioning of names, the second former's Tresparrett family possibly being one.

There are, however, ways around forbidden subjects. And I noticed in the school essays, particularly in those written for homework, that Charlotte Dymond was often referred to as 'Charlotte' and Matthew Weeks as 'Matthews'.

In his work entitled *THE TABOO,* Professor Charles Thomas has shown that, when it is not permitted to utter a particular word, a substitute name comes into use. So it might well be that 'Charlotte' and 'Matthews' were the chosen substitutes for Miss Dymond and Weeks. *9*

Professor Thomas also identified the cause of the taboo as invariably being fear - of retribution, ill luck, or whatever. So, if the Charlotte Dymond case has been taboo in North Cornwall, those who decided to maintain silence and who apparently warned the next generation to continue it must have been afraid of something.

They might have feared a come-back on them for having spoken against one of their own kind; after all, even the judge had said that it was only by piecing circumstances together that Matthew could be found guilty. They could have been afraid of the national spotlight which had been turned on them and were anxious to be rid of attention. Or might it have been that they feared retribution because they knew that Matthew Weeks was not guilty?

In one of the fourth form essays, it was stated that *the murderer was never found.* And, as the writer came from a traditional St. Kew family, I felt this was worth following up if only because David Watmough, well known in Canada for his plays, documentaries and short stories, is a native of St. Kew and, in his *TIME OF THE WIND,* had mentioned Charlotte Dymond's having been murdered by a butcher.

Hearing that Mr. Watmough was to visit Cornwall in March 1976, I asked his publisher, Donald Rawe, to enquire why a butcher had been implicated when everyone knew that the executed farmhand was the murderer. And Mr. Rawe accordingly did, during conversation at the St. Kew inn one evening; two other members of the company there - the Canadian playwright, Michael Mercer, and Terri Stacey, a C.B.C. news reporter - subsequently corroborating his version of the result.

It was that Mr. Watmough had grown up in North Cornwall being given to understand that a butcher was the murderer. And a St. Tudy man, who was also present, said that he, too, had been told that the wrong man had hanged for the Dymond murder.

Naturally, my thoughts returned to the bill hook Mr. Bragg had told me was reputed to have been the murder weapon. Certainly, farmers and butchers, I had asked, agreed that the so-called hook as sketched by my informant might well have been a butcher's implement.

Assuming that there has been a taboo on the Dymond case because of fear of retribution if the truth were known, we might ask by how much the collective guilt complex has influenced actions in the community. According to Professor Thomas, a taboo in speech often results in a taboo on actions. For instance, where fairies are referred to by substitute names like 'little people' and 'old men', ancient sites or monuments regarded as being their work or under their care may not be interfered with or removed.

If, as seems possible, Charlotte and Weeks have been referred to by euphemisms, we should find that something tangible connected with them has been held in undue respect. And there, at the murder spot near Roughtor Ford - the only site, apart from Penhale, with which both are associated - is a stone which has, in a sense, been revered. The locals have taken the trouble to keep it clean.

Charlotte Dymond

Should this sound far-fetched, it must be remembered that we are dealing with Bodmin Moor and with one of its remoter parts at that. Penhale farm is still not connected to a water main. Peat is cut between Trevilian's Gate and Lanlary Rock. Superstition dies hard in an area where many will still not cut hay on a Sunday, whatever the weather.

To answer the question, as to who or what is likely to bring about retribution, we cite the school essays again. A second form student wrote -

My parents have said that they have had friends that work down in the Stannon (clay)pit and they have heard strange noises on certain days and they turned round and caught a glimpse of a light figure vanish behind the bushes.
My mother asked if it was a horse, etc., but her friends said 'no'. They were sure it was a woman. My father has said that he has talked to friends when at work and they said that once, only once, when they went fishing, a day in November, they have heard a weird sound and seen a white figure with clothes on, best clothes. This could very well mean something and be perfectly true, as this lady, Charlotte, was supposed to have been killed on a Sunday in her best clothes.

From fourth form students came the following -

the suspicion is that, when it is misty, she is supposed to rise from the marsh and run down the slopes of Roughtor again to her death;

and

it is said she roams the (Rough) tor in the evenings if it is misty and dark and goes back to her grave when the light starts to come through; there is a story that says every night around 12 o'clock she walks along the road and, if a car comes along, you would not be able to catch her. If you go slow, she will, and if you go fast, she will.

Some fifth form students wrote -

I have heard many people are supposed to have seen a ghost and are afraid to go up to Roughtor at night; and

her ghost is supposed to walk on the moor on dark nights; and

the old people still will not go on to the moor at a certain time. I think it has something to do with Charlotte's ghost.

These extracts from essays written by members of traditional Davidstow, Camelford, Advent, Delabole and St. Breward families surely suggest that, if there is a fear, it is of Charlotte Dymond herself.

The belief that she has been seen since her death has been persistent for at least a century. And, irrespective of whether or not she has been seen, that belief has puzzled me. I would have thought that, if Matthew Weeks were really the murderer, it would have been his ghost haunting the area; that he would have been restless through remorse or grief.

It was this feeling, perhaps, that first made me suspect that all was not well with the case, or the accepted version of it. For, even if there is no such thing as a supernatural occurrence and it is 'all in the mind' of those who are supposed to have seen a ghost, it is Charlotte's ghost that has troubled them.

If we consider an extract from another essay, some logical explanations of the paranormal in the Roughtor area may be clarified -

people used to say that they used to see lights on the moor. These were minerals sparkling. They said it was the piskies. The ponies used to get their manes tangled up, they said this was where the piskies sat when they rode them. When the soldiers were on the moor, they always had two on guard because they were afraid of these lights. You could see these lights at Roughtor Ford. They also said that there is a streak of blood in the wall where Charlotte is laid (in Davidstow churchyard). They also said that a ghost of a man rides a pony across the moor at night.

I discussed these points with the late Mr. W. H. Cornelius of Trevivian and he accounted for them as follows. Lights at night are common phenomena in marshy areas, which emanate a methane gas that twinkles in the darkness. And the ghostly man story, he thought, probably originated with the one told about a huntsman, who left the Halworthy inn worse for drink and rode home across the moor where the hunt had been that day. Going along before him, he swore, was 'something white' that disappeared near 'Charlotte's stone'. Subsequent investigation, however, found this to have been a hound left behind by the hunt in the Roughtor area.

But the interesting thing about the lights is that, according to the essayist, they could be seen at Roughtor Ford, they were attributed to the piskies, and they terrified the soldiers. The last-named were probably those of the Callington 5th Corps, whom I mentioned in chapter one as having had difficulty keeping sentries posted. Yet there have been instances since, of Cornishmen from the eastern half of the county expressing reluctance to join their T. A. platoon on night exercises in the area, the reason being because 'it was haunted'. [10]

These things together, surely, lend credence to the taboo postulation. Piskies, the Cornish fairies, have been associated with this part of Bodmin Moor. It is therefore likely that there has been, since time immemorial, a 'funny feeling' about the area. The lights were feared. With the events of 1844, the lights took on a new shape, as far as clay workers and soldiers were concerned. The fear has since been more of Charlotte's ghost than of the piskies. Her affair, rather than theirs, is now taboo.

The fact remains, however, that it is Charlotte Dymond and not Matthew Weeks who walks the moor, although he, as a cripple and with teeth missing, would make the more frightening apparition. Yet people believe the lights to be her, never him. If there is, then, something that has not been included in the accepted story, it might well be that Charlotte alone knew what happened during the last few moments of her life, that Matthew Weeks might not have been there.

There is, without question, something extraordinary about this case. I was not a reader of murder stories, had little interest in crime statistics, and had no particular desire to study the affair. That said, I have worked on the case for a number of years as though compelled, having merely originally promised to look up my files for details for Colin Wilson.

It is not a pretty story. So it came as a relief to find that, while working on it at the dead of night, the only available time for the necessary concentration, there was no uneasy feeling. I never once felt eerie, not even when things began to happen.

From the time I started to write up my findings, just before Christmas of 1975, a number of incidents occurred for which there seems little logical explanation. My study, normally giving away the fact that I smoke, was heavily perfumed one morning. And, believing my husband to have freshened the air, despite the bouquet's being unfamiliar, I mentioned it. He, however, denied all knowledge and, search the premises for what might have left the scent though I did, there was nothing that matched.

It was my imagination, Tom maintained, for the perfume had gone by the time he reached the room. It became a family joke. That is until, in the presence of his mother one morning, I handed him coffee. Almost immediately he was handing it back 'because of the smell'.

There, wafting from the cup, was the aroma that had met me in my study. Every toilet and household commodity on the premises was tested but fell short of matching it. Even more disconcerting was the fact that the cup I'd given my husband was the one I normally used. The perfume had been meant for me. "

Several times after that, there was scented coffee. Other things happened which we are determined to call coincidence. And my husband has listened to the sound of my typewriter when I have been nowhere near my study.

There has also been a sequel to the perfume instances. On Wednesday, June 22, 1977, I took Donny MacLeod, one of the presenters of the B.B.C. television *Pebble Mill* programme, to the supposed site of the murder near the Roughtor monument. He climbed down the bank to a beach which is covered with water only when the river is in flood. And soon, in front of several witnesses, he was testing plants and the water for what could have produced the 'herbal aroma' which wafted by him as he stood on the spot which I now believe was the site of Charlotte's end.

Something seems to have stirred in Davidstow as well.

Although, to my knowledge, no other writer has recorded strange events as having taken place at Penhale, it would not be true to say that nothing has happened there before I started delving into the case. For obvious reasons, however, it is not advertised that the farmhouse attracts the phenomenal.

Up to the time I began researching the case, occurrences seem to have been infrequent and generally entailed the disappearance and re-appearance of household objects. In April of 1975, however, something more dramatic happened. A light slender female figure 'in old fashioned clothes' was seen in a bedroom one night.

Between then and the summer of 1976, when I paid one of my fact-finding visits, so much of an inexplicable nature occurred that the occupiers could scarcely remember to tell me it all. A rose tree, in particular, had given them trouble for it vanished, then re-appeared in unlikely situations, each time it was re-planted.

Although things had happened in my own household for which I could find no explanation, I was still fairly sceptical, I must admit. Yet two further incidents have made me wonder if the supernatural does not exist.

Apart from the rose tree, daffodils vanished from Penhale farm around April of 1976. This I noted and duly filed as just another statistic until, the following autumn, I had a 'phone call from someone I had never met. 'Who puts the flowers on Charlotte's grave?' enquired the caller from Davidstow [12] parish. 'It's not every year that it happens but, when it does, it's around April; and its always daffodils. They were there this year. It can give you quite a start going to church, when you've almost forgotten and there they are again.'

The second incident was connected with my visit to Penhale on Sunday June 27, 1976. My main object had been to discover the exact location of Higher Down Gate, as no-one I had asked had ever heard of such a place. The afternoon of that day, I walked up the lane and across the fields with some local residents until we came to what we thought must have been the place. A photograph taken, we returned to the farmhouse for tea and then drove over to Davidstow churchyard to find Charlotte's grave.

Some four months later, having worked on the Davidstow tithe map in Truro, I came to the conclusion that we had not walked far enough for, although the Gate is not actually named on the map, the field is marked and its entrance on to the then strip of common in the 1840s is obvious. The residents were not on the telephone, so I could not tell them that, what we had considered to be Higher Down Gate was in fact a breach in the hedge between Furze Down and Corner Down fields.

At the beginning of November, however, they paid me a surprise visit in Bodmin; and, proudly, I announced the exact location and showed them a copied extract of the tithe map. The wife turned pale and said to her husband 'I'll have to tell her now'. And she did, having hitherto felt odd about the affair and mentioned it to no-one.

Late in the evening of the day of my visit, she was almost asleep in bed at Moorhead, her home. Hearing laughter coming from fields below the house, she got up and went to the window in amazement, because there is no public thoroughfare on her smallholding. She saw nothing, but she *was* aware of a man and a woman near the gate between her property and another's. His words were drowned in the torrent of her strange laughter; then the woman was heard to say 'I don't want you to come any further. Go home.'

Up to the moment I showed her the map, the resident believed that the way to the moor from Higher Down Gate would have been through what is now Higher Penhale. She then learned, what I had discovered, that the place in question is across the yard from her bedroom window. She had heard what Matthew maintained Charlotte had said at Higher Down Gate, on that evening, in 1976. [13]

To lay the ghost

24. *As far as can be gathered, no attempts have been made to lay the ghost* of

Charlotte Dymond, wrote W. H. Paynter in his Old Cornwall journal article in 1967.[1] Her spirit, it seems, refuses to lie down.

Personally, I believe that she will continue to haunt North Cornwall until the true circumstances which surrounded her death are revealed. Such a revelation has not been possible up to now because writers have not been prepared to research more than the surface details. This book is the first attempt to discover the truth.

What I hope it has shown is that, when subjected to examination, the case against Matthew Weeks does not stand up, whereas the case in his defence is strong.

The knife and razor evidence given by John Stevens was unreliable. He admitted that one knife was really a pair of braces, John Peter let out in court that the other was unfit to kill a pig, and Matthew must have been seen with a razor before because Mrs Peter was aware of its existence, the honing incident was uncorroborated.

Weeks's possession of a murder story was immaterial, he could not read. The bad washing was obviously Charlotte's doing, not his. And the remark attributed to him, regarding Charlotte's mother being tried for her life if the girl were found dead, was on Elias Bettinson's word and therefore hearsay.

The so-called blood marks on the left sleeve of his jacket were never proven as such, let alone to be Charlotte's. And the blood on the handkerchiefs could not have existed unless planted - it was not noticed when the articles were found in his jacket on April 21; then the spot, which was said to have been on his red cotton handkerchief by April 25, had removed itself to Charlotte's green gauze handkerchief by August 2 when it was pointed out but discounted by the prosecution.

Similarly, the blood marks were obviously not on Weeks's shirt until after he had killed the pig, or John Stevens would have noticed them when he remarked about the missing button and torn front 'so early in the week'. That he did so remark indicates how usual it was for the farmhands' shirts to require mending most weeks, a reason presumably why Stevens himself possessed a needle and thread.

The boot print evidence, although failing miserably to incriminate Weeks, did cast a doubt upon the integrity of the prosecution. Were a case to be made that Weeks was deliberately framed, this would be one of the strongest points in favour of it.

The umbrella evidence, on the other hand, is disquieting. It was not noticed that Weeks and Charlotte set off with one, nor that Weeks return to Penhale with an umbrella on April 14. The one in his possession was presumably in the farmhouse until he left with it the following Sunday. The woman on the moor, however, was described by three witnesses as having sheltered under an umbrella although the article was discovered neither by the body nor in the clothes pit. The judge could 'not see much' in this point; but, then, the tenor of his charge to the grand jury and of his summing up was that of a believer in Weeks's guilt.

Other writers on this case have reached a similar conclusion because they, like the judge and the Cornish of 1844, accepted the verdict as foregone. But, had they started with the premise that Weeks was innocent until proved guilty, their opinions would surely have been different.

The evidence of the constables left much to be desired and the discrepancies between their and Weeks's versions of conversations are alarming. The glove evidence was conflicting in that Charlotte's friend thought the stripes should have been wider, while Mrs. Peter persisted with a contrary opinion. The bag evidence was inadmissable because, of the three people who watched Charlotte set off, only Mrs. Peter said she carried one and her memory was not to be relied upon without corroboration, and because Matthew's being in possession of it rested upon the witness of two young woman for the article itself was not produced.

In fact the bag evidence is highly suspicious. The only time in the case that black string was mentioned was in connection with its handle and that was found with the clothes in the turf pit. It is therefore probable that the bag and the letter and money it contained were found, despite the prosecution tale, and that the girls' story was spurious.

Similarly, the so-called turf-muddied stockings were inadmissible evidence. They had been washed by the time they were produced and their alleged state beforehand was on Mrs. Peter's word alone. It is also probable that the gloves in Matthew's possession were not Charlotte's.

If the prosecution could, to this point, be dismissed as having been based upon unreliable, uncorroborated, inadmissible, or very doubtful evidence plus hearsay, much of the rest of its case could in fact have been used by the defence to suggest Weeks's innocence, providing the necessary research had been undertaken.

It was alleged that Weeks's stockings and trousers were muddied to the knees and he had, therefore, been on the moor with Charlotte Dymond. As the trousers were dirty at the front and not at the back, the allegation is ridiculous. But, had the evidence been sure, it might just as well have corroborated Weeks's alibi as have pointed to his guilt. To reach Higher Down Gate, he would have had to cross part of Penminnies Marsh; and to visit Halworthy, he would have walked through Rosebenault Marsh.

According to Mrs. Peter's evidence in court as given by the *West Briton,* 'the moors were particularly wet around April 14 and the springs were all full then'; it was also, in the words of other witnesses, 'misty and foggy' on that day. Anyone acquainted with Bodmin Moor in that kind of weather will know that, from four o'clock in April, dusk can set in fast, impairing visibility so that even the surefooted can be up to his knees in no time on otherwise familiar ground. It was therefore quite unrealistic to expect Matthew Weeks the cripple to limp anywhere in the Davidstow area and return to Penhale immaculate.

Whether or not he went to Halworthy, as he said, may never be known. There is only the word of an elderly lady, Sarah Westlake, to deny that he did go; her son was out at his marsh and possibly did not return as early as he thought, the wife admitted that she had been unwell and had 'stepped just outside the door' probably to a lavatory. It is not beyond the bounds of possibility that, during the time she was 'outside', Weeks called and, finding no-one in, continued to the mother's. But, for some reason, she would not support his alibi; in any case, she also admitted to having been unwell on the day in question.

It was further alleged that, as Charlotte had three silver fourpenny pieces and had not been known to have spent any money since her Lady Day and Easter Monday payments, the fourpenny pieces seen in Matthew's possession by John Stevens were Charlotte's and he must therefore also have had her handbag. Cowlard, the solicitor for the prosecution, felt that this supported the case for murder premeditated. Weeks might have persuaded Charlotte to hand over the money, with the yarn about a new position in Blisland, saying that he would settle with Mrs. Peter after she had gone but really meaning to make the murder look as though it had been in the course of robbery, by a person or persons unknown.

On the face of it, Weeks would seem to have been short of money up to the time of Charlotte's disappearance. He himself said that she had asked to borrow the equivalent of 12½p but he could only let her have 7½p. While her shortage of money may be explained by the purchase of a new bonnet cap, and the three fourpenny pieces in his possession might well have been change given by Charlotte for a half-crown piece handed over by Weeks, his financial position seems extraordinary.

If we examine it, however, certain things become clear.

Pay days at Penhale seem to have been at fortnightly intervals. We know that there was one on Lady Day, March 25, and another on Easter Monday, April 8. On these dates, Charlotte received the equivalent of 20p and 25p respectively; and, although we are not told, Matthew, as a man and of longer service than the girl, would have received more than her. But, by April 14, he could not lend her the requested 12½p.

It may well be that the 'silver' noticed in his possession, after Charlotte's disappearance, by John Stevens comprised only the three fourpenny pieces assumed to have been the girl's. Nevertheless, within a day or so of this incident, he was in Plymouth spending money on new clothes and contemplating a trip to the Channel islands; money was about him when he was arrested; and he could write from Bodmin gaol that £5 was to be given to his mother.

Weeks, having been unable to assist Charlotte with more than 7½p on April 14, was in possession of as much money as the girl would have received for a year's work within days of her disappearance. It could not have been hers. She was short of cash, reputedly cut off from home and any assistance, and would hardly have saved that much in the few teen-age years she had been employed.

The truth is that Matthew Weeks had money

On March 26, 1842, he had put his mark to a document which read -

received of Richard Weeks, executor of the will of John Weeks late of the parish of South Petherwin, yeoman, deceased, the sum of £5.11.1d being the ninth part of our share of £50 bequeathed by the said testator which I am entitled to as one of the said children who has attained the age of twenty-one years. [2]

As Matthew's father had died in 1835, his share of the South Petherwin yeoman's estate was to be divided between his nine surviving children under the terms of the grandfather's 1836 will.[3] Matthew, having attained the age of twenty-one by November of 1841, thus received his ninth part of the £50 bequest from his father's brother, the executor, Richard Weeks.

But his grandfather left more than just money to Matthew. A ninth part of the house and garden occupied by his widowed mother at Larrick in Lezant was also his. As the average agricultural labourer received the equivalent of £23.40 per annum in the 1840s,[4] Matthew's £5.55 legacy amounted to almost a quarter of what he might have expected for a year's work; and with the prospect of receiving his ninth part of the proceeds, were the house and garden sold, he was indeed a cut above his own kind. Hence his having been able to dress well and to contemplate travel.

His fortunate position never came out at his trial. The inquest jurors had stated that *Matthew Weeks had not any goods or chattels, lands or tenements, within Cornwall or elsewhere* liable to forfeiture upon conviction. So the third son of John Weeks, who, had he survived Matthew's grandfather, would himself have been a South Petherwin yeoman,[5] was passed off by the powers that were as a penniless, unpropertied servant.

There is reason to believe that Charlotte Dymond was not as ignorant. If we accept Mrs. Peter's deposition, rather than what the press understood her to say in court, Weeks and Charlotte 'had kept company together for some time both before and since her last coming' back to Penhale 'about 18 months before her death'. She must therefore have returned to the farm during the autumn of 1842 - probably at Michaelmas, September 29 -and, if she had started courting Matthew just before her return, the chances are that she had been influenced by his coming into money at the end of March.

It can surely be the only explanation of an acknowledgedly attractive girl's falling for a pock-marked, sullen-looking cripple with teeth missing, who was some six years her senior.

Which of the two brought the courtship to an end on Lady Day, March 25, 1844, we cannot know; nor why. That it *was* finished, as Matthew told the constable, explains why Charlotte's clothes were in Mrs. Peter's care, although she stated that she had allowed Matthew to keep them in view of the romance; and why, when Prout threatened to move in to Penhale and claim Charlotte, Matthew was more interested in moving out, because he could not live with Prout, than in possibly losing Charlotte to him.

In order to discover what Matthew was probably up to on that fateful afternoon of Sunday, April 14, we return again to the point that, although he seems not to have had much money on that day when Charlotte wanted to borrow some, he had plenty the following week. **It is obvious that he did not keep his money at Penhale.**

As far as many Cornishmen in rural areas are concerned, even today, one's financial position is a closely guarded secret - particularly from banks. Examples of this attitude could be manifold, suffice two to explain. Margaret Leigh, who moved to Cornwall to farm Newton in Blisland parish in 1935, was fascinated to find that her neighbour kept his money in a pot which was buried in one of his fields.

And, in 1963, two men hanged for the murder of a Constantine farmer with the miserable knowledge that they had found only £4, when it was suspected that he really had thousands. He had. Directions written in Esperanto eventually led searchers to a jar full of banknotes in a field and to a safe buried beneath a cowshed floor. [6]

As Matthew Weeks had money just after Charlotte had left Penhale and him, and as he returned to the farm with his trousers muddied at the front but not at the back, there is every likelihood that during the afternoon in question he had been down on his knees somewhere to get his money.

No self-respecting Cornishman would reveal that, nor the whereabouts - not even to save his neck. Hence Matthew's seeming reticence about his movements.

Yet, despite allegations to the contrary, he never changed his tale. The girl probably did ask him for money and he offered what he had to hand. Whether or not she actually said where she was going, or he deduced it from the direction she took, she set off from the point on the moor, where Matthew said he left her and Cory saw him, towards Lanlary Rock which *is* on the way to Brown Willy and Blisland.

There *was* a letter which, of the two seen with it, only Charlotte could read. She *had*, albeit three weeks before, had notice to leave Penhale. And the boot print evidence supported his contention that he was not in the Roughtor area with the girl.

If the so-called confession is, as I'm sure it should be, discounted; and if Matthew's admission, that he went a little further than Higher Down Gate as he originally said, may now be accepted as an example of his understandable reluctance to reveal his movements on April 14, his story is essentially true.

As in the case of the jealousy charge, the conflicting tale-telling charge fitted witnesses for the prosecution rather than Matthew. Mrs. Peter, Cory, Stevens and Pethick in particular were guilty of changing their stories.

Counsel for the defence quite rightly pointed out that Weeks's conduct, after Charlotte had disappeared, was 'unsuspicious'. Nevertheless, much was made of certain of his movements by the prosecution and his attitude throughout the case puzzled even the press. It now seems, however, that Charlotte's having been given notice to quit Penhale on Lady Day could be the key to our understanding of these.

Charlotte Dymond remains an enigma.

She could read and write, her forename was middle to upper class, she probably carried her mother's surname because she was a bastard, and she was a native of Boscastle. This much we know from the records. And one more detail is fairly acceptable, she was unwanted at home, because she was put out by the time she was thirteen and no parent showed up even to attend her funeral.

Her birth and baptism seem not to have been recorded, however. The former was too early for civil registration and the latter appears neither in the parochial nor non-parochial registers of North Cornwall. [7]

The identity of her mother may therefore not be discovered. She must have been literate, surnamed Dymond, unmarried at the time of Charlotte's birth but associated with a man, connected with the Boscastle parishes, and in a situation which would keep her out of the workhouse but which would, at the same time, make her reluctant to own the child. Yet, such a woman is actually documented.

When the 1841 census was taken, a Miss Dymond, who had been born in the Boscastle parish of Forrabury at the end of the eighteenth century, was living in the hamlet of Tresparrett Posts in St. Juliot parish with a man who was some twenty years her senior and of independent means. They were still living together ten years later, when he was described as a widower and butcher of Poundstock parish and she as a dressmaker.

Parish registers reveal details of the woman's family. She had two brothers, one of whom moved with his growing family from Forrabury to farm in St. Juliot parish at some time between 1844 and 1847. But more extraordinary was the revelation that she and her brothers were bastard children, and their mother and her brother were also illegitimate.

We may not say that the woman was Charlotte's mother beyond doubt. But the coincidence of her details and those of the Dymond case are too close to be ignored. Charlotte was reputedly born in Minster or Forrabury parish during the 1820s, when this woman of appropriate age, surname and circumstance was probably still in the latter. The girl was illegitimate and so was the woman and her mother. Local tradition has associated a butcher with the case and the woman's consort was in that trade: there was even someone of his name in gaol in 1831, which might have connected with Matthew's paper story of a man in prison supported by his daughter. The letter Charlotte received might have reached her by means either of the dressmaker delivering the bonnet cap on the Saturday or of Thomas Prout who arrived the following day: Miss Dymond was a dressmaker by 1851, and Prout had journeyed from Helset some two miles from her Tresparrett home.

But the woman was more than a dressmaker. Her acknowledged profession in 1841 would explain why any child of hers could read and write and why she might not have been anxious to own a bastard daughter. **She was the village school mistress.** [8]

As Charlotte was unwanted at home, she had to make her own way in life. If she could have married well, she would have overcome a bad start. She was no doubt aware of this because she was literate; and the most sensible thing she had done had been to get in with Matthew Weeks who had money.

Having learned of his good fortune and returned to Penhale as his girlfriend, however, there is every likelihood that she saw an even better opportunity - of becoming mistress of the household. Being able to read, she could have discovered that Mrs. Phillipa Peter was not in fact the owner of one of the largest holdings in Davidstow parish, the 147 acres of Penhale and the 51 acres of Rosebenault.

It was held jointly by her sons, Edward and soft John Peter. [9]

The latter would have been an easy touch; and, as he was the elder son and was actually living and working on the farm, **whoever married him would have become its mistress.** It was hardly material that he was some twenty years her senior, he was unmarried; besides, she seemed to favour older men, Matthew was approaching twenty-four and Prout was almost thirty.

Had Phillipa Peter noticed what was going on, there was a reason for her to give the girl notice on Lady Day. Something certainly happened at Penhale on that day for it was also then that the courtship between Matthew and Charlotte ended. There had obviously been some kind of showdown, presumably when Matthew learned that Charlotte had been carrying on with someone else and Mrs. Peter served notice for it to cease.

What happened during the intervening three weeks up to Sunday, April 14, is uncertain; according to Matthew, Charlotte had been going out with 'some other chaps'; but on that day and, as she was leaving, he lent her some money and consented to accompany her a little way. It is even possible that the two were reconciled and Matthew agreed to collect her clothes from Mrs. Peter and to take or send them on when she was settled in her new position. Hence his fetching his money in readiness.

But, receiving no message from Charlotte the following week, he would have assumed that she had foregone her word, after all. Hence his miserably saying he'd 'drag' in her bonnet cap when asked to retrieve it from the thorn.

Nevertheless, he must have been puzzled as to Mrs. Peter's behaviour. It was common knowledge that she had given Charlotte notice on Lady Day; and, if what we suspect to have been the reason actually was, he must have wondered why she was making so much fuss when she had wanted to be rid of the girl.

But it was her turning against him that was really disturbing. She was at him even before the neighbours started. He would have to leave Penhale. Yet he could not do so without his mistress's permission, or he would be sought out and returned to her service by a constable, and she was hardly likely to let him go when she had accused him of being worthy of hanging in chains before anything had been known to have happened.

He had only one option - to flee the country.

The Channel islands were the obvious choice of destination when he left without permission. But he had overlooked his sympathetic nature and stayed on at Plymouth with his pregnant sister. His friendship with Charlotte Dymond had already caused him a lot of trouble. It was hardly suprising that, when the constable told him she was dead, he could not have cared less. And, knowing that he had not brought about her end, there was nothing for him to fear in going back, despite Davidstow's accusations. English Law would protect him.

If Matthew Weeks were not guilty of causing the untimely death of Charlotte Dymond, someone was. Already we have seen that at least two women had reasons for wanting to get rid of her and there is evidence to suggest that both had already taken action in that direction: the mother, by disowning her; and Mrs. Peter, by serving her notice to leave Penhale. It is also apparent that Charlotte was not easily put off: she must have persisted in visiting her mother for the rumour, that she would kill her if she went home again, to have circulated; and she did not quit Penhale.

In short, Charlotte was a menace to her mother and mistress.

There were also several men among the witnesses for the prosecution whose evidence left something to be desired. Thomas Prout was, as far as is known, never required to account for his movements on the evening in question ; but, in view of the fact that he apparently joined neither the concern nor search for Charlotte, when he was the first to notice her missing, he should have been.

His saying that he waited at Tremail chapel for her, as arranged, was accepted. Up to now, it has been assumed that the congregation would have challenged this statement were it false.

If the Wesleyan set-up in Davidstow parish is examined, in Thomas Shaw's study entitled *Methodism in the Camelford & Wadebridge Circuit 1743-1963*, however, we cannot be certain this would have been the case.

Ever since the Davidstow meetings had joined the Circuit Plan in 1815, the average membership had been only nine. By 1822, a local preacher had been reproved for failing to take his appointment there because 'but few people attended.' And, according to a vicar's report, even those were not dissenters but parish church attenders also.

Early meetings had been held at Tremail probably, Trewassa certainly, and even at Penhale in 1827. Then, as a result of the 1834-1835 disruption in the circuit, when the Reform Association broke away from the original Wesleyan Society, the Tremail chapel was built. Digory Hayne, for whom Charlotte worked in 1841, gave the land; and John Pethick, probably the inquest juror, was the class leader.

But, despite reform, Methodism in Davidstow - or, at any rate, at Tremail - seems to have left much to be desired. By 1853, a report on the situation there stated *this is one of the most unchurchlike churches we have (in the circuit) so far as attention to discipline is concerned'*. And it was fair comment for amongst the listed members was Elias Bettinson who had died, five backsliders, someone who'd left the area and another who'd gone to America.[10]

In view of all this, **Thomas Prout's alibi cannot be said to be supported by the Tremail congregation's silence.**

Of the three who gave evidence regarding the couple on the moor, the seemingly suspect behaviour of Isaac Cory and the involvement of William Gard may be explained in due course. But Richard Pethick, the cattle farmer on horseback, is worthy of immediate notice.

He was more Charlotte's age than any of the other men; and we have only his word that he was on the moor at 'about six o'clock' rather than half an hour earlier when Gard, the local preacher, saw the couple. As he was on horseback and if he were the man who joined Charlotte below Lanlary Rock, he would have left no boot prints until he had dismounted, tied up the animal, and accompanied her along the route where the marks appeared. Had he murdered Charlotte after Gard had left the area, he would have walked back to his horse past the turf pit where the clothes were buried.

As it was a Sunday, the chances are that Pethick was in 'best clothes' and might even have had an umbrella stuck in the top of one of his dress boots for he could have been checking his cattle either before or after going to a service. It would not have been unusual.

Moreover, as a cattle farmer, he was probably also a butcher like John

Chapman of Trevivian. And there is a local tradition, told to me by Mr. W.H. Bragg who gleaned it from a member of Constable Rickard's family, that the murderer 'came along behind Charlotte Dymond on horseback and, leaning over, caught her around the waist with one arm and galloped to the marshy ground. In a pocket, he carried a sharp bill hook. This was the murder weapon.' [18]

Examples in chapter twenty-three illustrate that local tradition cannot be overlooked. Of all the possible suspects, Richard Pethick is most likely to have been the man on the moor with Charlotte. But likelihood it remains for we know neither his height nor his boot size to compare with Matthew's.

Yet, in looking for suspects, we are assuming what the pathologist of the time was not totally sure of - that Charlotte Dymond was murdered.

In his deposition, Surgeon Good stated 'I do not think it possible that she could have inflicted the wound herself'. But, among notes on the back of the brief to prosecuting counsel was his comment 'it was the sort of wound a person might have inflicted on themselves'; and, as these notes were the basis of his formal statement, although that comment was omitted from it, that opinion was obviously held by him. This is clear, also, from his answers to questions put in court.

If the probability was not there, in the surgeon's opinion, the possibility certainly was, that Charlotte Dymond had committed suicide. And, in reviewing the evidence, it is not hard to discover the reasons and the method.

Consider the position in which she found herself. She was wanted neither at home nor at Penhale, if our deductions have been correct. The ulterior motive of her courting activities had been exposed, we suspect. And she might have fancied herself pregnant.

By April 24, the pathologist could report that her 'hymen was ruptured', it 'did not appear to be recent', and that, 'had any person connection with her, the time which had elapsed (between her disappearance on April 14 and the discovery of her body on April 23) and her exposure to water would have prevented its being discovered'.

'There were', wrote the doctor, 'no signs of pregnancy'; and the hymen could have been ruptured were Charlotte an horsewoman, of course. But, considering her reputed affairs with men, there is a likelihood that she was not a virgin. And she must have been well aware of what consorting with members of the opposite sex could lead to, not only from her suspected mother but also from someone else.

The *West Briton* understood Mrs. Peter to say in court that her niece, Rebecca Lanxon of Blisland, had been at Penhale for 'some days in the winter'. And, as documents of this case indicate that the farming community connected with it adhered strictly to the quarters when giving dates and seasons, the girl would have been at the farm during the period between December 25 and March 25.

Rebecca was eighteen, about the same age as Charlotte. And, assuming that the birth of her first child, baptised towards the end of September 1844, was normal, she must have been pregnant when she arrived at Penhale. It is, therefore, quite probable that her state was a topic of conversation between the two girls. And it is not beyond the bounds of possibility that, as her husband was almost thirteen years older, Rebecca suggested that Charlotte take up a new position with her at Metherin to help with the new baby.[1]

The letter, which Charlotte had by April 14, affected her. Matthew remarked about her running out after Thomas Prout that morning. Mrs. Peter was surprised that she went out at the time she did in the afternoon. Charlotte herself led Matthew to believe that it had come from Rebecca and invited her to a new position at Blisland.

It is possible, however, that it warned her not to go, after all; that Rebecca's plan had fallen through for some reason, even although she denied all knowledge of it when she knew Charlotte had disappeared. On the other hand, the letter might have contained her mother's final rejection.

If she fancied herself pregnant - and it is not unusual for menstruation to cease because of worry, or even wishful thinking - Charlotte was in a predicament. She could not turn to her mother. She had broken off relations with Matthew. And John Peter could not be held to ransom because she was already under notice to leave Penhale. Moreover, she appears to have had little or no money.

Thomas Prout, with an eye for her, might have been her solution. We do not know what really passed between the two that Sunday morning, his tale about meeting at Tremail chapel was told after he knew she was dead. But, if he turned her down when she considered herself desperate, the alternative to a workhouse in the mind of a girl like Charlotte could have been suicide.

She might even have planned it, for the eventuality.

Mrs. Peter remarked that she had stayed out late on the four Sundays previously, so she could have been choosing the location and testing its isolation. She wore no bonnet cap, her old one was crudely washed and the new one at home. Neither did she wear her best gown, that was left in her box with Mrs. Peter.

If Tom Prout's tale were true, Charlotte sent him in the opposite direction to which she intended to go so that, if he were waiting at the chapel, he would not be obstructing her in the afternoon. She asked Matthew for money to back up her story about going to Blisland, probably in the hope that he would accept and spread it so that searchers would be looking in the wrong direction when she disappeared.

But she underestimated Matthew's sympathetic nature. Although it was over between them, he was concerned for her and wished to accompany her. She probably did consent to his going as far as Higher Down Gate. But when, to what must have been her consternation, he continued on to the moor by Trevilian's Gate to watch her progress, she just had to walk in the direction of Lanlary Rock as though she were going to Brown Willy and Blisland.

Then, of all things, someone joined her at the Rock as she changed direction for Roughtor Ford. It may well have been Richard Pethick who came upon her as he searched for his cattle. The walking to and fro of the couple, which the local preacher saw, could have been occasioned by Charlotte's having told Pethick that she was out for a stroll as far as the ford and back, despite the weather , and in order eventually to get rid of the cattle farmer who insisted on joining her and lending his umbrella.

Imagine, then, his horror subsequently when Charlotte was found dead by the river, when he knew that the local preacher had seen him with her. But the distance and the misty weather saved his being identified. This would account for his reluctance to identify Matthew as the man on the moor, and for his seeming hesitancy as to whether or not the man limped and as to how near he was before noticing.

Having at last got rid of Pethick, or whoever it was, Charlotte set her scheme in action. Just under half a mile from her intended destination, she would have taken off her bonnet, collar, and shawl in order to bare her neck, and her shoes and pattens so that she would leave no prints. These buried in the turf pit, she would then have gone through the marsh, in which tracks were found, and down to the river.

There, she chose a good site downstream from the ford, probably calculating that the body would fall in to the river and so be hidden from passersby but, at the same time, thinking that she would be aware of any oncomers while she was on the bank. What she used as a weapon, we cannot know. It was never found. But, then, as John Stevens remarked, it was never looked for. It might be remembered, however, that when Matthew was seen with his razor, he was supposed to have remarked to Stevens that the hone was 'too hard to make a sweet edge on the blade'; and that, when Mrs. Peter looked in Matthew's box for the razor she knew he had, none was to be found.

The weapon had to be heavy enough to sever the cartilage, so a kitchen knife would have been the ideal choice. Yet the roughness of the wound and the two attempts at making it fatal might just have been achieved with Matthew's razor, if Charlotte had taken it without his knowing or if she had actually asked to borrow it on some pretext and requested him to hone it. [13]

Whatever she used, she probably knelt at the edge of the bank and, with her right hand, drew the weapon around her neck under her left ear towards her right. But she had forgotten to take off her coral necklace. This foiled her first attempt and the beads spilled on to the bank.

Nevertheless, her first try partially cut the carotid artery and blood would have spurted on to the bank as she leaned over it. It apparently collected in one of the pits formed by the kicking up of turves by the roaming animals of the moor, hence the local tradition recorded by the vicar of Altarnon in his article that 'the cattle had torn up the ground in a ring round the turf on which the victim had bled to death'. And it accounts for the discovery by Constable Rickard of 'a good deal of blood' in a pit 'of no great depth' from which it seemed 'as if a clat of earth had been removed and then put down again'.

Charlotte would have been fully conscious at this time and well able to have knocked the turf back into place. But, when she made the second and fatal thrust with the weapon, she probably fell back in to the river. The wound, which 'would have emptied nearly all the veins of the body' in the pathologist's opinion, would have spurted blood much of which would have washed away. The weapon, too, could have fallen in the water and slithered to obscurity.

Charlotte Dymond

In my humble opinion, only suicide fits what we know of the Dymond case. It alone answers all the questions. If Matthew's knife could 'shut', as his purported confession described it, it was but a pocket knife unfit to kill a pig, let alone a girl who would struggle; and his razor would not have been heavy enough to achieve the damage found on Charlotte's body, without the determination of suicide.

The moorland searchers almost missed the body because the patten marks ran out, which indicates that the girl did not have them on for the last half mile of her walk. And, if this fits the careful planning of a person bent upon suicide, so does the discovery of clothes from the top part of her body. She would hardly have bared her neck for it to be cut, nor would she have allowed it to be without a struggle. In any case, as there was no mention of blood on the discovered clothes, when they should have been saturated, she could not have had them on when her throat was cut.

The beads on the bank were the crucial evidence of suicide, although the prosecution discounted them because it could not 'in any way connect the prisoner (Weeks) with them'. It preferred, instead, to suggest that he would be fool enough to leave the beads and body for all to find yet bury the clothes and cover the pit of blood. Nevertheless, the roughness of the wound and the two cuts baffled the people of 1844. As they failed to add up neatly enough to murder, the 'great force' with which they were supposed to have been inflicted was emphasised.

Yet it may be wondered if North Cornwall suspected that it was suicide at the time but allowed the case to be treated as murder. The pathologist's behaviour in court, the absence of a church service at Charlotte's funeral, and insistence that the ghost is the girl's all point in that direction.

It is evident that North Cornwall suspected that a butcher, possibly the presumed mother's consort, was guilty rather than Matthew if it were murder. But, as far as Mrs. Peter was concerned, suspects would have been too near to home.

One had to be Thomas Prout because he was due to meet Charlotte, was the first to notice her disappearance yet seemed to do nothing, and because his alibi was uncorroborated. When, according to the press, counsel for the defence asked John Peter what his mother had said in reply to Matthew's having mentioned that Charlotte might have gone to the moor with Prout or his brother, the answer was 'mother said nothing'.

Yet she should have said something, surely, if only to remark that, for someone she described as 'a servant man of Helset in the parish of Lesnewth', Prout spent an extraordinary amount of time around Davidstow. He had had, moreover, an amazing cheek to announce in her hearing that he might move in to live at Penhale.

Now that we know that soft John Peter was joint owner of the farm, it may be imagined that anyone could do as he liked. But it was 1844 and, as far as everyone was concerned, Phillipa Peter was mistress of Penhale. Lapses of her authority were attributed, by such as counsel for the prosecution, to her being ' a remarkably kind person, whose conduct to all her servants appeared to have been marked with the most exemplary kindness'.

The truth was that Thomas Prout was not merely someone who had probably once worked for Mrs. Peter with Matthew, not just a servant man who visited from a neighbouring parish for old time's sake or to see Charlotte. **He was a Peter on his mother's side**, which made him Phillipa's nephew by marriage.[14]

Another suspect had to be Richard Pethick, the cattle farmer on horseback, whose apparent reluctance to identify Matthew so worried Mrs. Peter's solicitor. The fact that he had to add to the statement he made to the magistrates, albeit in seeming clarification, was most suspicious. Had he been paid to do so?

He probably had not.

If he were the man on the moor with Charlotte, he knew he had been seen with her by Gard, the local preacher. And if he did not leave the Roughtor area until almost seven o'clock as he said, it was not because he had been watching a couple. He had been watching Charlotte Dymond.

It is inconceivable, if the image of Mrs. Peter's extraordinary concern for her servants is accepted, that Charlotte could be missing from Penhale for a whole week before a search was undertaken. Yet that is what we have been expected to believe. That is what the court swallowed.

The truth, doubtless, was that the girl's body was found long before April 23. It was too near a popular river crossing for it not to have been. Why else, if no-one ever went near the spot, were direction posts erected between Watergate and Five Lanes? The ford was on that route, as is obvious from the 1840 tithe map. Like most people who commit suicide, Charlotte wanted to be found. She chose a site isolated enough to go through with it, but near enough to a thoroughfare for it eventually to be discovered.

If Pethick left Charlotte at Lanlary Rock and resumed on horseback his cattle search, he would have been amazed to see her retracing her steps towards the ford as he returned to Advent. 'My curiosity being excited', his statement ran, 'I got off my horse and went back a little to see what (she) was about'. Charlotte, bent upon her fatal deed, would have been oblivious to his being there.

No wonder he 'mentioned having seen' the event when he went home. He had some explaining to do, no doubt, for Gard who had seen him with the girl was probably there. The families of the two men were related through the Hockens of Trevivian, they and the Pethicks having been based in Gard's Boscastle parish before Richard was born.[15]

The cattle farmer was saved by the weapon which was never found. It was probably he who picked it up for, were it as is most likely a kitchen knife, he knew where it had come from. He must also have known Weeks, despite the press understanding him to say in court 'I did not know the prisoner before that time' on the moor, 'I never saw the man before'. He knew who Charlotte was - **the servant of his cousin by marriage,** Mrs. Peter of Penhale farm in Davidstow.[16]

It is significant that, in the depositions of the three witnesses to the couple on the moor, only Gard the preacher stated 'I did not know who they were'. Possibly, because of the weather, he really did not recognise the man at the time; but, as he lived in Charlotte's native parish and was going to Tresinney in Advent where Pethick lived, it would be too much to believe that he was not conversant with the truth when he gave evidence.

He obviously chose to be as non-committal as possible, saying he noticed no shawl nor limp. 'He simply speaks to seeing the parties', wrote Mrs. Peter's solicitor, 'without however being able to identify them and .. it may be questionable whether, (with) such uncertainty, he would be allowed to give any evidence at all although..he speaks of them..as described by Pethick'.

In reality, Pethick must have described the couple as seen by Gard, if the cattle farmer were the man on the moor with Charlotte and the umbrella were his. Gard might have been reluctant to commit himself but three times, at the inquest, the hearing, and at the trial, he accepted permission to corroborate Pethick's evidence. Moreover, his describing himself as 'an occasional preacher under the Wesleyan Association', instead of as the 'cooper' and 'glazier' he was happy to be known as for the 1841 and 1851 census returns, he was adding un-necessary weight to his witness against Weeks.

Within an hour of having broken the news to his family, Pethick probably rode across the moor to Penhale farm. With him he must have taken the kitchen knife, hence the weapon's never having been looked for nor found, and on the way he would have called at Trevilian's Gate to alert Isaac Cory.

That is doubtless why the farmer went down to Penhale that evening. **He, too, was related to Mrs. Peter,** being the husband of her brother-in-law's sister and, as such, **an uncle of Thomas Prout and John Stevens.** [17]

The family was in a predicament. If Charlotte had committed suicide and if the reason for Mrs. Peter's having given her notice on Lady Day was as we suspect and was known in the parish, vindictive gossip would soon start. Suicide was a disgrace to any family, to any household, and could take generations to live down. But this was not any family, nor any household. It was Mrs. Peter's.

As the former Phillipa Billing of St. Breward, Mrs. Peter belonged to the family whose principal seat between 1568 and the end of the 18th century had been Hengar in St. Tudy. Although her own line had sat at Great Lanke since the house had been built there in 1627, she was doubtless aware that amongst marriages of members of the main family had been those to such as Oliver Flamank of the famous Boscarne line, Richard Lower who performed the first English blood transfusion operation in the presence of Charles II, William Morice the son of that king's Secretary of State, and three into the Trelawney family to which belonged the grand jury foreman. [18]

If the main Billing family had been the more celebrated up to 1700, Phillipa's line came into its own in the 19th century. She herself was the daughter of Edward Billing of Great Lanke in St. Breward and Mary Lean of Trehudreth in Blisland. As such, she was closely related to the cousins Mary Billing of Lanke and John Lean of Trehudreth who married at Helland in 1835.

The year after the Dymond case, John Lean assumed the prefix 'Mac'; and he, it was, who became **Sir John MacLean of the War Office, author of one of Cornwall's greatest historical works,** the three-tomed 'Trigg Minor'. For reasons which may now be apparent, MacLean did not include his own lineage when dealing with genealogies nor, despite a marked preoccupation with curiosities, did he mention the Roughtor monument. [19]

Charlotte Dymond

Should we suspect a reluctance to be associated with the Dymond affair on the part of MacLean, his cousins Phillipa (Billing) Peter, soft John Peter, Mary (Peter) Westlake, and Rebecca (Billing) Lanxon must have been equally anxious to avoid connection. But they were inextricably bound up in it. Even were suicide covered up, tongues would wag when the body was officially found, probably against Thomas Prout or Richard Pethick. And they, as was doubtless well known, were cousins on the Peter side of the family.

A solution to the problem was on the doorstep, Cory possibly suggested at the Penhale meeting that evening. Matthew Weeks, who was known to have consorted with Charlotte, was due in any moment. The three at the farm could say he had left it with her; and Cory himself had seen the couple, although not together, on the moor. If Pethick tallied his tale with Gard's and the footprint evidence, Cory could say the woman he saw had an umbrella and could discover the clothes where Pethick had watched Charlotte bury them. The neighbours would do the rest.

They did.

But it was not just local gossip that brought about the conviction of Matthew Weeks for a murder that was in reality suicide. It was something noticed by Richard Carew of Antony in his 'Survey of Cornwall' published in 1602. *All Cornish gentlemen are cousins,* he had commented. And, if that could be said of the gentry of this remote south western county as the sixteenth turned into the seventeenth century, it still held good in the nineteenth century, the yeomanry and peasantry included.

Of the hundred and twenty-odd persons connected with the Dymond case, **a mere two dozen seem not to have been closely related to each other** or associated by virtue of employment, tenancy or locality. This was the key to the prosecution's success. If the table of relationships at the end of this book is studied, outstanding queries are answered. Constable FitzGerald got into trouble for repeating Bennett's version of the arrest and Constable Brooming had hardly anything to do because both men, being unrelated to the prosecution clique, were in the dark about what was really going on.

On the other hand, Elias Bettinson could be an authority on the attitude of Charlotte's mother to her, because he was a native of her presumed father's parish.

The case in court was a farce on the grand scale.

But for his father's death at the early age of forty-seven in 1835,[20] Matthew might not have been involved. Under the terms of a will his grandfather made in 1826, his father and uncle, Richard, were to inherit the family estate at Trecrogo in South Petherwin as tenants in common at the death of his grandparents; and, if one or both of the men died before that time, the children were to benefit instead. Matthew might therefore have been heir to a ninth part of half of the estate. [21]

Just over a year after his father died, however, Matthew's grandfather made another will. It was doubtless occasioned by the change in family circumstances and probably to safeguard the position of his widowed mother and the children who were still dependant upon her. Under the new terms, while the uncle, Richard, was to come into the main estate upon the grandparents' death, the nine children of Matthew's family were left the Larrick house and garden together with £50, the shares being obtainable at the age of twenty-one or upon marriage. [22]

Having no father nor ties of inheritance, Matthew and his brothers and sisters tended to disperse rather than to follow the pattern usual for children of first sons of yeomen, which was to serve on the grandparents' estate until it became their father's and, in turn, their own. The pay sheet photographed in this book does seem to indicate, however, that Matthew worked for his uncle, Richard, for a period following his father's death in February of 1835.

Richard Weeks was a blacksmith and carpenter at Trekenner in Lezant, which was not far removed from Matthew's home at Larrick. Whether or not, when the pay sheet ended, on February 18, 1836, Matthew left his uncle's employ is unclear. But, as it was just over two months after the death of Richard Weeks's wife, circumstances may have made a difference to Matthew's position, particularly since the blacksmith's eldest son came of age to take a wheelwright apprenticeship in February of 1836. [23]

Whatever happened, Matthew was probably somewhere other than at Trekenner during the two years prior to his arrival at Penhale in Davidstow around March of 1838. How he got there is uncertain but it was probably through his being in the blacksmith trade.

One of the leading families in it around Matthew's home area was the [24] Doney family, a member of which had settled in St. Clether parish adjacent to Davidstow. It is therefore possible because there were connections between the Weeks and Doney families that Matthew entered the service of this John Harvey Doney, whom he mentioned in his letter from Bodmin gaol. And this would account for his ending up at Penhale for Mrs. Doney belonged to the Davidstow Baker family, one of whom occupied Wringfords, a holding adjacent to Mrs. Peter's farm. [25]

As it turned out, the move was fatal for Matthew. By sheer chance, the Baker family must have been the means not only of his removal to Penhale but also of the arrival there of Charlotte Dymond. For, if she were the daughter of the Tresparrett school mistress and her butcher consort, she had Baker connections on her father's side. **Charlotte was a member of one of the close-knit families of the Davidstow clan.**

Thus, when those connected with the Peter household rallied to the standard of family honour, the related Bakers and their associates closed ranks around them against him who was thought to have caused the death of their cousin, Charlotte. It was Simon Baker who officially found the body; and his brother and brother-in-law were amongst the twelve who returned the verdict of wilful murder at the inquest.

Matthew Weeks, the crippled outsider, stood no chance when such a community needed a scapegoat. But he must have been thoroughly baffled. Everyone but he knew what was going on, hence his seemingly inexplicable attitude throughout the case. Hence, too, my trying to explain certain points throughout this book for it was not until writing this last chapter that I realised that everyone was related; and publication had to be delayed for a year while I proved it.

Charlotte Dymond

To readers of the newspapers, listeners in court, and those who have been fascinated with the affair ever since, it was all so above board. A beer shop keeper from Trevalga, a cattle farmer from Advent, a preacher from Minster and so on, were obviously independent witnesses. They all supported the Davidstow contention that Matthew was guilty. So he must have been.

Had it come out that they, almost everyone connected with the prosecution, and incredibly the solicitor for the defence, belonged to one clan, the case should have been dismissed. Whether or not it would have been is another matter. Unless the connections of the challenger matched Mrs. Peter's in the county set, he would have stood little chance of being listened to.

She might have been a daughter of a second son, but she was a Billing of St. Breward. In an age of preoccupation with genealogy, that would have meant something to the gentlemen of the magisterial bench. Moreover, her being fifth cousin to the coroners and seventh cousin to the grand jury foreman would have related her to at least half of the grand jurors and almost certainly to the gaol chaplain who must have written the so-called confession.[26]

If this book is re-read, the mechanics of the case for the prosecution may be blatantly obvious. Where it fell down was when such as William Northam, who was unrelated, gave evidence which pointed away from Matthew's guilt, his stick notched with the measurement of the moorland print broke a main plank of the prosecution. No wonder the solicitor, Cowlard, was thoroughly perplexed and of the opinion that the case required 'management'. Only because it was expertly handled in court, the defence was at a disadvantage, the jury had been brain-washed by press coverage, and the judge believed in Weeks's guilt, did it stand up.

Brief to prosecuting counsel has been the basis of Matthew's defence in this book. That is a measurement of the worthlessness of the allegations against him.

If there be those who must for ever insist upon his guilt, because they believe in British Justice, they must discover new evidence to prove their point. Those, too, who advocate the return of capital punishment might bear this case in mind. The parallels between it and that of *10 Rillington Place* are startling. Both Weeks and Evans were fatherless, lame, illiterate - and ignorant of what they were caught up in.[27]

It seems now ironic that Colin Wilson, author of *The Outsider,* was the means of drawing my attention to the Dymond affair, a real-life example of what can happen to an outsider when a community needs a scapegoat. My reading of the brief to ascertain an outline of the story for him made me feel that something was wrong.

Precisely because of this, it was incumbent upon me to establish why. The justice or injustice of a man's execution was at stake. When I thought I'd discovered a reason, I wrote to Dr. F. D. M. Hocking, the Cornwall county pathologist.

I needed an opinion of the 1844 pathologist's post mortem examination report, I told him, and some advice as to how much blood might issue from a wound as described and the type of weapon that could have inflicted it.

In reply, Dr. Hocking stated that he did *not know anything about the case*

Charlotte Dymond

but nevertheless he felt he *must congratulate the doctor who wrote the description as it couldn't be bettered today.* That was praise, indeed, for Thomas Good, the Lewannick surgeon who prepared the report in 1844.

But it was Dr. Hocking's final comment which really interested me for it confirmed my personal suspicion. *You know,* he wrote, *this could be a typical suicide cut! It is very rarely that a person intending to cut his throat does it first go off. There are almost always several essays, beginning with minor cuts and then, in increasing desparation, doing a final violent slash. This would explain the two cuts, and the roughness of the wound resulting from the initial attempts.*

Could this be the case, asked Dr. Hocking, *or would it completely botch the whole thing up?*

In the light of his admitted ignorance of the case details, Dr. Hocking's opinion did not botch the whole thing up. Such unbiassed advice of an acknowledged expert made sense triumphant of something that had hitherto been ridiculous, the brief to prosecuting counsel. I was then able to acquaint Dr. Hocking with the facts of the affair and to disclose to him that the possibility of suicide had been accepted by the 1844 pathologist also. [28]

Yet Surgeon Good would not admit the probability of suicide.

He popped up in court at the very last moment to ensure that that point was driven home before the summing up and verdict. Why he did so may never be known for ostensibly he, too, was an outsider and could view the whole proceedings with the disinterest his profession demanded.

Yet I am persuaded that in reality he was as much involved in the machinations of the prosecution as any. He may have been Somerset-born but his maternal grandfather was a Cornishman and, as both his family names, Magor and Good, were prevalent in the 'murder area', it is not beyond the bounds of probability that he was also part of the local clan of families. In any case, since his neighbours were members of the Peter, Westlake and Doney families, we may be forgiven for imagining where his loyalty lay.

His intervention was permitted. Matthew Weeks was convicted on selective circumstantial evidence. [29]

No wonder the spirit of Charlotte Dymond has not been able to rest. [30] Committed as she was to hallowed ground, when suicide victims rarely were. The only one upon whom she could rely hanged by the neck until he was dead for her murder. The circumstances of her death as illegitimate as those of her birth.

If the erection and preservation of the Roughtor monument have perplexed generations, they should baffle no more. The inscribed granite monolith had to be there, a durable reminder that Charlotte Dymond was 'murdered by Matthew Weeks'. It kept the record straight, no questions asked. [31]

Were that its purpose and if it has to remain there, it might well commemorate a miscarriage of justice.

For I believe that **to lay the ghost of Charlotte Dymond is to proclaim the innocence of Matthew Weeks, to ease the conscience of suicide is to stop calling it murder.**

THE END

Charlotte Dymond

Relationship of Case Personnel

21 Witnesses (Prosecution)

BAKER, SIMON - born 1789 Week St. Mary; brother of inquest juror James B., b-in-law of inq. j. Geo. Hayne, related to inq. j. Chapman.

BETTY/BETTISS/BETTINSON, ELIAS - born Poundstock 1769; related to the Pethicks.

BUTLER/BUCKLER, ELIZA - family emanated from Blisland/St. Breward area, branching to St. Neot by late 18th century; intermarried with Stevens family.

CORY, ISAAC - born Jacobstow c. 1781; uncle of Stevens thru' sister, uncle of Prout thru' wife, sister-in-law in common with Mrs. Peter.

GARD, WILLIAM - born Forrabury 1796, illegitimately; related to Hockens.

HOCKEN, WILLIAM - born Boscastle c. 1815; through Pethick mother, related to witness & inq. jurors; connected with Gard on father's side.

JEWELL, REBECCA - born Davidstow c. 1821; thru' Philp mother, related to Mrs. Peter's Billing fam. &,thru' it, to Con. Rickard (housekeeper to his brother by 1851)

LANXON, GEORGE - born Blisland 1812; married to Mrs. Peter's niece.

LANXON, REBECCA - born St. Breward 1825 nee Billing; daughter of Mrs. Peter's brother & Con. Rickard's sister.

* NORTHAM, WILLIAM - born Okehampton, Devon, c. 1811, married into Launceston Crocker fam; seemingly unrelated to others.

PETER, JOHN - born Davidstow 1806; son of Mrs. Peter; 1st cousin of Con. Rickard, witnesses Lanxon & Prout & inq. j. J. Pethick; 2nd cousin of defence solicitor.

PETER, PHILLIPA - born St. Breward 1783 nee Billing; 7th cousin once removed to grand jury foreman Trelawney; 5th cousin to coroners Hamley; aunt of the Lanxons; aunt-by-marriage of Con. Rickard, Prout & inq. j. J. Pethick; related to others as shown in these tables.

PETHICK, RICHARD - born Advent c. 1824; related to Davidstow Pethicks & Hockens.

PROUT, THOMAS   born Davidstow 1814; nephew-by-marriage of Cory & Mrs. Peter.

SPEAR/SPARE, HEZEKIAH - born St. Breward c. 1813; thru' Brent wife related to Pethicks & Fords.

STEVENS, ELIZABETH - untraced in so far as Northill girls of this name seem too old (30 plus); but families of this surname connect with N. Cwll Steven's. Possible that girl was a Lewannick Stevens &, if so, was related to Cons. Bennett & Dingle.

STEVENS, JOHN - born Davidstow 1824, nephew of Cory.

VOSPER, HUMPHREY CRADDOCK - born Northill 1785; connected with Con. Bennett's family, the Peter fam. thru' Dawe marriages & Mrs. Peter's Billing family thru' Lean.

WESTLAKE, JOHN - born Davidstow 1805; married to Mrs. Peter's daughter.

WESTLAKE, MARY - born St. Breward 1815, daughter of Phillipa (nee Billing) & Richard Peter of Davidstow.

WESTLAKE, SARAH - born Davidstow c 1774; mother of Mrs. Peter's son-in-law John.

6 Police Constables

BENNETT, JOHN - born South Petherwin 1780; related to Vosper, Rickard, & Lewannick Stevens (thru' Whale) families.

* BROOMING, JOHN - born outside of Cornwall c. 1806, non-Cornish wife. Seemingly unrelated to others.

DINGLE, WILLIAM - born Northill c. 1801; related to Doneys, & to Stephens's thru' Coombes.

* FITZGERALD, JOHN - born Cork, Ireland, c. 1811. Seemingly unrelated to others.

HAYNE, GERRANCE - born Davidstow 1814; related to Baker, Bennett, Pethick, Prout & Peter families.

RICKARD, THOMAS - born St. Breward 1788; nephew-by-marriage of Mrs. Peter, uncle of Rebecca Lanxon, cousin of Thomas Prout & inq. juror Pethick.

Pathologist

⊛ GOOD, THOMAS - born Taunton, Somerset, 1804; but, as his maternal godfather (Magor) came from Gwennap in Cwll & both Magor & Good are also N. Cwll fams., he was probably related to prosecution members, particularly the Haynes.

2 Coroners

HAMLEY, JOSEPH - born Bodmin 1782; 5th cousin once removed to Mrs. Peter.

HAMLEY, EDMUND GILBERT - born Bodmin 1817; 6th cousin to Mrs. Peter.

12 Inquest Jurors

BAKER, JAMES - born Davidstow c. 1806; brother of witness Simon B., b-in-law of inq. j. Geo. Hayne, related to inq. j. Chapman.

BENNETT, JOHN - born Davidstow c. 1811; his Pethick mother had sister-in-law in common with Mrs. Peter; cousin to inq. j. Pethick, related to Earl, Hayne & Jewell families.

Charlotte Dymond

CHAPMAN, JOHN - born Davidstow 1812; related to Baker, Pethick, Westlake, Earl & Parsons families.

EARL, ROBERT - born Davidstow 1797; cousin to inq. jurors Pethick & Bennett, related to Chapman & Hayne families.

FORD, RICHARD - born St. Breward c. 1784; related thru' Hawken to Spear, Best to Stevens, Cowling to Good, & Kingdon to Mrs. Peter's Billing families.

HAYNE, DIGORY - born Davidstow c. 1790; brother of inq. j. Geo., related to Con. Hayne, & Bennett, Prout, Pethick, Baker & Peter families.

HAYNE, GEORGE - born Davidstow 1791; brother of inq. j. Digory & similarly related.

HOCKEN, WILLIAM - born St. Gennys c. 1814; related to witness.

JOLLOW, EDWARD - born St. Juliot c. 1801; related to Peters thru' Pearse family.

PETHICK, GERRANCE - born Davidstow 1780; sister-in-law in common with Mrs. Peter; uncle of inq. j. Bennett; related to Hayne, Chapman & Earl families.

PETHICK, JOHN - born Davidstow 1801; nephew of Gerrance & of Mrs. Peter; cousin to inq. j. Bennett; related to Hayne, Chapman & Earl families.

WESTLAKE, JOHN - unclear which of several namesakes but the family related to Peters, Dymonds, Chapmans, Doneys.

3 Magistrates

BRADDON, JOHN - born Bridgerule c. 1778; thru' Spettigue mother related to Gillard & Rowe, thru' Kingdon wife connected with Mrs. P's Billing family.

CHILCOTE/CHILCOTT, SAMUEL - born outside of Cwll c. 1781; but almost certainly connected with Tintagel fam. of this surname & related to prosecution families.

LETHBRIDGE, JOHN KING RENNALL - born Launceston 1789; uncle of prosecution solicitor; related to Rowe family thru' Cudlip & King.

2 Solicitors

COWLARD, JOHN LETHBRIDGE (Prosecution) - born Totnes, Devon, 1812, nephew of the chairman of the committing magistrates.

PETER, RICHARD (Defence) - born Bodmin 1809; second cousin to John Peter, Mary Westlake, Con. Rickard, Thomas Prout & inq. j. John Pethick.

Charlotte Dymond

4 Counsel

* COCKBURN, ALEXANDER JAMES EDMUND (Pros.) - seemingly unrelated to others.
* OXENHAM, GEORGE NUTCOMBE (Pros.)   born Paul 1799; seemingly unrelated to others.

ROWE, WILLIAM CARPENTER (Pros.) -   born Launceston after 1795, related to Lethbridge thru' Cudlip & King families.

* SLADE, FREDERICK WILLIAM (Defence) -   born Somerset 1801; seemingly unrelated to others.

23 Grand Jurors

All members of the Cornish gentry to which Mrs. Peter belonged.

12 Petty Jurors

* All from West Cornwall & seemingly unrelated to others.

Judge

* PATTESON, JOHN -   born Norwich 1790; seemingly unrelated to others.

2 Gaol Officers

* EVEREST, JOHN BENTHAM (Gov.) -   born outside of Cwll 1782; seemingly unrelated to others.

KENDALL, FRANCIS JOHN HEXT (Chaplain) -   born Lanlivery 1805; related to members of Cornish gentry to which the 23 grand jurors & Mrs. Peter belonged.

Miscellaneous

ARNALL/ARNOLD, CHRISTOPHER (moorland searcher) - born Camelford c. 1821; related to Rickard & Pethick thru' Browning, Hayne & Bennett thru' Ruby, Parsons, Peter & Chapman thru' Saltern.

CORY, MARIA (found Charlotte's clothes)-   born Warbstow c. 1785 nee Prout; wife of Isaac C., aunt of Thomas Prout.

DONEY, JOHN HARVEY (blacksmith mentioned in Weeks's letter) - born Lewannick 1797; b-in-law of inq. jurors Geo. Hayne & James Baker & witness Simon B.

DONEY, MARIA (Weeks's gaol letter) - born St. Clether c. 1824; daughter of J. H. Doney & Thomasine Baker.

Charlotte Dymond

DONEY, SUSAN (Weeks's gaol letter) - born St. Clether c. 1826; sister of Maria D.

DYMOND, CHARLOTTE (the deceased) - born Boscastle c. 1828; if the daughter of the Tresparrett schoolmistress & Poundstock butcher, related to members of the inquest jury, constabulary, bench & prosecution.

⊛ FOWLER, JOHN (court mapper) - born outside of Cwll c. 1801; but married into Cornish family, & a namesake married a Gard at Minster 1780.

⊛ GILLARD, JOHN (Charlotte's funeral officiate) - born Brixham, Devon, c. 1799; but probably connected with N. Cwll fam. of this surname & related to Braddon & Rowe thru' Spettigue, & the Pethicks.

HAYNE, MARIA (Weeks's gaol letter) - born c. 1823; d-in-law of inq. juror Digory Hayne.

HAYNE, THOMASINE (gaol letter) - born Davidstow 1829; daughter of inq. j. D. Hayne.

PARSONS, CHARLES (alleged vendor of knife) - born Davidstow 1759; related to Prout & Chapman, & Hayne thru' Saltern.

PROUT, JOHN (mentioned as having gone to moor with Charlotte) - son of Mary Peter & Digory Prout; brother of Thomas; nephew-by-marriage of Mrs. Peter.

⊛ WEEKS, MATTHEW (convicted) - born Lezant 1820; thru' Hicks mother related to Fowler fam; & Weeks family in general connected with Doney, Pethick & Spear fams. Matthew's family in particular unrelated immediately to others in the case however.

WESTLAKE (mentioned children) - Eliza Jane born Davidstow 1835, Rebecca born D 1838, Richard Peter born D 1836; issue of John Westlake & Mary Peter; grand children of Phillipa Peter & Sarah Westlake.

Acknowledgments in Appreciation - 1973/1978

Colin Wilson - for initiating the project.

Bodmin Old Cornwall Society - for the loan of the prosecution brief.

The Editors who carried Appeals for Information - Western Morning News, West Briton, Cornish Guardian, Cornish & Devon Post, Camborne-Redruth Packet, Cornish Life, Falmouth-Helston Packet, Cornish Times, Western Sunday Independent, Cornwall Family History Soc. Journal, B.B.C. (T.V.) Pebble Mill.

Charlotte Dymond

Responders to Appeals - Mesdames F. T. Stanley (Nanstallon), B. J. Carter (Swindon), M. M. Spear (Plymstock), H. B. T. Pearce (Tregoodwell), A. J. Statton (Halworthy), M. Barrett (St. Dennis), E. M. Mitchell-Fox (Falmouth); Miss S. Cornish (St. Ives); Messrs. G. Brown (Tintagel), O. E. Dickinson (St. Austell), W. M. Chiswell (Bodmin), C. Selby (Blisland), R. Norden (Hayle), M. C. Browning (St. Breward), W. H. Bragg (Wadebridge), A. J. Penfound (Delabole); Ms. P. Moodie (Lond.)

The Archivists - Messrs. W. H. Paynter (Looe Museum), I. P. Collis (Somerset Record Office), E. C. Harris (Lord Chancellor's Office), A. Venning & J. G. Lang (Launceston Museum), L. E. Long (Bodmin Museum), W. B. Harris & J. R. Elliott (Plymouth Central Library), R. W. Chell (Devon Record Office), H. L. Douch (Truro Museum), J. L. Walford (Public Record Office), P. Gaudin (Bar Council), W. Breem (Inner Temple Library), D. W. G. Dancy (Met. Office), G. Dalton (Middle Temple Library), R. Walker (Lincoln's Inn Library), M. G. Thomas & staff (Bodmin Library), P. L. Hull & staff (Cornwall Record Office); Exeter City Librarian; British Newspaper Library Superintendent; Mesdames the Registrars C. Abbott (General), E. Hedger (Camelford); the Misses F. M. Hulse (Pitmans Colleges), A. Broome (R.I.C. Truro); R. Coll. Surgeons, Edin. & Eng.

Search Assistants - Mesdames E. Arch (C.R.O.), B. Disley (Somerset press), J. M. Symons (Forrabury & Minster registers), R. Chadburn (C.R.O.); Messrs. D. J. Offord (P.R.O.), N. Brown (prison records), C. J. Kerr (P.R.O.), C. H. Haimes (Sheviock registers), C. R. Clinker (railway records); the Reverends T. Shaw (Methodist records), H. Gribble (Lezant & Lawhitton registers), P. R. F. Sanderson (Poundstock registers); Wing Comdr. A. R. G. Bax (St. Juliot registers); Sgt. E. J. Burgess (police archives).

Typescript Checkers - Mrs. A. B. Yeo (Halworthy detail, chap. 3), Mrs. E. M. & Mr. P. Waldron, Mr. & Mrs. J. Hayne (Davidstow detail, chaps 1-15), Prof. C. Thomas (taboo detail, chap 23), Dr. F. D. M. Hocking (path. detail, entire work), Mr. L. E. Long (history, entire), Mr. F. W. Weeks (family detail, entire), Mr. and Mrs. J. Arch (footprint & medical detail respectively, entire), Mr. & Mrs. L. Perry, Mrs. C. Mettam (literary detail, entire) Mrs. M. M. Hill (legal detail, entire).

For Access to Case Properties &/Or Information - Mr. & Mrs. J. H. Parsons (Alldrunkard Inn, Halworthy), Mr. W. H. & Mr. & Mrs. P. H. Cornelius (Penhale & Trevivan), Messrs. D. C. Keast & C. T. Dowton (Trevilian's Gate), Rev. J. Kirby (Tremail Chapel), Rev. F. J. W. Maddock, Messrs. J. Sleep & G. Wicket (Davidstow Church & records), Messrs. F. W. Weeks & Mr. & Mrs. G. S. Congdon (wills & other docs.), Mrs. & Mr. Waldron, Mr. & Mrs. Hayne (Penhale house & Higher Down Gate, resp.), Mr. D.J. Brookham (handcuffs); Messrs. C.G. Peter, R.M.B. Parnall; Major J. Lethbridge; Mesdames E. D. Riley, D. M. Rickard, P. Arnold; Miss C. M. Cowlard (biog. details).

Sir James Smith's School, Camelford - Messrs. D. G. E. Haynes (head), R. A. Kitching (history), students & parents for undertaking the survey.

For Other Help - Mesdames R. M. Barton (Falmouth), P. Geen (Bodmin), E. Rundle (Blisland); Messrs. D. W. Bogle (Camelford), M. Mercer (Canada), D. R. Rawe (Padstow), G. Chisholm (Bodmin), J. Theobald, S. Reynolds (Sunday Independent), R. Crossley (St. Teath), W. H. Boney (Tintagel), E. Dangerfield (Bodmin), J. H. Parsons (Trevone), C. Clemens (photography); Dr. C. Causley (Launceston); Col. J. Hayward (Prisons Dept.); Miss T. Stacey (C.B.C.); Insp. Quick, Con. J. Brown (Bodmin Police); my husband Tom, son Simon, Mesdames G. M. Barton & T. E. M. Munn our parents; Rev. A. S. W. Barrie (Bodmin); Cwll. County Library Info. Dpt.

Charlotte Dymond

Bibliography

Documents, Extant

◊ *Meteorological records: 1840-1849:* Pencarrow observed by T. Corbett, St. Breock obs. by Wm. Molesworth - Met. Office, London Rd., Bracknell, Berks, RG12 2SZ.

◊ *Charlotte Dymond's death entry:* Camelford Registration District, Cornwall; 1844, no. 84.

◊ *Matthew Weeks's death entry:* Bodmin Registration District, Cwll.; 1844, no. 439 (Gen. Register Office, St. Catherine's House, 10 Kingsway, London, WC2B 6JP)

◊ *Brief to the prosecution, 1844:* Bodmin Old Cornwall Society Library, Guildhall, Fore Street, Bodmin, Cornwall.

◊ *Coroner's Inquest Indictment:* Assizes 25/31, Western Circuit: Public Record Office, Chancery Lane, London, WC2A 1LR

◊ *Indictment:* Assizes 25/31, Western Circuit: P.R.O.

◊ *Home Office Register of Indictable Offenders, 1844 Cornwall:* HO 27/72: P.R.O.

◊ *Crown Minute Book:* Assizes 21/60, Western Circuit: P.R.O.

◊ *Other documents mentioned* in the source references are to be found where indicated, abbreviations being as follows -

    brief - to prosecution, as above.
    census - Public Record Office (P.R.O.) as above, or film in Cornwall Record Office, Old County Hall, Truro, Cornwall.
    conversations - with author who retains notes.
    C.R.O. - Cornwall Record Office, as above.
    ibid(em) - in the same place
    letters/notes/essays - in the author's files.
    op(ere) cit (ato) - in the work cited
    private collection - known to author who has copy
    P.R.O. - Public Record Office, as above
    registers, of baptism, marriage, burial - located in relevant parish church or C.R.O. as above.
    tithe maps & directories, c. 1840 - C.R.O. as above.
    wills & pay sheet - private, as above.

Newspapers, Contemporary

THE TIMES, LONDON - May 1, 10; Aug. 5, 8, 1844. (British Newspaper Library, Colindale, London, NW9 5HE).

MORNING POST - May 1; Aug. 6, 1844. (ibid).

MORNING CHRONICLE - April 30; Aug. 5, 1844 (ibid).

MORNING HERALD - Aug. 5, 1844 (ibid).

BELL'S NEW WEEKLY MESSENGER - May 5; Aug. II, 1844 (ibid).

PLYMOUTH, DEVONPORT, STONEHOUSE HERALD - May 4; Aug. 10, 1844 (ibid).

FALMOUTH PACKET - Aug. 10, 1844 (ibid).

ILLUSTRATED LONDON NEWS - Aug. 10, 1844 (ibid).

WEST BRITON - April 26; May 3; Aug. 2, 9, 16, 1844 (R. I. Cwll. Museum, River Street, Truro, Cornwall).

ROYAL CORNWALL GAZETTE - April 26; May 3; July 5; Aug. 2, 9, 16, 1844 (ibid).
TREWMAN'S EXETER FLYING POST - May 2; Aug. 8, 15, 1844 (City Library, Castle Street, Exeter, Devon.)
WESTERN FLYING POST - April 27; May 4; Aug. 10, 17, 1844 (Western Gazette Offices, Sherborne Road, Yeovil, Somerset).

Other newspapers, mentioned in the text &/ or source references, are to be found as follows - *BODMIN (CORNISH) GUARDIAN,* Reference Room, Passmore Edwards Library, Lower Bore Street, Bodmin, Cornwall.

CORNISH & DEVON POST, Western Buildings, Launceston, Cornwall.

SUNDAY INDEPENDENT, Burrington Way, Plymouth, Devon, PL5 3LN

WESTERN MORNING NEWS, Leicester Harmsworth House, New George Street, Plymouth, Devon PL1 1RE.

CORNWALL COURIER, Poole House, Pool Street, Bodmin.

Journal Articles

Murray's Handbook, pp. 205-210, London, 1865 (new ed. David/Charles, 1969)

Royal Institution Of Cornwall Journal, pp. 345-346, Oct. 1888 (R.I.C. Library, River St. Truro, Cornwall.)

Federation Of Old Cornwall Societies Journal, pp. 532-536, Spring 1967 (O.C.S. Library, Guildhall, Fore St., Bodmin, Cwll.)

Features In Books

Charles Causley, 'The Ballad Of Charlotte Dymond', Johnny Alleluia collection, pp. 44-47, Rupert Hart-Davis, 1961.

James Turner, 'Ghosts In the South West', Bodmin Moor chapter, David/Charles, 1973.

Colin Wilson, 'Murder In The Westcountry', intro. p. 14, Bossiney Books, 1975.

L. E. Long, 'Executions In Bodmin', title essay, Bodmin Books Ltd., 1979.

Source Notes

1 the ghost of Charlotte

1. Mr. W. H. Paynter, notes to author, 1974
2. Disputes & tributary name: J. Maclean, 'The History Of the Deanery Of Trigg Minor', vol. 1, Bodmin section, Liddell, 1870s.
3. W. H. Paynter, Old Cornwall, vol. VI, no. 12, pp. 532-536, Fed. O. Cwll. Socs., 1967.
4. Mr. W. H. Paynter, notes, 1974: story confirmed by Col. E. L. Marsack, Callington Volunteers.
5. J. Maclean, op. cit., vol. I, p. 350.
6. Sir James Smith's School pupils, Camelford, essays to author, 1973.
7. Michael Williams, 'Supernatural In Cornwall', p. 38, Bossiney, 1975.
8. Sir James Smith's School pupils, op. cit.
9. Mr. W. H. Paynter, Old Cornwall op. cit.
10. J. Maclean, op. cit, vol. I, p. 376; & plate XI, fig. 9.

2 what they belonged to do

1. Oxford or Cambridge histories of England, or similar, may be used as a framework into which details, from early 19th century surveys of Cornwall, can be fitted for the period background.
2. C. Redding, 'Illustrated Itinerary Of Cornwall', pp. 245, 225/6, How & Parsons, 1842.
3. W. T. Lawrence, 'Parliamentary Representation Of Cornwall', Netherton & Worth, 1920s.
4. C. Redding, op. cit., p.I.
5. Kelly's Directory, p. 799, 1883.
6. West Briton, February 17, 1843.
7. J. Rowe, 'Cornwall In The Age Of The Industrial Revolution', p. 248, Liverpool, 1953.
8. D. B. Barton, 'Tin Mining & Smelting In Cornwall', pp. 1-85, Barton, 1967
9. West Briton, March 3, 1843.
10. West Briton, February 17, 1837.
11. R. M. Barton, 'Life In Cornwall In The Late 19th Century', intro., Barton, 1972.
12. Inspector Hutchings, 'Cornwall Constabulary', Blackford, 1957.
13. L. E. Long, 'An Old Cornish Town', p. 56, Bodmin Books, 1975.
14. West Briton, May 15, 1812.
15. C. Carter, "The Blizzard Of '91", David/Charles, 1971
16. J. Webb, Cornish Nation, lyver 3, nyver I, pp. 12-18, Mebyon Kernow, Summer, 1975.
17. West Briton, May 29, 1840. J. G. O'Leary (ed.), 'Autobiog. of Joseph Arch', pp. 97-8, MacGibbon/Kee, 1966.
18. J. Pearce, 'The Wesleys In Cornwall', Barton, 1964.
19. L. E. Long, op. cit., pp. 48 & 51.
20. In the 1840s, one tenth of a labourer's 40p weekly wage would have been spent if he bought the West Briton (1¾p) & sent one child to dame school (1p to 2½p).

3 all worthy & all drunkard

1. J. Wallis, 'Cornwall Register', pp. 9-13, 172-175, Liddell, 1840s.
2. C. Henderson, 'Essays In Cornish History', p. 19, Oxford, 1935.
3. J. Wallis, op. cit., pp. 173-175.
4. C. Henderson, 'Cornish Church Guide', pp. 83-84, Blackford, 1925 (Barton, 1972)
5. J. Wallis, op. cit., pp. 263-266
6. 1841 & 1851 census returns (P.R.O.); Davidstow Baptisms 19/4/1838 (C.R.O.: DDP/46/1/3).
7. J. Wallis, 'Bodmin Register', p. 120, Liddell, 1827-1838.
8. Brief; Mesdames A. B. Yeo, A. J. Statton, notes to author, 1973/4; Bodmin Guardian 'Whispers', 16/10/1930; H. L. Douch, 'Old Cornish Inns', Barton, 1966; English/Cornish Dictionaries, Cornish Lang. Board, 1970s.N. B: we have adhered to local tradition re. the pronunciation & spelling of 'Halworthy'.

9. Mrs. A. B. Yeo, Mr. W. H. Cornelius, notes to & conversations with author, 1973/4.
10. 1841 & 1851 census (ibid). Davidstow Baptisms 12/6/1842 (ibid., op. cit.).
11. Brief; West Briton, Oct. 6, 1820.
12. Murray's Handbook, pp. 205-210, London, 1865 (David/Charles, 1969).
13. Rev. T. Shaw, Letters to author, 1974 & 1976.
14. St. Breward Baptisms 13/6/1783 (C.R.O.: DDP/20/1/1); Brief.
15. Davidstow Baptisms 16/7/1806 (C.R.O.: DDP/46/1/1); Brief.
16. Lezant Baptisms 5/11/1820 (C.R.O.: DDP/124/1/6); Brief; Sherborne Mercury 4/5/1844, p 3 ; Royal Cwll. Gaz. 26/4/1844, p. 3; West Briton 9/8/1844, p. 4; 1841 census (ibid).
17. Davidstow Baptisms 20/3/1824 (C.R.O.: DDP/46/1/3); census 1841 (ibid); N. B. namesake baptised 25/6/1826 but former more likely (see final chap.; & family, p.164). Brief.
18. Brief; 1841 census (ibid); London Times 5/8/1844, p 6; Sherborne Mercury 27/4/1844, p. 3.
19. Personal observations - & conversations with Mrs. E. M. Waldron, Messrs. P. Waldron, D. C. Keast, Mr. & Mrs. J. Hayne, Mr. & Mrs. P. Cornelius - on location; Brief; 1841 tithe maps (C.R.O.) for Davidstow & St. Clether parishes; 1841 census (ibid).
20. Mr. D. W. Bogle, weather observer, Camelford.
21. Mr. D. C. Keast; Lewannick baps 12/9/1785 (C.R.O.: DDP/123/1/1); J. MacLean, 'Trigg Minor' vol. 1, p. 376 & plate XI fig. 9.
22. Northill baps 25/3/1811 (C.R.O.: DDP/166/1/3) names Mary as wife, 1841 & 1851 census names Ann.
23. 1841 tithe maps, Davidstow & St. Clether (C.R.O.)
24. 1851 census; St. Breward baps 27/11/1814 (C.R.O.: DDP/20/1/3); Davidstow baps, C.R.O. DDP/46/1/1; 1841 census.
25. Brief.

4 a letter in his hand

1. Brief.
2. 1841 Census: Davidstow & Lesnewth parishes (P R.O.); Lesnewth parish registers (C.R.O.); Davidstow Baptisms 22/10/1814 (C.R.O.: DDP/46/1/3); tenement by Peter property, Rosebenault, known variously as Rose-by-Note (St. Clether tithe map), Rosebenitt, Rosebenald, & today s Rosebenote (census returns).
3. The entire chapter follows & quotes the brief unless otherwise stated.
4. Met. Office, Pencarrow & St. Breock rainfall, 1844; Exeter Post, April, 1844.
5. Brief; West Briton 9/8/1844, p. 4.

5 her mother would kill her

1. West Briton, 9/8/1844, p 4 gives 'white skirt' instead of 'bonnet cap'.
2. Davidstow Marriages 3/8/1835 (C.R.O.: DDP/46/1/4); St. Breward Baptisms 24/7/1814 (C.R.O.:DDP/20/1/2).
3. Locations of shute, trough & thorn verified by Mrs. E. M. Waldron with former Penhale owners: shute stopped c. 1910, trough still there, thorn cut down 1973/4; West Briton, op. cit. It was never clarified as to what "little maid" was sent to

4. Poundstock baps 24/9/1769 (C.R.O.: DDP/193/1/2;) Lanteglos baps 8/4/1797 (C.R.O.: DDP/115/1/3); 1841 & 1851 census returns, Davidstow.
5. St. Breward Baptisms 21/8/1825 (C.R.O.:DDP/20/1/2); 1841 census, Penquite, St. Breward (P.R.O.)
6. West Briton, op. cit.
7. The entire chapter follows & quotes the brief unless otherwise stated.
8. West Briton op. cit.
9. Davidstow Baptisms 30/1/1812 (C.R.O.:DDP/46/1/1); 1841 & 1851 census returns (ibid).
10. West Briton & Royal Cwll. Gaz., 9/8/1844, p. 4.

6 the neighbours are saying

1. Long Valderns field 1248, Davidstow tithe map (C.R.O.); 1841 & 1851 census (P.R.O.); Royal Cwll. Gaz., 9/8/1844 p. 4.
2. The entire chapter follows & quotes the brief unless otherwise stated.
3. H. R. Williamson, 'The Silver Bowl', p. 152, Michael Joseph, 1948 (1975 ed.)
4. St. Breward baps 18/7/1778 (C.R.O.:DDP/20/1/1),18/10/1812 (20/1/2); 1841 & 1851 census (P.R.O.); St. B. tithe map (C.R.O.); Rev. T. Shaw, letters, 1976. Poladrick = Bolatherick.
5. George: Blisland baps 20/12/1812 (C.R.O.: DDP/11/1/3); Metherin: 24/9/1844; Rebecca: St. Breward baps 21/8/1825 (C.R.O.: DDP/20/1/3).

7 small marks of blood

1. The entire chapter follows & recapitulates evidence as given in the brief.
2. Half-a-crown or 2/6d coin (12½p), less eighteen pence or 1/6d (7½p) = one shilling or 1/- (5p). If a 12d or shilling piece were not available, the following coins could be used in 1844: 48 copper farthings, 24 halfpences, 12 pennies, 4 silver threepences, 3 fourpences, 2 sixpences. As Charlotte was known to have had fourpences & Weeks not to have had, although seen with some, they are the likely coins of change.
3. J. G. O'Leary (ed.), 'Autobiography Of Joseph Arch', MacGibbon/Kee, 1966, pp. 97/8 cites the 1875 case of Luke Hills imprisoned for breach of contract under the Master & Servant Act. This is relevant to Weeks himself in connection with his submitting to arrest without warrant: see chap. 10, source note 9.

8 the body of a woman

1. Davidstow Baptisms 17/3/1805 (C.R.O.: DDP/46/1/1) & Marriages 3/8/1835 (46/1/4).
2. Route between farmhouse & H. D. Gate: 1257, 1254, 1253, 1251, 1249, Davidstow tithe map (C.R.O.).
3. A. K. Hamilton Jenkin, 'Mines & Miners of Cwll', vol. XVI, 1970: Lanlary Rock is part of a quartz reef, the back of an immense copper lode in which tin & blende also occur.
4. 1851 census, Lanteglos (P.R.O.); Poundstock baps 18/6/1789 (C.R.O.: DDP/193/1/2)
5. West Briton, 9/8/1844, p 4.

Charlotte Dymond

6. ibid.
7. 1841 & 1851 census returns, Lewannick (P.R.O.); Puriton, near Bridgwater, Som. bap. 7/1/1805 per Mr. I. P. Collis, Somerset County archivist.
8. G. Thurston, 'Coronership', p. 3, Barry Rose, 1976; 'Coroner's Practice', Butterworth, 1958. Good eventually became Cwll. East Div. Coroner.
9. West Briton ibid.
10. The entire chapter follows & quotes the brief unless otherwise stated.

9 seduced by the Devil

1. The entire chapter follows & quotes the brief, unless otherwise stated, the inquest having been reconstructed from details contained in this and press reports.
2. Census returns, 1841 & 1851 (P.R.O.); St. Breward Baps. 27/4/1788 (C.R.O.: DDP/20/1/2)
3. Radcliff & Cross, 'The English Legal System', Butterworth, 1937 (1964 ed.)
4. Brief, punctuated by Dr. F. D. M. Hocking, Cornwall County Pathologist.
5. Bennett: Lewannick baps 1/11/1780 (C.R.O. DDP/123/1/1); Dingle: 1841 census; FitzGerald: 1851 census; Brooming: 1841 census, St. Mary Magdalene (P.R.O.)
6. Radcliffe & Cross, op. cit.
7. Mr. A. Venning, letter to author, 1974 (citing A. Robbins, 'Launceston', 1885)
8. G.Thurston, 'Coroner's Practice', Butterworth, 1958
9. J. Maclean, 'Trigg Minor', vol. 2, pp. 540-553; mayors, M. P.s & Gilberts: vol. 1, Bodmin; Wymond: vol. 1, p. 170 annot. by Wm. Iago (private collect.); Royal Cwll. Gaz. 26/4/1844.
10. Observations - & conversations with Mrs. E. M. Waldron - on location.
11. Coroner's Inquest Indictment (P.R.O.: Assi. 25/31)
12. Indictment (ibid); D. Hayne, 1841 & 1851 census returns (P.R.O.); R. Ford, ibid.; W. Hocken, ibid.; G. Hayne, Davidstow Baptisms 9/12/1791 (C.R.O.:DDP /46/1/1); J. Bennett, census; J. Chapman, David. Baps. 30/1/1812; J. Pethick, Baps. 8/11/1775 or 23/7/1801; R. Earl, Baps. 14/5/1797; E. Jollow, census; J. Baker, ibid; G. Pethick, Baps. 12/11/1780 (as namesake,31/5/1808 of Trewassa, at Liskeard 1837 & Lanteglos 1851 acc. to census); J. Westlake, census.
13. Tresoke Marsh, Davidstow tithe map 418 (C.R.O.)
14. Treneglos census returns, 1841 (P.R.O.); Eliza Jane, Richard & Rebecca.
15. Sherborne Mercury, 27/4/1844, p. 3.
16. Advent census, 1841 & 1851 (P.R.O.); tithe map, c. 1840 (C.R.O.)Minster, ibid. Gard, also C.R.O.: MR/CW/7, MR/CW/21, MR/CW/33; Rev. T. Shaw, letters, 1976; Minster bap. 9/1/1796 (C.R.O.: DDP/153/1/1).
17. Royal Cwll. Gaz. 9/8/1844, p. 4.
18. 'the man was lame' inserted between lines on brief at this point, whereas, in court, Pethick said he 'did not observe the man's gait' till within 39 yds. of him (West Briton 9/8/1844, p. 4) which would have been when he spoke to him.
19. 1841 census; brief; West Briton, ibid.
20. Royal Cwll. Gaz. 26/4/1844, p. 3.
21. Morning Chronicle 30/4/1844; London Times & Morning Post 1/5/1844.
22. Indictment (ibid)

23. Radcliffe & Cross op. cit.
24. Death Cert.: Camelford district, no. 84, 25/4/1844.
25. West Briton, 26/4/1844, p. 3.

10 across the Tamar to Plymouth

1. Wills, of Richard Weeks (1800) & John Weeks (1836), per Mr. & Mrs. G. S. Congdon.
2. Lezant registers C.R.O.: DDP/124/1/2-9). Landrake=Landlake.
3. The entire chapter reconstructed from the brief unless otherwise stated.
4. West Briton, & Royal Cwll. Gaz., 26/4/1844, p. 3.
5. Radcliffe & Cross, 'The English Legal System', Butterworth, 1937 (1964 ed.)
6. West Briton, 9/8/1844, p. 4.
7. W. Brit., 16/8/1839 (St. Columb constable); Hutchings, 'Cornwall Constabulary', pp. 18, 19; Police Sgt. E. Burgess, letter, 1974.
8. Lewannick marriages 25/4/1780, baps. 1/11/1780, burials 14/2/1837 (C.R.O.: DDP/123/1,3,6).
9. J. G. O'Leary, 'Autobiog. Of Joseph Arch' - see source note 3 to chap. 7.

11 King John, the Doctor, & the master of the hounds

1. T. F.T. Plucknett, 'A Concise History Of The Common Law', Butterworth, 1929 (1956 ed.) Radcliffe & Cross, 'The English Legal System', Butterworth, 1937 (1964 ed.)
2. J. Wallis, 'Cornwall Register', pp. 38, 49, Liddell, 1840s; 1841 census (P.R.O.)
3. Mr. R. Braddon Parnall, letter, 1976.
4. London Times, 10/5/1844, p. 7; Laneast census, 1841 (P.R.O.); Mr. A. Venning, letter, 1976; J. Wallis, op. cit., pp. 265, 274. Royal Cwll. Gaz. 24/5/1844 p. 2.
5. J. Wallis, ibid,; Miss C. M. Cowlard & Mrs. E. D. Riley, letters, 1976; Mr. A. Venning, ibid.; Directories: Pigot's 1844, Kelly's 1883. Gurney signed the eventual indictment.
6. London Times, op. cit.
7. The entire chapter reconstructed from the brief unless otherwise stated.
8. Mr. J. Arch, bespoke shoemaker, Bodmin, surgical footwear specialist.

12 the constable denied it

1. R. M. Barton, 'Life In Cwll. In The Mid-19th Century', intro., Barton, 1971.
2. Rev. T. Shaw, letters, 1974 & 1976.
3. Sherborne Mercury, 4/5/1844, p. 3.
4. The entire chapter reconstructed from the brief unless otherwise stated.

13 the road to Bodmin gaol

1. The entire chapter reconstructed from the brief unless otherwise stated.
2. London Times, 10/5/1844, p. 7; West Briton, 3/5/1844, p. 2.

Charlotte Dymond

3. T. F. T. Plucknett, 'Concise Hist. Of Common Law', Butterworth, 1929 (1956 ed) Radcliffe & Cross, 'The English Legal System', Butterworth, 1937 (1964 ed.)
4. Sherborne Mercury, 4/5/1844, p. 3.
5. C. Redding, 'Illustrated Itinerary Of Cornwall', p. 245, How/Parsons, 1842: 33% men & 54% women could not even sign own names when married.
6. Plucknett, Radcliffe/Cross, op. cit.
7. Royal Cwll. Gaz., West Brit., 9/8/1844, p. 4.
8. London Times, West Brit., as 2 above.

14 something black showing

1. West Briton, May 3, 1844. Times, London, May 10, p. 7.
2. Brief: Penhale to Higher Down Gate (H.D.G.) = ¾ mile 220 yds. (1540 yds.); H.D.G. to Trevilian's Gate (T.G.) = ¼ mile (440 yds.). So, Penhale to 60 yds. beyond T. G. between 4 p.m. & 4.40 p.m. = 2040 yds. in 40 mins. (51 yds. per min.)
3. Brief: H.D.G. to Lanlary Rock (L.R.) = 1½ miles (2640 yds.); & T.G. is ¼ mile (440 yds.) from H.D.G. towards L.R. So, T. G. to L. R. = 1¼ miles (2200 yds.). Cory said couple 60 yds. beyond T. G., when first seen, & walked further ¼ mile in next 20 mins. So, their pace = ¾ m.p.h. (22 yds. per min). As couple 500 yds. from T.G. when last seen at 5 p.m., still 1700 yds. to L.R. & would need 77 mins.
4. Brief: L. R. to Roughtor Ford (R.F.) = 1¼ miles (2200 Yds.) If one gun shot = 60 yds., 3 = 180 yds. from R.F. Subtract 180 yds. from 2200 yds. between R.F. & L.R. = 2020 yds. + 1700 yds. to L.R. when Cory last saw couple = 3720 yds. (Repeat method if one gun shot = 80 yds)
5. Penhale to T.G. timed with local residents 27/6/1976; T.G. to L.R. by Messrs. T. & S. Munn 25/1/1976; L.R. to R. Ford takes longer now because of forestry.
6. Brief: Penhale to H.D.G. = 1540 yds; H.D.G. to T.G. = 440 yds; T.G. to L.R. = 2200 yds. So, Penhale to Rock = 4180 yds; 2½ m.p.h. = 4400 yds per 60 mins. (73.33 yds. per min.)
7. Brief: L.R. to R.F. = 2200 yds; Gard saw couple either 180 or 240 yds. from R.F. so they'd walked either 2020 or 1960 yds. from L.R. If L.R. left at 4.57 p.m., they'd 33 mins to achieve Gard's position (61.2 or 60 yds. per min. = over 2 m.p.h.)
8. 2½ m.p.h. = 73.33 yds. per min. At this pace from Penhale, T.G. passed at 4.27 p.m. &, by 4.40 p.m., couple would be 953.29 yds. beyond T.G. (880 yds. = ½ mile)
9. Gard said couple were 2 gun shots from him & 3 from R.F. If gun shot = 60 yds., they're 120 yds. from him; or, if 80 yds., they're 160 yds removed.
10. Cory from T.G., in one direction = 440 yds., couple from T.G. in other = 953.29 yds. (1393.29 yds. between Cory & couple if he's at Moorhead, or 953.29 yds. if he's at T.G.)
11. The entire chapter follows and quotes the brief unless otherwise stated.

15 dropped into the grave

1. 1841 Davidstow tithe map, 1226-1229, 1254/5, 1258 (C.R.O.); field 1254 ankle-deep in mud even in 1976 heat wave, personally verified 27/6/1976.
2. The entire chapter follows & quotes the brief unless otherwise stated.
3. Cornish & Devon Post, 29/4/1967 (Mr. S. J. H. Brookham's letter); Davidstow Bap. 23/9/1799 at Forrabury by 1851 when Egloskerry-born 39-year-old at Lam-

brenny. So Constable probably Davidstow bap. 25/6/1814.
4. Sherborne Mercury 4/5/1844, p. 3; Davidstow burials 25/4/1844 (per Mr. J. Sleep)
5. Press cutting per Mrs. A. B. Yeo, probably Western Morning News, 1973. Another cutting probably from same paper c. 1950s of an article by Ashley Rowe, mentions a ballad of 51 six-line verses by Joshua White of St. Wenn, printed by W. Drew of St. Columb (per Mr. L. E. Long).
6. Location in James Turner's 'Ghosts' (David/Charles, 1973) & photo in Sunday Independent 4/11/1973 incorrect. However, photo & location in Cornwall Courier 31/3/1977 correct, since its feature writer conferred with the resident who was present when the author deduced the location on 27/6/1976.
7. Sir James Smith's School pupils, Camelford, essays, 1973.

16 this fire of iniquity

1. West Briton 7/7/1843. Dunstan was Wadebridge-Bodmin Railway superintendent.
2. West Briton 28/6/1844, p. 2.
3. West Briton 5/7/1844 (letter dated 26/6/1844)
4. West Briton 28/6/1844, p. 2.

17 the case requires management

1. Radcliffe & Cross, 'The English Legal System', Butterworth, 1964 ed.
2. Royal Cwll. Gaz. 9/8/1844, p. 4; E. Foss, 'Judges of England', vol. 9, pp. 167-171; Middle & Inner Temples librarians.
3. R. Cwll. Gaz., op. cit.; Inner Temple librarian; Mr. A. Venning, letter, 1974; E. Foss, op. cit., p. 168.
4. R. Cwll. Gaz., op. cit.;Inner Temple & Lincoln's Inn librarians; R. B. Gardiner (ed.), 'Registers of Wadham College, Oxon', part II, pp. 274-5, 1895.
5. 1841 census, St. Mary Magdalene (P.R.O.)
6. Distance given by Pethick differs from report to report: left blank, brief p. 13; 'within about a stone throw', brief p. 43; '39 paces (3 feet) only', brief p. 44; '39 yards', R. Cwll. Gaz., op. cit.
7. The entire chapter follows & quotes the brief unless otherwise stated.

18 a strong opinion

1. Lincoln's Inn librarian, letter, 1974. T.W. Sanders, 'Law & Practice - Bastardy', 2nd ed., London 1850: under 1844 Poor Law Amendment Act, an attorney cost 1 gn. & counsel 2 gns. (£2.10p); but costs would have been higher for criminal cases.
2. West Briton 9/8/1844, p. 4; J. L. Vivian, 'Visitations Of Cornwall', pp. 608-9, Pollard, 1887.
3. Mr. C. G. Peter, letters, 1976; Directories: Pigot's 1844, Kelly's 1883.
4. Royal Cornwall Gazette. 9/8/1844, p. 4.
5. Burke's Peerage, pp. 2462-3, 1970 ed.; Middle Temple Librarian, letters, 1974.
6. Mr. C. G. Peter: practice papers destroyed 1911-12 removals, inter-war period, & since .
7. J. Wallis, 'Bodmin Register', pp. 81-133, Liddell, 1833; J. Maclean, 'Trigg Minor', vol. I .

8. R. Cwll. Gaz., 2/8/1844, p. 2; Bodmin Tithe Map c. 1840 (C.R.O.); Wm. Iago, Western Morning news, 30/7/1891.
9. B. Nield, 'Farewell To The Assizes', Garnstone Press, 1972.
10. R. Cwll. Gaz., op. cit.; Nield, op. cit.; Maclean, op. cit.; 'Cathedral For Cornwall', Truro, 1960s; Burke's Landed Gentry, p. 478, 1871 ed. (Fursdon).
11. E. Foss, 'The Judges Of England', vol. IX, pp. 235-9; West Briton, 2/8/1844, p. 2
12. West Briton op. cit.; Radcliffe & Cross, 'English Legal System', Butterworth, 1964 ed.; Mr. H. L. Douch, letters, 1974; Lanhydrock & Bocconoc pamphlets; Maclean, op, cit, 3 vols; J. L. Vivian, op. cit.
13. West Briton, R. Cwll. Gaz., 2/8/1844, p. 2; Morning Herald, 5/8/1844, pp. 6-7

19 his wretched position

1. Lightfoots executed for murder of Nevil Norway, 13/4/1840 (W. Brit. 17/4/1840)
2. Radcliffe & Cross, 'English Legal System', Butterworth, 1964 ed.
3. Times, Morning Herald, 5/8/1844, pp. 6, 7, resp.
4. Chronicle, Herald, 5/8/1844; Fal. Packet, Mercury, 10/8/1844, pp. 3, 4, resp.
5. Brief; Coroner's indictment & indictment (P.R.O., Assi 25/31)
6. Birth regis. from 1837; Lezant Baptisms now C.R.O., DDP/124/1/6
7. Times, Herald, op. cit.; E. Foss, 'Judges Of England', vol. IX. pp. 167-171
8. Reconstruction of trial based upon R. Cwll. Gaz. & W. Briton reports, 9/8/1844, p. 4, in conjunction with sources cited above.
9. Despite Bennett's reported evid., brief mentions no caution re. arrest.

20 there is no hope

1. Radcliffe & Cross, 'English Legal System', Butterworth, 1964, ed.
2. Chronicle, Times, 5/8/1844, pp. 3, 6, resp.
3. Reconstruction of defence based upon R. Cwll. Gaz. & W. Brit. reports, 9/8/1844, p. 4, in conjunction with sources cited.
4. Times, op. cit.
5. ibid.
6. Herald, 5/8/1844, p. 7.
7. T.F.T. Plucknett, 'Concise History Of Common Law', Butterworth, 1956 ed.
8. E. Foss, 'Judges Of England', vol. IX, pp. 235-238; Fal. Packet, 10/8/1844.
9. Times, op. cit.; Exeter Post, 8/8/1844, p. 3.

21 all but cut off

1. West Briton, 9/8/1844, p. 2.
2. Sherborne Mercury, 17/8/1844, p. 2.
3. West Briton 16/8/1844, p. 2.
4. J. Wallis, 'Bodmin Register', pp. 111-116; J. Maclean, 'Bodmin', p. 77, Liddell, 1870.
5. West Briton. 5/1/1844; 12/10/1847
6. ibid, 19/10/1838; 30/6/1843

7. ibid, 16/8/1844, p. 2; J. L. Vivian, 'Visitations', Pollard, 1887.
8. West Briton op. cit.
9. R. Odell, 'Exhumation Of A Murder', p. 191, Harrap, 1975. Mrs. Peter had son, William (Davidstow Baps. 3/12/1824, C.R.O.) who might have been this one; or, as Jane Peter was assistant matron at Bodmin gaol, her husband could also have been on the staff there (Quarter Sessions Mins., 1843, C.R.O.)
10. Lezant Burials 25/2/1835 (C.R.O., DDP/124/1/7); G. E. Fussell, 'The English Rural Labourer', p. 145 Batchworth, 1949.
11. 1841 & 1851 census: Forrabury, St. Clether & Davidstow.
12. W. Brit., R. Cwll. Gaz., 16/8/1844, p. 2.
13. W. Brit., 6/10/1820
14. W. Brit., 16/8/1844, p. 2; subsequent observations discussed with Dr. F.D.M. Hocking, 1976.
15. A. Pierrepoint, 'Executioner: Pierrepoint', Coronet, 1977, pp. 71-4: 'The authorities have always been gratified when they could get a confession of guilt from a prisoner, and.. they gladly published these.. some prison chaplains became over zealous.' The observations at the end of this chapter are more fully discussed in chapter six of 10 Rillington Place' by L. Kennedy dealing with Timothy Evans; I came upon this after my own chapter had been researched & written, & was startled by the similarity of the cases & of our treatment of them.

22 firmly grasped in death

1. Bodmin Guardian, 29/1/1904, p. 3; hence also 'Trevilian's Gate' in Davidstow.
2. Mr. C. R. Clinker, conversations, 1976.
3. Mr. W. H. Paynter, letter, 1974: a Liskeard solicitor's father related having met the lady en route. Mr. W. H. Bragg, conversation, 1975: a Wadebridge man walked along railway for the event.
4. Sherborne Mercury, 17/8/1844, p 2.
5. R. Cwll. Gaz., 16/8/1844, p. 3.
6. Bodmin Guardian, op. cit.
7. R. Cwll. Gaz., op. cit.
8. Bodmin Guardian, op. cit.
9. R. Cwll. Gaz., op. cit.
10. West Briton, 16/8/1844, p. 2.
11. West Briton, 25/10/1844
12. W. H. Paynter, Old Cornwall, vol. VI, no. 12, p. 536, Spring, 1967.
13. Bodmin Guardian, op. cit.
14. R. Odell, 'Exhumation Of A Murder', p. 193, Harrap, 1975.
15. G. Thurston, 'Coroner's Practice', Butterworth, 1958.
16. 1840 broadsheet, 'Confession & Dying Behaviour Of James & Wm. Lightfoot', private collection.

23 strange to say

1. W. H. Paynter, Old Cornwall, vol. VI, no 12, p. 535, Spring, 1967 & letter, 1974; Kelly's Directory, pp. 78-9, 1897; Mr. Wickett, Davidstow cemeteries superinten-

dent. Per Mrs. P. Arnold: Mrs. Peter's grandson suggested the cross should be placed on the grave.

2. Mrs. Peter's sister, Elizabeth, married Henry Bastard of St. Breward (Maclean, vol. I, p. 391); A. H. Malan, R.I.C. journal, part III, p. 345, Oct. 1888.

3. Colin Wilson, 'Murder In The Westcountry', Bossiney, 1975, p. 14: 'the murder of Charlotte Dymond deserves mention largely because there is a monument to her near Rough Tor, which has intrigued many tourists and hikers. I became interested in the case after seeing the monument, and infuriated at the general lack of information about it. Accordingly, I wrote to Mrs. Pat Munn, the author of the best guide book on the (Bodmin Moor) area...'

4. Murray's Handbook, pp. 205-210, London, 1865; W. H. Paynter, op. cit.; Charles Causley, 'Johnny Alleluia' collection, pp. 44-47, Hart-Davis, 1961 & letter, 1974.

5. Colin Wilson, op. cit.; James Turner, 'Ghosts In The South West', David/Charles, 1973.

6. Mr. W. H. Boney, letter, 1974; Sir James Smith's School pupils, 1973; Mr. E. Dangerfield, conversation, 1976: recollected having met an elderly man in a Camelford inn, during the 1950s, who said his grandfather was a search party member & saw the crows.

8. Mr. W. Weeks, conversation, 1974.

9. Charles Thomas, 'The Taboo', 1951.

10. Professor C. Thomas, letter, 1976.

11. Mr. D. C. Keast, conversation, 1976: when his family lived at Penhale, there was a scent bottle reputed to have been Charlotte's .

12. Mrs. E. M. & Mr. P. Waldron, Mr. J. Sleep, conversations, 1976.

13. Mr. & Mrs. J. Hayne, conversations, 1976.

N.B. since this chap. was written, another series of strange events has taken place - on Sundays Nov. 13, 20, 27, 1977 a large white window-sill in my bathroom turned bright pink. The first time, it was daubed; the second, smeared thickly; the third, smeared thinly. No household substance matched the appearance or perfume of the 'pinkness'. On each of these Sunday evenings, I turned from working on this book to preparing lectures I was giving to the local teaching fraternity; &, it was during the time of the changeover, that my husband discovered the colouration which also coincided with the disappearance & re-appearance of items belonging to him.

24 to lay the ghost

1. Vol. VI, no. 12, p. 535, spring 1967.

2. Per Mr. F. W. Weeks.

3. Per Mr. & Mrs. G. S. Congdon.

4. G. E. Fussell, 'The English Rural Labourer', p. 145, Batchworth 1949.

5. 1826 will, per Mr. F. W. Weeks, shows eldest son John Weeks joint heir & executor.

6. M. Leigh, 'Harvest Of The Moor', Bell 1937; D. Mudd, 'Murder In The Westcountry', pp. 99- 100, Bossiney 1975.

7. Mr. W. H. Boney, letter, 1974, suggested a domestic baptism, as his was in 1900 & a neighbour's in 1918. Such as I remember in 1946, however, was registered.

8. C.R.O. Forrabury registers & census films. West Briton 20/5/1831.

9. C.R.O. Davidstow tithe map & directory c. 1841.

10. Rev. T. Shaw, letters, 1976; C.R.O., Wesleyan registry MR/CW/33.
11. Letter 1974; during subsequent discussion, June '75, informant said 'the bill hook was small, as used for pea-stick cutting, & would have fitted into a man's jacket pocket'. Dr. Hocking, however, letter '76, wrote 'a hatchet of any kind is ruled out completely by the sharpness of the cuts that would cleanly divide the carotid artery & the larynx'. But see last sentence, italics section, p.143.
12. Rebecca bap. 21/8/1825, St. Breward; Catherine Jane bap. 24/9/1844, Blisland; George bap. 20/12/1812, Blisland. C.R.O. registers.
13. Dr. Hocking, letter Feb. 1976, 'A cut-throat razor is a possibility, but the fact that the weapon entered the cartilage between vertibrae would suggest a rather more robust kind of knife, more like a bread or kitchen type'; May 1976 after discussion, 'the cuts appear to have been made with a sharp, but not razor-sharp, weapon because of the rough edges described by the doctor. The nature of the cuts suggested a sharp knife being used'. See no. 28 below. There are numerous instances of cut-throat suicide: one took place outside Bodmin gaol (W. B. 16/8/1839).
14. Assuming he was bap. 22/10/1814, son of Digory & Mary Peter (sister of Mrs. Peter's husband). C.R.O. Davidstow registers.
15. Minster marriages 1801 Pethick-Hocken, 1811 Gard-Hocken; baps 1802-1811 Pethick; 1841 & 1851 census Trevivian, Davidstow. C.R.O.
16. 1841 & 1851 census, Advent; Tithe map & direc.; son of Cath & Abraham,who was s. of Thomas Pethick & Ann Bennett m. Davidstow 1752. Last 2 related to Mrs. Peter's brother-in-law's grandparents. C.R.O.
17. Cory m. Maria Prout 1811 Davidstow. Sister m. Sam Stevens 1810. Wife's brother m. Mary Peter, Mrs. Peter's sister-in-law, 1806. C.R.O.
18. J. MacLean, 'Trigg Minor', vol. I, pp. 385-391; vol. 3, 359-64.
19. Wm. Iago, annotations to his autographed copy of 'Trigg Minor' lent to me by Miss K. & Mr. J. Pethybridge, vol. I, pp. 44, 62,390. Iago knew MacLean's pedigree.
20. Lezant burials 25/2/1835 (C.R.O. DDP/124/1/7); bap. 12/12/1787 so 47, not 48 as recorded.
21. Per Mr. F. W. Weeks.
22. Per Mr. & Mrs. G. S. Congdon.
23. Lezant registers & census, C.R.O. Mr. F. W. Weeks, conversations, 1977.
24. Lewannick & Northill registers; St. Clether tithe map & census. C.R.O.
25. Davidstow registers, census, tithe map. C.R.O.
26. No. 18 above; with J. L. Vyvyan, 'Visitations', pp. 477-9; & MacLean, vol. 2, pp. 551-3.
27. L. Kennedy, '10 Rillington Place', pp. 60-2, 90-1, 103, Panther 1977. (Timothy Evans, hanged for murder 1950, granted a free pardon & remains removed from gaol 1966.)
28. My letter 4/2/76; Dr. Hocking's reply 12/2/76; mine 19/2/76; we discussed case 26/5/76; his 28/5/76; mine 4/6/76; script to him 4/10/76; discussion resumed end Oct. 76; final chap. to him mid-June 1977.
29. Russell, 'Deadman's Hill' (Hanratty case), Secker 1965, p. 153: 'circumstantial evidence is quite good but all of it must point to one inevitable conclusion, the guilt of the accused'; p. 139: 'the real test is, does it exclude every other reasonable possibility?' It must not be selective. 1841 & 1851 census returns, Lewannick parish.

30. Crossing, 'Guide To Dartmoor', 1909 (new ed. David/Charles 1965, p. 295): female bones found at a crossway, by James Bryant of Hedge Barton 'over 40 years ago' were said to have been of Kitty Jay, an unmarried girl who committed suicide by hanging herself in Canna Farm barn near the foot of East Down. No-one could recollect the occurrence, presumably in 1860s, but 'according to the barbaric rule of her time, a suicide had to be buried at a crossway'.

31. When, in 1888, the vicar of Altarnon organised the re-erection of the monument and, with two friends, 'guaranteed the needful sum', he commissioned the granite mason 'to collect the remainder in St. Breward' in order to retrace the inscription. It must therefore have been reinstated by public subscription in Mrs. Peter's home parish within forty-four years of its erection, which seems to indicate its importance to the neighbourhood.

Charlotte Dymond

Index

A
Abscondence - 33,35,36,38,56,62,80,121,152
Acreages - 14,15,19,20
Advent - 17,40/42,47,84,96/99,142,158,162,164,175,182
Africa - 13
Agnes, St. - 113
Alan, River - 9,40,42,97,99,130,131,136,144,155
Alfred, Prince - 10
Alibi - 27,28,35,46,50,70,117,148
Alldrunkard - 16,58,96,102,143,172
Allegations - 7,8,53,146/163
Allen, River - 11
Altarnon - 17,19,20,24,40,63,68,70,95/98,136,156,183
America - 12,13,153
Animals - 9,10,16,19,23,33,47,57,136,142,143,153,155,156
Archer, E. - 109,126
Arnold, C. - 40,41,44,49,167
Arrest - 14,51/57,62,64,66,78,80,101,179
Arundell, W. - 109
Assize - 50,58,69,75,103,106/124,179
Atlantic - 12
Austell, St. - 109
Australia - 13
Autopsy - 42,44,45,135

B
Bakehouse - 17
Baker fam. - 40/42,45,46,63,83,84,95,116,161,164,165
Balkans - 10
Bar - 16,57,62,83,106,108,111,112
Barn - 19,42,45,91,93
Baron, E. - 58
Barn Park Rd. - 107
Barristers - 83/106,112/123
Bastard - 18,39,150,151,163,164,178
Bastard, S. - 136,181
Beads - 41,44,61,63,131,139,156,157
Bedroom box - 20,26,34,37,56,85,88,127,155,156
Beer Act - 20
Bell's Weekly - 81,170
Bennett, J. - 43,45,51/58,61,64,66,67,88,105,118,127,160,165,175,179,182
Bennett, R.G. - 109
Bettinson, E. - 18,28,31,34,36,37,49,63,77,117,146,153,160,164
Bible Christian - 17
Bill hook - 115,137,141,154, 182
Billing fam. - 159/162, 164/166
Blacksmiths - 127,128,161
Blazey, St. - 11
Blisland - 28/36,40,46,56,61,62,70,78,97,109,114,122,138/142,110/130,154,155,139,164,182
Blood (& hounds) - 30,35/37,41/44,53,57,60,68,77/79,115/119,130,131,136/139,143,146,156/159,162,174,176
Boconnoc - 109,179
Bodmin - 4,7,9,12,14,44,58,66,69,80,83,97,102,104,107/135, 138, 144,145,148,161,165,166,178/180,182
Bodmin Moor - 4,8/10,17/19,40/44,70/79,96,97,107,124,129,137,142,143,147,181,191

Body - 40/46,55,58,61/66,70,73,75,77,79,82,83,99,115,120,124,130,135/139,156,161.
Body, P - 110
Bonnet (& cap) - 6,9,22/28,36,37,41,49,66,69,75,114,116,130,151,152,155,156,173.
Boots - 6,23/25,30,40/42,53,54,58,61,63,65,69,74/77,80,81,87,94,98,118,119,146,153,154.
Boscarne - 159
Boscastle - 16,18,40,80,96,140,150,151,158,164,168
Braddon, J. - 57,139,166,176
Braddon, W. - 109
Bragg, W.H. - 137,141,154,180
Bray, R. - 108
Breton - 13
Breward, St. - 17,20,34,40,41,84,97,99,138/143,159,162,164/166,173/175, 181/183
Brewery Lane - 107
Bridgwater - 15,106
Brief - 7,56,75,78,83/88,105,106,112,120,154,162,163,168,170,173/176, 179
Bright, J - 12
Britain - 10,11
Brittannia Inn - 20,31,40,58,83,95, 98,
Brooming, J. - 44,45,61,160,165,175
Brown Willy- 24,28,33/36,40,46,47,61, 62,70,71,78,122,136,150,155
Brush, R. - 113
Bullocks - 20,33
Burials - 75,79,123,135,163,176
Burton, P. - 133
Buryan, St. - 113
Butchers - 30,31,36,43,54,79,117,141,151,153,157
Butler, E. - 52,119,164
Butson, I. - 113
Butter - 16
Butters Tor - 47,97
Buttons - 22,27,29,35/37,114,139,146

C
Callington - 9,137,143,171
Camborne - 4,109
Cambridge - 83
Camelford - 13/20,24,40/46,51,54,58,62,63,68/70,80,81,95/98,138/143,153,167,171,173,181
Camel, River - 9,96,97,134
Capital Pun. Act - 135
Cardew, M. - 113
Cardinham - 20
Carew, R. - 160
Carnanton - 109
Carolld - 42,115,130,156
Carpenter, J. - 109
Cathedral - 108,179
Catshole Tor - 47,97
Causley, C. -137,171,181,192
Caution - 55,57,118,179
Cemetery - 79,107,135,143,145,180,
Census - 18,21,33,127,151,159,170/176,180/182,
Channel (& Isles) - 12,54/58,64,105,106,148,152
Chapel - 10,14,16,20,23,34,49,63,66,68,75,80,88,100,105;117,152/155

Chaplain - 108,123,126/135,162,167 180
Chapman, J. - 30,31,36,45,79,95,128, 129,154,166,175
Charabanc Trippers - 137
Charge - 53,55,150
Charles II - 159
Chatham - 125
Cheshire - 16
Chilcote, Rev. S. - 57,166
Chronicle, Morning - 15,77/78,112/125,170,175,179
Church (& St.) - 14/17,23,36,51,72,79,82,95/97,100,106/108,112,116,126,134,135,145,153,159
Circumstantial Evidence - 36,50,66,86,108,122/124,163,182
Civil Court - 107,110,111
Clay - 10,142,143
Clements, W.B. - 109
Clerk (court) - 108,112
Clether, St. - 95,96,161,167,168,180,182
Clothes - 6,10,14,19,23,24,30,33,35,37,42/44,53,56,67,70,74,75,80,84,88,101,112,114,115,118,119,121,127,130,131,135,137,142,146,148,152,153,157
Coads Green - 52,54,56,64,67,71,73,118,128,136
Coal - 11,16
Coat - 23,30,33,36,47,60,61,64,112,114,127,146
Cockburn, Q.C. - 83,105,110/124,157,167
Coincidences - 7,138,151
Collins fam. - 109
Colquite - 109
Commission - 106/110
Confession - 80,124,125,129/133,162,180
Congdon, J. - 51
Congdons Shop - 54
Conservative - 11,62
Constantine - 150
Convict - 123/135, 149
Copper - 13
Coral Necklace - 41,44,61,63,131,139,156,157
Cornelius fam. - 91/93,137,143,173
Cornelly - 109
Corner Down - 39,95,145
Cornish Lang - 13,15,16
Corn Laws - 11/13
Coroners (& Acts) - 42,44/51,61,108,162,165,175,179,180
Cortege - 79,100
Cory fam. - 20/24,28,30,31,34,36, 37,40,45,47,63,65,66,69/75,84/87,95,98,116,122,137,150,153,159,160,164,167,177,182
Counsel - 83,106,167
County Town - 44,107,191
Courtship - 19,25,37,39,56,62,65,120,123,136,149,152,154
Cowland fam. - 58/64,67,76,83/88,105,112,114,120,148,162,166,176
Criminal Court - 103
Cross Exam. - 57,64,88,114/119
Crowan - 113
Crowds - 69,70,76,81/83,107/111,124,133/135
Crowdy Marsh - 40,96,136

184

Charlotte Dymond

Crows - 139,181
Cuddra - 109

D
Darlington Inn - 69
Davey, S. - 109
Davey, W. - 113
Davidstow - 9,15,17,18,20/24,28,31, 34,36,38,40,42,45,53,57,70,79,81, 84,95,96,100,116,128,135,137/145, 157,161,162,164/168,173/175,177, 180/182
Deafness - 43,54,58,88,108,119
Defence - 69,87,103/106,110/113, 119/121,150,162,179
Delabole - 13,16,96,138/143
Denials - 20,65,68,158
Deputies Lieut - 57,58
Description - 52,78,81,112
Devonport (& paper) - 54,64,81,118, 170
Devonshire - 16,52,57,58,65,83,101, 137,166,168
Dingle, W. - 43,45,54,58/61,63,65, 69,76,77,118,119,127,165,175
Distances - 15/21,24,35,39/42,47,48, 52,63,70/74,84,85,116,117,145, 175/178
Doctors - 42,44,57,176
Doney fam. - 127,128,161,163,167, 168
Dorset - 65
Downhead - 20
Downinney - 57
Dressmaker - 14,22,151
Drowning - 84,112,131
Dungey, T - 104
Dunstan, Lieut. - 81,178
Dymond fam. - 6/10,18/41,79,117, 140,150,151,168,170

E
Earl, R. - 45,166,175
E. Cwll. Hosp. - 107
Easter - 22,36,148
E.India Co. - 13
Elizabeth, Queen - 106
Emmigration - 13
English - 11/15,159
Enys, J. - 109
Erme, St. - 109
Esperanto - 150
Essays - 7
Evans, T. - 162,180,182
Everest, gov. - 126/135,167
Evidence - 42/50,57/69,75,84/88,105, 146/163
Ewe, St. - 109
Executions - 11,32,58,133/135,150, 163,182,191
Exeter (& St.) - 58,79,107

F
Falmouth (& paper) - 4,12/15,77, 78,81,112/125,133,168,170,179
Farming - 12,14,16,19,20,127
Fentondale - 17,97
Fernacre - 20
Fishing - 9,10,12
Fitzgerald, J. - 43,45,51,54,62,64, 66,69,88,105,160,165,175
Five Acres - 19,95
Five Lanes - 17,96,158
Flamank, O. - 159
Ford, R. - 45,166,175
Forrabury - 96,140,151,164,177, 180,181

Fortesque, G. - 109
Foss, E. - 108
Fourpenny pieces - 18,23,32,36,38, 50,148,174
Fowey - 13,97
Fowler - 84,116,168
Foxhole - 47,97,117
Fox, J. - 113
Franciscan - 107
French (& Rev.) - 11,15,16,58
Funeral - 79,100,106,157
Fursdon, Rev. E.- 108
Furze Down - 95,145

G
Gaol - 14,69,75,80,83,102,104,107, 124/135,148,161,180,182,191
Gard, W. - 47,63,69,72/74,87,117, 130,153,158/160,164,175,177,182
Ghost - 9,10,142/145,157,171,178, 181
Gibbon, E. - 12
Gilbert, D. - 109
Gilbert, W.R. - 44,175
Gillard, Rev. J. - 16,79,168
Glanville, Rev. J. - 16
Globe Inn - 107
Gloves - 23,41,48,53,56,61,114,118, 130,147
Good, Dr. T. - 42,43,46,62,63,66, 115,121,154,163,165,175
Gown - 9,23,26,41,47,155
Grave - 79,100,106,135,136,145,181
Greenwhich Time - 13
Gregor, W. - 109
Grylls, C. - 58
Guernsey - 54
Gullet - 43,112
Gulval - 109,113
Gurney - 11,58,176

H
Hale, T. - 6
Halworthy - 16,19/21,26/28,30,31, 33,39,40,46,50,54,57,63,69,70, 83,95,96,102,109,117,138,143,147, 172
Hamley fam. - 44,51,164,165
Handbag - 23,29,41,52,56,64,118, 130,147
Handbills - 110,124,129,134,178,180
Handcuffs - 16,57,62,101,137
Handkerchief - 26,33,36,37,41,56,60, 63,112,114,119,122,127,146
Hangman - 134
Harriers - 57,139,176
Hayne fam. - 18,45,76,88,101,118, 119,128,137,153,165,166,168,169, 175
Haynes, D.G.E. - 138
Headlines - 15,62,65,77/82,124
Hearsay - 50,146
Heligan - 109
Helland - 9,97,109, 159
Helset - 21,85,96,151,157
Helston - 12
Hendraburnick - 43,45,96
Hengar - 97,136,159
Herald, Morning - 110,112/125,170, 179
Hext, Cap. W. - 109, 126
Hicks, J. - 51,127
Hicks Mill - 42,43,54
Higher Down - 19,20,23,24,27,29, 31,33,39,46,63,84,91,92,95,122, 145,147,150,155,174
Hitchens, T. - 113
Hoblyn, D.P. - 109

Hocken, W. - 31,45,46,48,63,79,95, 117, 158,164,166,175,182
Hocking, Dr. F.D.M. - 162,175,180, 182
Hoe, Plymouth - 52,80,101
Honey St. - 107
Horndon, W. - 109
Horse & cart - 14,41,42,54,69,70, 81,107,133,142
Horseman - 47,48,72,81,84/87,153, 154,158
Howard, J. - 125
Huguenots - 58
Huntsman - 57, 139, 143
Huskisson - 12
Hymen - 43, 154
Hymns - 14,79,81,100

I
Identification - 25,41,42,47,52,64, 66,69,121,122,156
Illogan - 113
Illustrated Lond. News - 110/126, 170
Income Tax - 13
India - 13,44
Indictable Offs. Act - 68
Indictments - 67,83/88,105,109,112, 170,175,179
Inner Temple - 83,178
Inney, River - 19,96
Inns - 16,20,31,40,58,83,95,96,98, 102,107,133,143
Inquest - 43,45,55,65,66,70,93,112, 135,161,165,175
Ireland - 12,165
Ives, St. - 12,108
Ivey, H. - 113

J
Jacka, C. - 113
Jacobstow - 16,20,96,164
Javelin Men - 107
Jealousy - 7,21,23,29,36,37,62,80,81, 85,88,120/123,129,150
Jersey - 54,86
Jewell, R. - 48,61,118,147,164
John, H. - 113
Johns, C. - 110,120,124
Johns, T. - 51
Jollow, E. - 45,166,175
Judge - 107,146,162,167,178,179
Juliot, C. - 140,151,166
Jurors - 44/50,57,66,78,108/113, 119/123,162,165,167
Just, St. - 113

K
Kenegie - 109
Kendall fam. - 109,126/135,167
Kestell Mill - 137
Kew, St. - 138/143
Kitching, R.A. - 138,139
Knives - 20,30,34,36,37,50,62,66, 85,115,117,129/131,146,156/158

L
Lady Day - 18,20,21,28,36,61,88, 115,148,150,152,159
Lady Huntingdon's - 107
Lake, Lord - 44
Landrake - 51, 176
Lands End - 12
Laneast - 58,176
Langmaid - 134
Lanhydrock - 109,179
Lanke - 97,159

185

Lanlary Rock - 10,24,28,34,40,47, 50,63,65,70/76,85,96,98,117,122, 142,150,153,155,158,174,177
Lanteglos - 15,96,174,175
Lanxon Fam. - 28,29,33/37,46,50, 61,70,71,114,121,154,160,164
Larrick - 17,51,149,161
Launceston - 12,16,17,20,44,58, 83/85,97,106,107,115,125,127, 140,164,166,167
Lean fam. - 159
Leap Year - 17
Leigh, M. - 149,181
Lesnewth - 16,21,96,157,173
Lethbridge, J.K. - 52,57/66, 107, 109,166
Letters (& patent) - 22, 29,34,61, 107,114,117,121,126/129,132,150, 151,170,173,182
Levan, St. - 113
Lewannick - 42,109,163/167,173,175, 176,182
Lezant - 17,21,35,43,51,80,112,149, 161,168,173,176,179,180,182
Liberals - 83,106
Lightfoots - 111,135,179,192
Lights - 142
Lime - 16
Limp - 17,24,34,35,38,47,48,50,59, 73,74,76,85,85,86,112,117,118,131, 143,147,149,156,161,175
Lincoln's Inn - 84,178
Linkinhorne - 66
Liskeard - 10,12,133,137,175,180
London (& Inn) - 14,107,124
Long, L.E. - 7,171,172,191
Long Valderns - 46,95,174
Looe - 137
Lord Chancellor - 44
Lord Chief Just. - 83
Lostwithiel - 109
Lovett, W. - 11
Lower, R. - 159
Ludgvan - 113
Lunatic asylum - 107
Lyne, J. - 109

M
Mabyn, St. - 44,109
Maclean, Sir J. - 159,160,171,173, 175,178/180,182
Macleod, D. - 144
Madford - 58,84
Magistrates (& Acts) - 16,28,36,50, 53,54,57/68,75,79,80,84/88,102,108, 118,139,158,162,166
Malan, Rev. A.H. - 136,137,139,181
Malaya - 13
Markets - 14,16
Marshes - 9,16,19,36,40,46,74/77,80, 95/98,114,130,131,137,147,154,156, 177
Marsland - 12
Master & Servant Act - 14,174
Maunsel House - 106
Mawgan-Pyder - 109
Mayors - 17,44,58,106,108,109,175
Mediterranean - 10
Menabilly - 109
Mending - 22,27,29,35,37,114,121, 139,146
Mercer, M. - 141
Merino wool - 14
Messenger, J.B. - 109
Methane gas - 143
Metherin - 35,97,155,174
Methodist - 14,17,47,153,159,172

Michaelmas - 149
Michael, St. - 10,20
Middle Temple - 83,106,108,178
Milking - 23,24,122
Minster - 47,96,140,151,162,175, 182
Minver, St. - 138/143
Mitchell, G. - 134
Mitchell, J. - 113
Mitchell, T. -113
Molesworth, Sir W. - 11
Money - 11,13,14,16,18,20,22,32, 36,38,39,50,56,66,68,82/85,88/90, 127,147/150,152,155,174,178,183
Moorhead - 19/23,63,177
Moorland monument - 82,83,99,136, 137,141,144,159,163,183
Morice, W. - 159
Morshead, W.W. - 109
Motives - 65,66,69,80,81,85,120/123
Mount Folly - 107
Mowhay - 19,21,45,91,93
Municipal Act - 44
Munn, S.& T. - 4,10,144,177
Murray, J. - 137,171,173,181
Mylor - 109

N
Nankivell - 136
Necklace - 41,44,61,63,131,139,156
Neot, St. - 15,164
Newlyn - 11
Newspapers - 14,15,46,52,56,57,62, 64/66,68,70,76/82,105,110/126,161, 162,168,170,177,179,180
Newton - 149
Noble, J. - 9
Norman - 15
Northam, W. -16,27,39/42,46,63, 65,69,83,87,118,162,164
Northill - 20,43,52,54,58,76,106, 108,109,164,165,173,182
Northumberland - 106
Norway, W.K.- 82
Norwich - 67,108
Notice - 18,28,38,61,68,152,155, 159
Nova Scotia - 83

O
Onslow, Sir W. - 136
Otterham - 57,96
Oxenham, G.N. - 83,105,116,167
Oxford - 83,106

P
Padstow - 11,13
Palmerston - 11
Parishes - 15,17,20,84,109
Parliament - 11,12,44,58,69,83,106, 108,175
Parsons, C. - 20,36,62,85,168
Pathologists - 42,50,61,66,112,137, 156,157,162,163,165
Pattens - 23,24,39,41,45,50/58/60, 69,70,73,78,87,94,98,130,156,157
Patteson, Sir J. - 107/125,167
Paul - 83,113,167
Paupers - 12,13,106,178
Paynter, J. - 109
Paynter, W.H. - 137,146,171,180,181
Pearce - 14,79,109
Peat - 14,16,26,74/77,142
Pebble Mill - 6,73,130,144
Peel, Sir R. - 11/13
Pelyn - 109,126
Pelynt - 109

Pencarrow - 11
Pencrebar - 109
Pendarves - 109
Penhale - 17/52, 56,63,66,79,84,85, 91/93,95,96,117,122,128,140,142, 144/160,173,177
Peninsula Wars - 106
Penminnies Marsh - 96,147
Penrice - 109
Penrose - 109
Penryn - 12,79
Penzance - 83,167
Perfume - 144,181
Perry J. - 134
Peter fam. 17/52, 103, 105,124/132, 145/163,180,182
Pethick fam. - 45,47,63,69,74,84/87, 116,119,120,130,131,153/160,164, 166,175,178,182
Petroc, St. - 107,108
Phenomena - 9,10,142/145,181
Pig (& kill) 19,30,35/37,68,85,93, 117,146
Pillow makers - 16
Piskies - 141/143
Plan - 84,85,116,155
Pleading - 112
Plymouth (& papers) - 12,51,54, 56,62,64,66,67,78,80,101,105,118, 122,122,148,152,170,176
Poladrick - 34
Police - 13,14,42,49,51,53,58/60, 64, 66,67,78,80,101,105,111,119,120, 127,137,147,152,165,176
Pool - 11
Poor Law - 13,178
Population - 12,15,19
Port Isaac - 138/143
Postal system - 11
Post, Morning - 78,170,175
Post mortem - 42,44,45,63,135,162
Potatoes - 12,127
Poundstock - 151,160,164,168,174
Preacher - 16,47,63,70,81,117,153, 155,159,162
Pregnancy - 43,53,56,152,154,155
Pretty Billy's - 133
Prima facie - 50,57,62,75
Princess Royal - 18
Prints - 24,39/41,45,50,51,54,58/60, 63/65,69,70,73/78,87,94,98,118/120, 146,153,156,157,160,162
Prisons - 11,124,151
Prosecution - 64,65,76,83/88,105, 106,113/119,146,150,157,162/164
Prosecutrix - 58,60,67,83,106
Prout fam. - 20,21,25,31,49,50,56, 62,66,75,79,85,95,100,105,113, 117,120,122,151,152, 155,157/160, 164,168,182
Psalms - 134
Publicans - 16,40,46,58,81/83,133, 162

Q
Quarrels - 20,21,27,29,36,37,74
Quarter days - 18,22,43,46,58,149, 154,180
Queen's Counsel - 83,106

R
Railway - 11,13,14,107,133,178,180
Raleigh, Sir W. - 12
Rashleigh, C. - 109
Ravens - 136, 139
Rawe, D.R. - 141
Rawlings, H.P. - 109

Razor - 22,34,36,37,50,66,88,146,156,157,182
Reform (& Act) - 11, 12,69,83,153
Register, Cornwall - 15,97,172,176
R.I.C. Journal - 136,171,181
Rickard, T. - 42,45,61,74/77,86,116,118,119,131,137,154,165
Rivers - 9,10,19,40/42,69,77,82,99,114,130,131,136,144,155
Robartes, T.A. - 109
Rodd, F. - 108,109
Rogers, Cap. F. - 109
Rosebenault - 19,21,95,96,147,151,173
Roughtor - 9,10,20,24,40,47,49,58,63,69,70,72,78,81/83,85/88,98,99,116,122,136,138,141/144,150,155,158,159,163,181
Rowe, W. - 83,105,115,120,167
Royal Cwll. Gaz. - 14,62,78,80/82,110/126,133/135,171,173/178
Russell, Lord - 108
Russia - 10

S
Sabbath - 16,22/24,27,28,32,35,42,47,70,82,100,142
Saltash - 52
Sandys, W. - 109
Sawle Pam. - 109
School (& teacher) - 14,38,108,126,138,143,151,161
Scott, F.W. - 79
Search - 39/41,136,139,155,157
Sedge - 16
Sentence - 123,128
Sessions - 58,180
Settle - 22,24,49
Sex, intercourse - 43,88,154
Shaw, T. - 153,173/176,181
Shawl - 6,9,23,24,41,47,64,69,70,73,75,130,156
Sheep - 16
Sheerness - 125
Sherborne Mercury - 65,67,79,80,112/125,170,173,175,176,179
Sheriff - 107,108
Shire Hs/Hall - 107,111
Shirt - 22,23,27,35/37,44,78,84,89,114,118,119,121,127,146
Shoes - 23,41,69,75,94,107,130,156,176
Showery Tor - 10,40,41,48,97
Shute - 27,92,173
Sightseers - 69,70,76,81/83,107/111,124,133/135
Sikh Wars - 44
Simonward - 40
Sir James Smith's - 7,138/143,171,178,181
Skittles - 16
Slade, F.W. - 106,110/124,167
Sladesbridge - 137
Slate - 13,16
Smile - 17,112,119
Soldiers - 9,13,16,143
Solicitors - 44,58/61,67,103,106,127,166
Somerset (& Militia) - 15,16,42,65,80,106,134,163,165,175
Southampton - 83
Southill - 109
South Petherwin - 43,51,54,58,66,118,148,149,161,165
Spear fam. - 28,33/37,46,50,61,70,71,117,164
Spermaceti - 12

Spry, R. - 109
Stacey, T. - 141
Stannon - 10,97,142
Statements - 66,68,85,86,105
Stevens, E. - 52,64,117,164
Stevens, H.L. - 108
Stevens, J. - 18/24,27/30,32/37, 39,42,45,61,66,68,69,78,85,115,122,146,148,156,159,182
Stockings - 22,23,26,27,36,37,41,61,75,118,127,147
Story - 21,34,36,37,137,146,151
Strangulation - 84,112,131
String - 52,75,147
Struggle - 41,43,78,84,157
Subscriptions - 82,83
Suicide - 62,63,66,115,116,121,154/163,182,183
Sum-up - 121,122,147/163
Survey(or) - 84,116,138/143

T
Taboo - 140/143
Tamar, River - 12,51,176
Teath, St. - 138/143
Teetotallers - 81/83
Temperance - 81/83
Territorials - 143
Thomas, Prof. C. - 140/143,181
Thompson, H. - 109
Thorn - 27,92,152,173
Throat - 41,42,84,112,115,118,120,130,131,156,157,163
Times, London - 78,81,111,132,170,173,175,176,179
Tin - 13,172
Tintagel - 138/143,166
Tithe map - 19,33,73,95/97,102,145,170,174,175,177,179,181,182
Toll gates - 20,133,180
Tories - 14
Town clerks - 52,106,108
Trebartha - 108,109
Trecrogo - 51,160
Tredethy - 9,109,126
Tregeare - 58
Tregenna - 108
Treglith - 57
Tregoney - 15
Trehane - 45,96
Trehundreth - 97,159
Trekenner - 161
Trelaske - 109,126
Trelawne - 109
Trelawney, Sir W. - 109,110,159,164
Tremail - 17,18,28,31,45,49,62,66,76,79,95,96,100,152/155
Tremayne, J. - 109
Treneglos - 16,57,96
Trenewth - 18,96
Treseat - 17,96
Tresinney - 47,97,158
Treslay - 45,96
Tresoke - 45,96,
Tresparrett - 96,140,151,161,168
Treswallock - 34,97
Trevalga - 40,83,96,162
Trevanters - 19,95
Trevilians Gate - 19,21,24,31,40,58,63,70/76,83,95/98,116,142,155,159,177,180
Trevithick - 11
Trevivian - 30,45/48,79,95,96,137,143,154,158,182
Trewardale - 109
Trewarthenick - 109

Trewassa - 17,28,45,96,153,175
Trewinnow - 45,96
Trewmans Post - 79,171
Treworra - 45,96
Trial - 103, 110/124,179
Trousers - 23,30,33,36,37,48,53,69,75,78,112,114,118,127,147
Truro - 12,145,179
Truthan - 109
Tucker, J. - 6
Tudy, St. - 109,136,138/143,159
Turf - 26,27,61,74/77,88,107,119,130,131,136,142,147,153,156
Turner, J. - 137,138,171,178,181
Tywardreath - 109

U
Ullacombe - 58
Umbrella - 23,24,33,35,37,47,50,116,118,121,122,127,146,153,156,159,160
Uny Lelant - 113

V
Verdicts - 36,49,57,62,65,66,78,122,123,146,161,163
Victoria - 8,19,15,45,49,83,107
Vosper farm - 20,40,41,46,58/60,63,65,72,83,95,98,165

W
Wadebridge - 14,16,96,133,137,153,178,180
Wages - 12,14,18,22,36,38,89
Waistcoat - 22,23,27,28,33,36,37,53,66,112,127
Wallis, Rev. J. - 15,97,172,176,178,179
Warbstow - 57,167
Ward, J. - 108
War (& Office) - 10,159
Warrant - 51,53,54,57,88
Washing - 22,26/28,32,35/37,66,146,147,174
Watergate - 17,97,158
Watmough, D. - 141
Weapon - 38,41,43,49,69,84,112,115,120,130,137,141,154,156,158,162
Weather - 12,19,22/24,27,33,41,47,48,63,73,78,81,89,114,116,122,133,142,147,170,173
Weeks fam. - 6,17/38,51,57,69,89,90,104,111/134,145/163,168,170,176,181
Welsh - 12,13,15,16
Wentworth - 12
Wesley, J. - 14,16
West Briton - 14,62,80/82,111/126,132/135, 147,154,168,170,172/178,191
West. Flying Post - 65,171
West. Sun. Independent - 138,168,171
Westgate - 106
Westlake fam. - 26,27,31,33,39/41,44/46, 60,63,65,66,72,117,118,128,129,147,163,165,168,175
Wheat - 24,31
Whiff - 26,75,156
Whigs - 14,62,82
White, J.T. - 113,123
Wightman, Judge - 107/111
Wills - 90,127,148,149,160,170,176
Williams, Rev. M. - 136
Willyams, H. - 109
Wilsey Down - 16

Wilson, C. - 7,137,144,162,168, 171,181,191
Witnesses - 46/50,55,57/67,69,83/ 88,105,114/122,146,162,164
Workhouse - 11,13/15,151,155
Wound - 43,49,63,112,115,120, 130,154,157,162
Wringfords - 96,161
Wymond, W. - 44,175

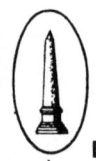

Other softback books by the same publishers

L. E. LONG

Bodmin Gaol (& other essays & anecdotes on) An Old Cornish Town - 90p

Praised for its humour & scholarship, this collection of 14 essays interspersed with 7 anecdotes on bygone Bodmin also contains 10 photos, a gaol plan, source notes & appendices. Subjects include leather & wool workers, the Basset funeral, inns, mayors, schools, field names, Bery Tower, Finn V.C.'s diary. (80 pages)

..*absolutely fascinating.. I began reading it again as soon as I'd finished it..*
Colin Wilson

Executions In Bodmin (& other essays & anecdotes) - 1978/9

The second of the Old Cornish Town series should include the advent of gas, electricity & a cinema, St. Lawrence Fair & Hospital, tinners, traders & suffragettes, the Post Office, French prisoners, the Gilbert monument, & Bodmin in verse & song.

ROGER BUTTS

A Walk Around Kynance - 45p

Although ostensibly an introduction to the flora & fauna of the Lizard cove, this smart little production is really an eye-opener to the Cornish countryside in general. The walk is in 14 stages with map, there are 5 graphs showing bird & plant seasons, sections on the history, geology, & study of the area, a glossary, bibliography, & colour photo cover spread. (30 pages)

..*a splendid, fact-filled book to enrich any visit..*   West Briton

PAT MUNN

The Story Of Bodmin Moor - £1.50

Reprinted within weeks of its appearance in July 1972, & now in its revised & indexed clear-print edition, this work continues to enjoy a rare popularity. Tracing 7000 years of human activity in the towns, villages & countryside of north, south-east, & mid-Cornwall, it includes maps & references, source notes, bibliography, tour routes & 16 photos. (118 pages)

..*it is a work of meticulous research..*   Tom Salmon, B.B.C.

Introducing Bodmin, The Cornish Capital - 70p

Demand was such for this, the only detailed guide to the county town, that its price was reduced from the original 85p. Now in its revised & indexed edition, it has 13 area maps under which places & items of interest are alphabetically listed & explained, town plan with refs, 15 photos, historical resume, bibliography, lists of celebrities, customs, dates, documents, regalia, & an additional information section. (120 pages)

..*this is a work of some scholarship..*   Joe Pengelly, B.B.C.

Bodmin Riding & Other Similar Celtic Customs - £1

The applaud of academics & folklorists, as well as of general readers, greeted this first-ever study of the custom that was revived in 1974. There are versions of the tune, photos of the revival, records from 1469 with refs., examples of similar events elsewhere in Cornwall & in Ipswich, Bath, Scotland & Brittany. (100 pages)

..the very model of what a study in local history should be..   *Charles Causley*

obtainable from booksellers or, add 15%, direct from

BODMIN BOOKS LTD., 45, FORE STREET, BODMIN, CORNWALL,

PL31 2JA, UNITED KINGDOM.

Pat Munn is now researching 'The Lightfoot Murder - Cornwall 1840'. She will be grateful for information via the address above.